Performances of Violence

Performances of Violence

Edited by
Austin Sarat,
Carleen R. Basler,
and
Thomas L. Dumm

University of Massachusetts Press
Amherst & Boston

Copyright © 2011 by University of Massachusetts Press
All rights reserved
Printed in the United States of America
LC 2010037344
ISBN 978-1-55849-857-0 (paper); 856-3 (library cloth)

Designed by Jack Harrison
Typeset in Scala
Printed and bound by Thomson-Shore, Inc.

Library of Congress Cataloging-in-Publication Data

Performances of violence / edited by Austin Sarat, Carleen Basler,
and Thomas L. Dumm.
     p. cm.
 Includes bibliographical references and index.
 ISBN 978-1-55849-857-0 (pbk. : alk. paper) — ISBN 978-1-55849-856-3
(library cloth : alk. paper)
 1. Violence. I. Sarat, Austin. II. Basler, Carleen. III. Dumm, Thomas L.
 HM1116.P46 2011
 303.6—dc22

                      2010037344

British Library Cataloguing in Publication data are available.

To my son Benjamin Joseph Sarat,
for the countless joys he brings to my life (A. S.)

Contents

Acknowledgments

This book is the product of a wonderful year of collaborative inquiry under the auspices of Amherst College's Copeland Colloquium. We are grateful: to Copeland Fellows Amy Huber, Maple Raza, Mark Doyle, and Leo Zaibert as well as to our Amherst colleagues Catherine Epstein and Laure Katsaros for their intellectual companionship during this year. We also want to thank Tovah Ackerman for her skillful research assistance and Amherst's Dean of the Faculty, Greg Call, for his generous support.

Performances of Violence

Introduction
How Does Violence Perform?

Carleen Basler,

Thomas L. Dumm,

and Austin Sarat

"*Homo homini lupis est,*" wrote Plautus in the second century BC, "Man is a wolf to man." History, alas, seems to have borne him out. Violence is ubiquitous; its performances surround us. In every age, bodies are broken, blood is spilled for good causes and bad and, all too often, for no discernible cause whatsoever.

To provide just a few examples of our embeddedness in a history of violence: Aeschylus writes of the violence of the house of Atreus, the *hubris* of Agamemnon, his wife Clytaemnestra's terrible revenge for his sacrifice of their daughter, the demands of the Furies for the head of Orestes when he in turn kills her, and on and on, the violence of blood justice, and its eventual replacement with the enlightened, but no less terrible, justice of Athena, daughter of Zeus. The test of Abraham's faith by God was his willingness to kill his son Isaac. (Isaac, his favored son of his old age, displaced the illegitimate Ishmael, who, driven into exile, founded the lost tribe, the violent outliers of Israel.) Indeed, Freud tells us that the foundation of civilization itself rests on the killing of the father by the sons.[1]

Legal historians and classicists teach that the oldest of sovereign powers concern the ability to decide whether to kill or let live.[2] Vishnu's mace possesses the power to destroy the universe.[3] Tzvetan Todorov describes the sacrificial culture of the Aztecs and their destruction at the hands of the avatars of a culture of killing, the Spanish conquistadors.[4] It seems safe to say that the origin myth in many cultures has a tale of violence at its core.

But what is violence? As ubiquitous as violence is, it is notoriously difficult to define. To make a question of Supreme Court Justice Potter Stewart's famous statement concerning pornography, do we know it when we see it? Or is it something more elusive than we may initially think?

When we speak of violence, we are not asking about something that is external and objective, that which becomes comprehensible to us only through modern, scientific, understanding, but rather of a phenomenon that is deeply connected to what it means to be human, in structure, intent, and consequence. Justice, power, repression, revolution, all key concepts of political theory, are intertwined with various concepts of violence—its relationship to action, its silencing of speech, its potential existence as a form of speech, its pre-political cast, its central role in what Clausewitz once called the continuation of politics by other means, war.[5]

Moreover, these examples remind us that violence is not something that can be isolated from its context. Violence is *performed*. It is an action, even though it may be an act of destructive power, something that lets loose in the world the terrible powers of annihilation. As we imagine ourselves to come into being *ex nihilo*, out of nothingness, through violence we exit *an nihilo*, into nothingness. We are rightly frightened by violence to the extent that it succeeds in communicating to us this terrible destructive power. This is why we begin by thinking about violence and killing. While not all acts of violence are acts of killing, there is a touch of the killer in all violent acts.

But in every act of violence more than physical force is involved. Violent deeds are embedded in elaborate rituals and enactments, performances. Violence is at once grim and gruesome and yet theatrical and spectacular. Violence is both self-creating and self-denying, enacted by, and on, particular socially situated actors. Yet, as the essays in this book by Corey Robin and Ruth Miller attest, the relationship between violence and agency is unclear. Understanding the meaning and significance of violence requires, we believe, attention to rituals and enactments as well as to displays of force, to both the private and public life of violence, to the ways violence both constitutes and suppresses particular ways of being in the world.

Violence communicates. Through its effects it informs us of danger, power, weakness, strength. But it is also performative in a sense that is not unrelated to how language itself performs. When the philosopher J. L. Austin suggested that there are performative speech acts—I marry you, I promise you, I forgive you—he showed how utterances can be actions, even though there is not any immediately visible sign of the action itself beyond the utterance.[6] The performative character of language extends to certain passionate utterances, as Stanley Cavell has noted, and the passionate, in its articulation, can lead to violent acts, especially when the means to voice the passion are thwarted or suppressed.[7]

One of the great difficulties in thinking about the performance of violence has to do with the close association that violence has with language. Is it possible to claim that some utterances are themselves violent, that there are, as the famous title suggests, words that wound?[8] Violent acts *initially* seem to be the opposite of speech acts. They are immediately visible, and while performative utterances are a way to project our present into the future, violent acts incline toward truncating a future. We might want to say that violence is destructive, not constructive, and yet we also know that there may be such a thing as creative destruction.

Performances of Violence seeks to promote understanding by examining violent deeds and their cultural surround. It focuses on the relationship between the performances of violence and the subjectivity/subjecthood of its performers as well as on how performances are represented. While scholars often study particular kinds of violence, e.g., crime, war, terrorism, separately, we bring them together, hoping, in so doing, to learn about their underlying connections. We also bring scholars from different fields together—anthropology, history, political theory, law, and social thought. Doing so helps to unearth some of the subterranean cross currents of the cultural lives of violence. Expressions of violence and the forms they take that may previously have gone unnoticed or unilluminated here gain an unexpected but welcome resonance.

With respect to public performances of violence, much scholarly energy has been devoted to examining the conditions under which nations and governments deploy and depend on violence. Moreover, we can ask how and why states have been able to mobilize their citizens to carry out acts of violence.

But, as we use it, the phrase "performances of violence" also refers to conditions of violence beyond the immediate purview of nations and governments. Here we are interested in the psychic and cultural life of violence. *Performances of Violence* seeks to encourage inquiry that crosses conventional disciplinary lines, inquiry that takes up the invitation of some of the most important theorists in the social sciences and humanities to study violence for what it can tell us about our selfhood and our society.

The difficulty of containing our understanding of what is and is not violent might be suggested by the etymology of the word, "touch." "Touch" is a word that comes from the Old French "*toucher*" which is related to the Italian "*tocco*," to knock, stroke, and "*toccare*," to strike, or hit, both of which emphasize the violence of contact. The violence of touch, this immediate contact with our corporeal existence, would seem to confirm that we are embodied beings, in refutation of Descartes. And while Emerson once said, "Souls never touch each other," it would seem that there is a way in which there is a constant touching of the soul, to the extent that we understand the soul to be the seat of the mind.[9]

Of course, we don't usually think that touching is violent (though context is crucial—there is the violent touching of the sexual harasser, for instance, in which the most subtle grope is a violation). But what the example of touching suggests is that there are degrees of violence, that when we think through the performance of violence we need to be prepared to imagine an enormous range of potential acts. One of the great struggles of the late modern state has precisely to do with this difficulty. When Max Weber famously defined the state as having the monopoly of the legitimate use of violence, he sought to engage in what we might think of as a definition of containment.[10] A line is drawn, on one side of which is legitimate violence, on the other side all those terrible crimes that we outlaw. Such is the domain of law.

Law, as Robert Cover noted, seeks to unify language and violence, to be a felicitous union of violence and the word. For Cover, it is the capacity of language to govern violence, to tame and domesticate it, to channel and direct its performances, that marks the dividing line between law that is legitimate and has a chance to be just and law which is but an imitation of the extra-legal world of violence which it purports to displace. Law provides a stage, one stage, on which violence can be performed.

If the law represents one face of the state, war, which predates the modern state, and even predates history itself, is now supposed to be within the power of the modern state to control. Indeed, in her 1963 study, *On Revolution*, Hannah Arendt suggested that the balance of terror between the two major nuclear powers, the United States and the Soviet Union, would inevitably lead to the end of war.[11] Of course, that has not been the case. Though every declaration of war in the modern era seems to be aimed at ending war, the paradox of security is, as Michel Foucault famously noted, that we seem to have become an animal that will risk the planet itself in order to protect ourselves.[12] And the dissolution of the bipolar world seems to have unleashed ever greater levels of violence, as witnessed by the spread of civil wars, the increased proliferation of nuclear arms, and the rise of terror as a primary weapon of warfare.

Indeed, terror, as Veena Das's essay suggests, is in some ways the quintessence of the performance of violence. By design terror is staged in public—the larger the stage, the more effective it is in its primary goal, which is to terrorize. All secondary goals of terror, to kill targeted enemies, to incite a destructive response by those who are the target of terror, to inspire those who are on the side of the terrorists, to cause the enemy to withdraw or surrender, flow from the inculcation of fear in those who are the audience of the act of terror.[13]

If we confine ourselves even to state violence and violence against the state, we are addressing an enormously wide range of human behavior. But to speak of violence primarily in relationship to the state, the law of the state, and the relationships that exist among states is to deny its ubiquity, even as we acknowledge, if only negatively, its force. When our examination of violence focuses on crime, on the power of the state to kill, on war, we are on what appears to be solid ground. But it may be that we are like the drunken man who searches for his car keys under the street lamp because that is where the light is. In other words, the ground can suddenly shift.

For instance, consider the baby bottle. While there have been devices for feeding babies since prehistory, the invention of a vulcanized rubber teat in 1845, and later, the invention of the "banana" bottle in 1894 which allowed for the degree of cleaning needed to make bottles sanitary and hence safe led to the gradual overtaking of breast feeding by formula feeding. Among the earliest formula makers was Henri Nestle, who in the late nineteenth century began promoting a formula that he claimed was healthier for babies than breast milk.[14] By the late twentieth century, Nestle Corporation was marketing formula to mothers in many poorer countries, places where there were often no good sources of clean water. Between the lack of clean water and the need of poor mothers to dilute formula to stretch it, a combination of diarrhea and malnutrition caused by bottle feeding became endemic in developing countries. Baby bottles thus contributed to the deaths of millions of infants, an estimated (by the UN) one million in 1986 alone.

We found many of the facts of this story in an article in the April 1987 issue of *Multinational Monitor* devoted to the issue of "Corporate Crime and Violence."[15] But was this violence? And if it was violence, was it criminal? Obviously the editors of the journal must have thought so. And yet this violence, like the violence of asbestos companies that once suppressed knowledge of the deadliness of this toxic material in order to remain in business, or the violence of manufacturers who knowingly dump PCBs into streams which results in the deaths of many people who are exposed to their poisons, is difficult to trace. It is a violence that is calculated and performed within the accounting sheets of profit and loss. And despite the fact that there have been many tort actions against corporations, it is rare for anyone to be accused, let alone convicted, of murder for what is done in the name of profit. Often such actions are not deemed violent at all.

The question of corporate violence raises yet another question for us. Does there need to be an identifiable agent in order for a performance of violence to have occurred? The great Italian Marxist philosopher Antonio Gramsci developed the idea of "structural violence" to explain how the very organization of society itself can, without any particular person being charged as responsible, wreak violence on those who live under the society's strictures. Mass poverty and its attending depravations—drug use and alcoholism, domestic abuse, all of the illnesses associated with poor diet, high stress, and bad laboring conditions—for Gramsci these are clear signs of structural violence, and in their injustice must be remedied by . . . "the violence of revolution."[16]

We tend to examine these symptoms, if indeed that is what they are, usually by looking at crime and punishment. As Mary Atwell's essay indicates, the jewel in the crown of punishment, so to speak, is the crime of murder and its concomitant punishment, the penalty of death. Scholars from various disciplines study capital punishment in order to focus more intensely on the problem of understanding violence and its relationship to law, to the psychology of the violent offender, to the semiotics of power, and to a host of other problems. How violence is performed by the state, its rituals, its techniques, its judgments, have come under increased scrutiny in recent years. And there is much to be learned from this scrutiny, especially what it might mean for the state to kill its offending citizens.

There may be a brutality, a coarsening of selves in a society in which there is so much violence. Since 9/11 approximately 120,000 Americans have died from gunshot wounds.[17] Every day, it seems, news comes of the latest mass murder. American prisons hold more inmates, proportionately and absolutely, than those of any other country in the world. We also spend more on our military annually than all of the other nations of the world combined. And, disclaimers and denials notwithstanding, our highest officials did not simply ignore the torture of prisoners from our wars in Iraq and Afghanistan, but actively promoted it. Back in the 1960s, in the midst of deep social turmoil, a member of the Black Panther Party,

H. Rap Brown, infamously declared, "Violence is as American as cherry pie." In the succeeding decades, there has been little evidence to refute his claim, and much evidence to support it.

But we are not only concerned with the violence of American culture, though that is sufficient cause for concern. We are also interested in the connection between culture and act, the link between the two being *performance*. The various examples that we discussed so far—law, terror, ritual, fiction, speech acts—all occur at a peculiar intersection, that of the crossing of publicity and secrecy. Sometimes violence is performed in secret, whether by the state or by the criminal, or by the criminal state. Sometimes it is performed publicly, as in terror or riot. And, Anne Norton's essay in this book suggests, sometimes the exposing of a violent act is itself designed to stage a counter-violence, to incite people to act against injustice, or against an enemy. In all cases, performing violence involves a quest to move the hearts and minds of people, every bit as much as, or perhaps even more than the staging of a play or the production of a film or novel. The staging of violence sometimes glamorizes, sometimes degrades, those who are its purported agents. When violence is performed we are moved.

It is clear that when we think about performing violence we are opening up an enormous subject. In this volume, we have not attempted to be comprehensive, but instead, intensive in our examination of this subject. *Performances of Violence* seeks to explore the relationship between selfhood, agency, and violence. It focuses on the psychic life of violence and its expression in the performances of particular selves, all the while calling into question the adequacy of ideas of agency in the face of those performances.

In addition, we are interested in the way performances of violence are represented in the mass media and in everyday life. Are those performances inflated, distorted, made into spectacle in their media representations? How and when do those performances become embedded in our taken-for-granted worlds? How are everyday practices of violence linked to larger political and cultural contexts?

To pursue these questions requires an interdisciplinary approach of the kind this book provides. For example: the theme of *monstrosity* plays a profound role in many performances of violence. Monsters have served as convenient metaphors for evil and as embodiments of the mysterious and terrifying effects that performances of violence have on their audiences. In this book when Mary Welek Atwell investigates the characterizations of Aileen Wuornos as a monster, when Corey Robin gestures toward the terrifying aspects of monstrous sublimity, and when Ruth A. Miller notes how parrhesiastic speech on the part of suffragettes was characterized by Francis Parkman and others as monstrous, they are all helping us understand the varying roles monstrosity plays in the ways we culturally receive and process our understandings of violent acts.

In their essays, Veena Das and Miller address the strange ways in which temporality is perceived under the sign of violence when terrorists attack and when performative speech acts simultaneously are violent in character and disavow that violence. Here they bring to our attention the structural commonalities underlying what we may think of as being dramatically different expressions, a bomb and an order.

When Anne Norton notes the strange relationship between witnessing and distance in the spectatorial frames of tourism and pornography used by prison guards at Abu Ghraib to domesticate the violence they performed, when Paul Steege describes the blurring of lines between collaborators, witnesses, and bystanders in postwar Berlin, and when Corey Robin cites Edmund Burke on how "it's always best to enjoy pain and danger at a remove," they are all raising crucial questions concerning how we are able, or in some cases, unable to experience the very violence we are witnessing.

To underline serious difficulties that attend our attempts to understand violence, the work collected here does not counsel despair, but serves as a prod to better ways of knowing how violence operates within the context of cultural meanings. Paradoxically violence seems to obscure its meanings by the very power of its presence. The work gathered here shares a respect for, and a willingness to struggle with, that paradox.

We begin by taking up the complex connections among selfhood, agency, and violence. Corey Robin initiates our exploration by examining the way violence is portrayed in the writings of prominent conservative political thinkers. There he finds that the performance of violence is often regarded as essential, life-affirming, enlivening for those who witness it. As Robin puts it, "Far from being saddened, burdened, or vexed by violence, the conservative has been enlivened by it."

Robin traces this enlivening in Edmund Burke's *A Philosophical Enquiry into the Origin of Our Ideas of the Sublime and the Beautiful*. There Burke develops a view of the self "desperately in need of negative stimuli of the sort provided by pain and danger which Burke associates with the sublime. The sublime is most readily found in two political forms: hierarchy and violence." According to Burke, "Curiosity leads to weariness, pleasure to indifference, enjoyment to torpor, and imitation to stagnation . . . Suicide, it seems, is the inevitable fate awaiting anyone who takes pleasure in the world as it is."

Such sentiments, Robin argues, pose a challenge to conservative theorists, since the conservative self is, traditionally, "partial to things as they are not because he thinks they are just or good but because they are familiar . . . But should the self of *The Sublime and the Beautiful* be assured of his attachments and familiars, he'd quickly find himself confronting the specter of his own extinction, more than likely at his own hand." Robin theorizes that this "lethal ennui" just below the surface of conservative discourse is what causes conservative politicians to opt for violence and activism when conservative theorists would opt for "quiet enjoyments and secure attachments." Pain and danger are the most generative and generating experiences of the self for they fulfill the imperative confrontation with non-being.

The experience of ruling another weakens the sublime. As a result, Robin describes the tendency of conservatives to worry that hierarchies have gone soft. More recently they have directed their concern about "going soft" to "the liberal obsession with the rule of law." This obsession has led to "a culture of rules and laws slowly disabling and devitalizing American power. These are signs of a Nietzschean unhealthiness, and 9/11 was its inevitable result." If another 9/11 is to be prevented, conservatives say, the movement needs to be reversed.

But, as Robin rightly notes, the great irony of the War on Terror is that law and lawyers are now far more critical than they were before 9/11 since lawyers in the White House insisted on justifying increased violence *through* the law. Thus, "far from minimizing state violence—which was the great fear of the neocons—lawyering has proven to be perfectly compatible with that violence." Far from being the modality for containing violence, law has enabled its ubiquitous performances. But there is a danger in this staging of violence. As Robin puts it, "So long as the war on terror remains an idea—a hot topic on the blogs, a provocative op-ed, an episode of *24*—it is sublime. As soon as it becomes a reality, it can be as cheerless and tedious as a discussion of the tax code."

Robin notes that in the conservative imagining of subjectivity, especially the subjectivity of those who wish to rule, violence plays a key role. In that imagining "If the powerful are to remain powerful—if they are to remain alive at all—their power,' Robin writes, "indeed the credibility of their own existence, must be continuously challenged, threatened, and defended."

Ruth Miller's essay broadens the context in order to consider the linkage between the performances of violence and our assumptions about the subjectivity of those who engage in those performances. Miller asks what it might mean to say that someone performs an act of violence—but to say this without invoking agency. In her view, doing away with agency would open up the possibility that being the object of assault might be as much an act of violence as initiating an assault. Though this way of understanding violence is arguably distasteful, Miller's essay indicates that, despite the pervasive rhetoric of agency, this is very much where existing theories of violence in fact leave us. In her view, abandoning agency might help get at the peculiarly physical nature of linguistic violence as well as the peculiarly linguistic nature of physical violence and leaving agency out of narratives of violence might also open up a space for alternative interpretations of the violent act.

Miller begins by highlighting some problems and questions that arise when agency is central to narratives of violence, particularly focusing on the speech act as an act of violence. J. L. Austin's discussions of the speech act, Miller writes, "indicates a relatively coherent narrative of the sovereign individual at work." In other words, he presents a narrative of agency. But "the illocutionary act is necessarily an act of *repetition*, an act that can only construct and situate a subject within an already existing linguistic realm. In order for speech to *be* an act, therefore, the intention and will—individual agency—must disappear." Butler's theories, Miller writes, separate the subject and language. Miller explores a disintegration of spatial and temporal boundaries which occurs when violent speech acts occur, and argues against trying to articulate such acts or the responses to them in a vocabulary of agency.

Miller argues that not only is it possible to narrate violence without invoking agency, narratives of speech acts already have done so. Butler writes that the interaction between linguistic and physical violence is far more than metaphorical since, to the extent the body is constituted by language, speech puts physical existence at stake. While Butler's theories provide a useful account of the physical and bodily effects of speech, Miller believes that Butler does not get at the physicality of the speech act itself. Miller tries to rectify this shortcoming.

Miller writes that the violent speech act is not only a type of modern "*parrhesia*" [the Foucauldian concept of speaking freely], but that this type of *parrhesia* is the most common sort of political speech in the modern period. Miller believes that Foucault's theories can serve as a starting point for thinking about another major implication of the performance of violence absent agency—namely the coming together of speaking, hearing voices, hitting, and being hit. Miller argues that certain narratives of violence (particularly those introduced by the state) which rely on agency reduce the complexity of violence and leave us with an incomplete understanding of the violent act.

Contra the beliefs of the conservative thinkers whom Robin surveyed, Miller concludes by reiterating her belief that "agency is irrelevant to the performance of the violent act." In Miller's view, when agency enters the picture, it undermines the political goals of critical scholarly engagement, and is very foreign to performative speech, to illocutionary speech, itself.

Mary Atwell continues the discussion of the way subjectivities get framed in performances of violence and raises the question of how mass media frame and shape those performances. She presents an intensive examination of a single case, the case of serial killer Aileen Wuornos. Atwell treats serial killing and capital punishment as distinctive, though linked, performances and regards Wuornos as both perpetrator and victim of violence, focusing particularly on the way gender played out on both dimensions. "In discussing the story of Aileen Wuornos," Atwell argues, "there is an analogy with Judith Butler's discussion of gender not as integral but as shifting, as a reiterated social performance. So it is with the offender/victim nexus. Status as a victim or as an offender is related not to a fundamental identity but to the performance of acts deemed criminal. Wuornos provides a case study that highlights the gaps between the performance of violent acts and the master status of 'serial killer,' a status defined by the perception of others."

Wuornos was a prostitute who was accused of murdering several of her clients. Atwell reminds us that although her lover, Tyria Moore, was strongly suspected as having taken part in the murders, the FBI focused on Wuornos. After Wuornos was caught, Moore was used to elicit a full confession from Wuornos. Wuornos confessed to the killings but claimed all were in self-defense. At her trial both the prosecution and the defense tried to sway the jury by using sex-role stereotypes. The prosecution seemed to imply that Wuornos's crime was even more heinous because it subverted the "natural order of male dominance." The defense argued that Wuornos was only responding in self-defense to being repeatedly raped and victimized. The jury convicted Wuornos of first-degree murder and armed robbery and sentenced her to death.

She subsequently pleaded guilty to five other murders, though, Atwell writes, she was assisted by an attorney who—by his own admission—was incompetent to defend a capital trial and had only agreed to do so in exchange for the rights to sell her story to the media. Here we can see a crucial moment in which one performance of violence bleeds into and feeds another, in which the gruesome becomes the spectacular, in which subjectivity is constituted through its legal and media portrayal.

Atwell's essay places these performances in the context of Wuornos's life (of sexual and physical abuse) leading up to the murders and considers what it was about the Wuornos case that so fascinated journalists and filmmakers. Perhaps they were attracted to the notion of the female outlaw exacting revenge on perpetrators. Following Judith Butler, Atwell concludes that "it is the presence of outsiders, those whose behaviors defy categories that threaten hierarchy. The criminal justice system seems especially ill equipped to deal with such multiplicity of meaning. Perhaps this discomfort helps to explain the attention to the case of Aileen Wuornos. Not only does her story blur the simple categories of victim and offender, that very blurring creates the uneasiness that engrosses our attention."

Like Atwell, Anne Norton takes up the media framing of performances of violence, in this case in the context of America's war on terror. For her, terrorism and responses to it are crucial violent performances, but they also serve as the staging ground for other performances. Norton focuses on the violence performed by American soldiers on Abu Ghraib and Guantanamo prisoners marked as Muslim. She notes, "The violence is performative in two senses. First, it is theatrical and spectacular. Much of the violence at Abu Ghraib was staged for the camera . . . The drive to see, to be seen, to see oneself seen, informed the staging of violence, the photographic records of the violence, and impelled the circulatory vortex into which the photographs were cast . . . There is also, in the taking and circulation of these photographs, in testimony concerning them, in the quiet speech of shamed refusal, another drive: the drive to record, to confess, to bear witness."[18]

Norton discusses the reader's and viewer's roles as critics in the performance of violence. She argues, "The reader and critic are, however, not always in the service of justice." As she sees it, certain of the readings and critiques of the violence at Abu Ghraib served to reaffirm and reinforce structures of dominion and subjection.

Abu Ghraib, Norton writes, was already known for abuse before the American government took over. The American takeover was both a practical and symbolic act of conquest, of stepping into Saddam's place. Guantanamo, alternately, "is the material expression of an America which does not wish to be seen as American." Much is concealed from Americans concerning the geography of violence in the post-9/11 world. "In this context," Norton suggests, "the Abu Ghraib photographs seemed to offer unmediated access to the previously hidden: sudden, unexpected stolen knowledge that had escaped governance." Thus, Norton, like Atwell, calls us to think about the mediated image as fundamental to contemporary performances of violence.

The pictures and videos of Abu Ghraib are clearly influenced by pornography, leading fundamentalist Christian groups to bemoan the cultural depravity in America. Thus fundamentalists were able to condemn Abu Ghraib without condemning torture or questioning the deployment of mercenary forces. As Norton observes "defenders of the Bush administration deployed tropes of pornography and pleasure to render torture benign and defensible."

Norton, again like Atwell, also is interested in the gendered nature of performances of violence. Here Norton analyzes Lynndie England's role, the woman whose face is most prominent in many of the Abu Ghraib pictures, writing, "England became an icon for abuse: the abuse she did and the abuse she endured. The ambivalence of her role, abuser and abused, captures a familiar strategy in the architecture of power and oppression, and alters it, subtly [sic] and effectively." The photographs tended to "affirm narratives of female weakness, and to conceal the political processes that so elegantly served several chauvinisms simultaneously." Media accounts of the photographs also affirmed the narrative of female weakness, reporting stories of her childhood special education classes and failed romances; asking if England was a victimizer or a victim.

Norton also discusses the now-iconographical picture of the man in the black hood for its religious meanings: the black hood (a dark version of the hoods of Klansmen), the crucifixion posture, and the religious representations of the image in recent artwork by Fernando Botero. She concludes, "Three figures animate this essay: the woman, the dog, the divine. They are bound together in the suffering of the body, the sweetness of life, the passion of incarnation. Perhaps it is the experience of life in the flesh that opens to the divine. Life, bare life, and the sweetness of life testify to a divinity indiscriminately incarnate."

Veena Das's essay continues the exploration of terrorism and its mediated representations while also asking her readers to think about the embeddedness of performances of violence in everyday life. She concentrates her attention on the November 2008 terrorist attacks in Mumbai. Some, Das contends, characterized this event as part of a pattern of revenge for anti-Muslim violence around the country. According to this narrative, the terrorists are exacting vengeance for the country's failure to provide justice. Das writes, "This is a comforting narrative that would somehow domesticate the violence within well-recognized categories of rights, justice, revenge, but it is difficult to know how the motives of the terrorists were discerned since there was little communication from any known militant or terrorist outfit claiming any responsibility for the attacks." She argues, "It seems necessary therefore to pause, to hesitate before reading motives, or even to fix this event into stories that rely on a framework of causes and consequences. Let us, instead, pay close attention to the kind of spectacle that violence created and the affects that circulated around the event."

Das, like Atwell, calls our attention to the way that spectacle plays out in the mass media. For her the media create one of the important conditions for contemporary performances of violence. Thus Das examines the coverage of the Mumbai attacks by India TV, which broadcast a conversation between the police and two of the attackers. Many who listened to the conversation simply did not believe that the dialogue was anything other than simulated and delivered with "the burning hotels as the mis-en-scene." While rhetorical excess and melodramatic special effects "were the order of the day in media reports and discussions, generating a deep skepticism about what was being observed, there were real effects of the attacks in both [India and Pakistan]. India passed antiterrorism legislation, the threat of nuclear war between India and Pakistan heightened, both countries began to rely more heavily on their armies."

Das asks "how we might understand the relation between aesthetic and political representation considering the modality through which the real was portrayed." To answer this question, she looks at Stanley Cavell's work on expressed and tacit political consent. Das writes, "Simply because you are a Muslim, your tacit consent in acts of terrorism is taken for granted. How one expresses one's distance, or gives a different rendering of the simultaneous sense of having been unjustly treated within the Indian polity and yet feeling distant from those who assume to represent your grievances through acts of violence, is the key issue to many Muslims." Some Muslims do so by staying quiet, afraid their words will be used against them. In the context of terrorism, a "performance of non-consent had to be repeated and public in order for Muslims in India to signal their distance from the acts of the killers."

Das concludes by predicting, "The sense of 'irreality' I noted in the creation of media representations and especially the sense that the internal states and their expressions had become unhinged from each other, continue to hold the possibility that Muslims will have to perform their allegiance to India in more strident terms even as the grief of a community that does not recognize itself in what is propagated in its name finds little expression." For Das, performances of violence, like the terror attacks in Mumbai, put the status of particular subjects into question, raising the issue of their very belonging to a national community, forcing them to prove allegiances in a public way, matching the intensity of the performance of violence with an equally intense performance of loyalty.

Performances of Violence concludes with Paul Steege's exploration of perceptions of and responses to violent "incidents" on the sector borders in Berlin from 1948 until the 1980s. His title, "Ordinary Violence on an Extraordinary Stage: Incidents on the Sector Border in Postwar Berlin" derives from the language of daily events reports which the municipal police submitted to the mayor's office in West Berlin in early 1949. Nearly every report included discussion of an "incident on the sector border," which served to enact physically the political divide between East and West Berlin, within the everyday practices of border-crossing. In these reports of vehicle assaults, physical attacks on policemen, shootings, and street-corner brawling, Steege contends, the "ordinary" work of surviving in an economy of scarcity (especially but not only black marketeering) is increasingly staged within the rhetorical and physical rituals of an emerging Cold War.

Of course, even after the construction of the Berlin wall, incidents on the border continued, if at times with new variations. By examining the period before and after the construction of the Berlin wall in August 1961, this essay blurs the lines between the explicit acts of extraordinary violence associated with the wall (e.g., state-sponsored shootings) and "ordinary" acts of violence on and around the sector borders in the period before the wall fractured Berlin's urban geography.

Building on Walter Benjamin's distinction between experience (*Erfahrung*) and lived-through time (*Erlebnis*), Steege again draws attention to the connection between the public life of violence and the constitution of the self. He argues that we need to recognize the continuities of practice within the acts of violence on Berlin's sector borders before and after the construction of the wall. The performance of "extraordinary" acts of violence on the wall, which ostensibly sealed the border with concrete, depended on meanings articulated by those contesting its crossing in the years before. The people, Steege argues, who crossed the sector border after the wall was built—licitly and illicitly—confronted the "normalcy" of the (potential) violence it marked and joined in a complicated performance that asserted the wall's total control, even as their very practices undermined those claims.

Taken together, the work collected in this book explores the contingencies of violent performances. Here media representations and the scene of everyday life play key roles. Through performances of violence identities are fashioned, subjectivity constituted, agency affirmed or denied. Our book illuminates historical continuities as well as breaks in the way performances of violence are understood by some as life-affirming even as they mark the physical end of life. Membership and belonging are sometimes put into question and at other times affirmed in and through performances of violence. Finally, political power and its meanings permeate those performances. The work collected here helps to open a space where acts of violence can be connected to their performative dimensions and where practices of representation can be interrogated for what they call forth in the way violence is performed and in the way those performances are received and understood.

NOTES

1. 1. Sigmund Freud, *Totem and Taboo*, Authorized translation with an introduction by A. A. Brill (New York: Random House, 1946).

2. See especially Carl Schmitt, *Political Theology*, trans. George Schwab, foreword by Tracy Strong (Chicago: University of Chicago Press, 2005), and Giorgio Agamben, *Homo Sacer*, trans. Daniel Heller-Roazen (Stanford: Stanford University Press, 1998).

3. Devi Chand, *The Yajurveda*, Sanskrit text with English translation, 3rd thoroughly revised and enlarged edition (New York: AMS Press, 1980).

4. Tzvetan Todorov, *The Conquest of America*, trans. Richard Howard (New York: Harper and Row, 1984).

5. Carl von Clausewitz, *On War*, introduction by Anatol Rapoport (Baltimore: Penguin Books, 1968).

6. J. L. Austin, *How to Do Things with Words* (Cambridge: Harvard University Press, 1962).

7. See Stanley Cavell, "Passionate and Performative Utterances," in *Philosophy the Day after Tomorrow* (Cambridge: Harvard University Press, 2003).

8. See Mari Musata et al., *Words That Wound: Critical Race Theory, Assaultive Speech, and the First Amendment* (Boulder, Colo.: Westview Press, 1993).

9. Etymologies are from the *Oxford English Dictionary* (OED) (Oxford: Oxford University Press, 2001 edition). The Emerson quotation is from "Experience," in Essays: Second Series, in Joel Porte, ed., *Selected Writings of Ralph Waldo Emerson* (New York: Library of America, 1988).

10. Weber, "Politics as a Vocation," in *From Max Weber: Essays in Sociology*, ed. Hans Gerth and C. Wright Mills (New York: Oxford University Press, 1958).

11. Hannah Arendt, *On Revolution* (New York: Viking Press, 1963).

12. Michel Foucault, *The History of Sexuality: Volume 1, The Will to Know*, trans. Richard Howard (New York: Pantheon, 1976), 184.

13. For a trenchant study of contemporary terrorism, see Talal Asad, *On Suicide Bombing* (New York: Columbia University Press, 2007).

14. For a fascinating review of the history of the baby bottle, visit the website for the Baby Bottle Museum of London, England, www.babybottle-museum.co.uk/.

15. See Russell Mokhiber, "Infant Formula: Hawking Disaster in the Third World," *Multinational Monitor* 8, no. 4 (April 1987), special issue, "Corporate Crime and Violence." multinationalmonitor.org/hyper/issues/1987/04/formula.html.

16. Antonio Gramsci, *Prison Notebooks*, trans. Joseph Buttgieg (New York: Columbia University Press, 1992).

17. See George Herbert, "American Slaughter," *New York Times*, April 17, 2009, A19.

18. The theatrical nature of the violence at Abu Ghraib resembles what is recorded on the postcards of lynching in the American South, which included hundreds of spectators smiling for the camera, posing with burned, mutilated bodies, knowing these images would be circulated. See James H. Madison, *A Lynching in the Heartland: Race and Memory in America* (New York: Palgrave Macmillan, 2001).

1

Easy to Be Hard
Conservatism and Violence

COREY ROBIN

> I enjoy wars. Any adventure's better than sitting in an office.
> —HAROLD MACMILLAN

Despite the support among self-identified conservative voters and politicians for the death penalty, torture, and war, intellectuals on the right often deny any affinity between conservatism and violence. "Conservatives," writes Andrew Sullivan, "hate war."

> Their domestic politics is rooted in a loathing of civil wars and violence, and they know that freedom is always the first casualty of international warfare. When countries go to war, their governments invariably get bigger and stronger, individual liberties are whittled away, and societies which once enjoyed the pluralist cacophony of freedom have to be marshaled into a single, collective note to face down an external foe. A state of permanent warfare—as George Orwell saw—is a virtual invitation to domestic tyranny.[1]

Channeling a tradition of skepticism from Oakeshott to Hume, the conservative identifies limited government as the extent of his faith, the rule of law his one requirement for the pursuit of happiness. Pragmatic and adaptive, disposed rather than committed, such a sensibility—and it is a sensibility, the conservative insists, not an ideology—is not interested in violence. His endorsements of war, such as they are, are the weariest of concessions to reality. Unlike his friends on the left—conservative that he is, he values friendship more than agreement—he knows that we live and love in the midst of great evil. That evil must be resisted, sometimes by violent means. All things being equal, he would like to see a world without violence. But all things are not equal, and he is not in the business of seeing the world as he'd like it to be.

The historical record of conservatism—not only as a political practice, which is not my primary concern here, but as a theoretical tradition—suggests otherwise. Far from being saddened, burdened, or vexed by violence, the conservative has been enlivened by it. I don't mean that in a personal sense, though it's true that many a conservative, like Harold Macmillan quoted above or Winston Churchill quoted below, has expressed an unanticipated enthusiasm for violence. My concern is ideas and argument rather than character or psychology. Violence, the conservative intellectual has maintained, is one of the experiences in life that makes us most feel alive, and violence, particularly warfare, is an activity that makes life, well, lively.[2] Such arguments can be made nimbly—as in the case of Santayana, General MacArthur, and the Imperial War Museum[3]—or laboriously, as in the case of Treitschke:

> To the historian who lives in the world of will it is immediately clear that the demand for a perpetual peace is thoroughly reactionary; he sees that with war all movement, all growth, must be struck out of history. It has always been the tired, unintelligent, and enervated periods that have played with the dream of perpetual peace . . . However, it is not worth the trouble to discuss this matter further; the living God will see to it that war constantly returns as a dreadful medicine for the human race.[4]

Pithy or prolix, the case boils down to this: war is life, peace is death.

In this essay, I analyze the source of that belief in Edmund Burke's *A Philosophical Enquiry into the Origin of Our Ideas of the Sublime and the Beautiful*. There Burke develops a view of the self desperately in need of negative stimuli of the sort provided by pain and danger, which Burke associates with the sublime. The sublime is most readily found in two political forms: hierarchy and violence. But for reasons that shall become clear, the conservative—again, consistent with Burke's arguments—often favors the latter over the former. Rule may be sublime, but violence is more sublime. Most sublime of all is when the two are fused, when violence is performed for the sake of creating, defending, or recovering a regime of domination and rule. But as Burke warned, it's always best to enjoy pain and danger at a remove. Distance and obscurity enhance sublimity; nearness and illumination diminish it. Counterrevolutionary violence may be the Everest of conservative experience, but one should view it from afar. Get too close to the mountaintop, and the air becomes thin, the view only fair. At the end of every discourse on violence, then, lies a waiting disappointment.

The Moral Psychology of the Conservative

The Sublime and the Beautiful begins on a high note, with a discussion of curiosity, which Burke identifies as "the first and simplest emotion." The curious race "from place to place to hunt out something new." Their sights are fixed, their attention is rapt. Then the world turns gray. They begin to stumble across the same things, "with less and less of any agreeable effect." Novelty diminishes: how much, really, is there new in the world? Curiosity "exhausts" itself. Enthusiasm and engagement give way to "loathing and weariness."[5] Burke moves on to pleasure and pain, which are supposed to transform the quest for novelty into experiences more sustaining and profound. But rather than being a genuine additive to curiosity, pleasure offers more of the same: a moment's enthusiasm, followed by dull malaise. "When it has run its career," Burke says, pleasure "sets us down very nearly where it found us." Any kind of pleasure "quickly satisfies; and when it is over, we relapse into indifference."[6] Quieter enjoyments, less intense than pleasure, are equally soporific. They generate complacency; we "give ourselves over to indolence and inaction."[7] Burke turns to imitation as another potential force of outward propulsion. Through imitation, we learn manners and mores, develop opinions, and are civilized. We bring ourselves to the world, and the world is brought to us. But imitation contains its own narcotic. Imitate others too much and we cease to better ourselves. We follow the person in front of us "and so on in an eternal circle." In a population of imitators, "there never could be any improvement." Such "men must remain as brutes do, the same at the end that they are at this day, and that they were in the beginning of the world."[8]

Curiosity leads to weariness, pleasure to indifference, enjoyment to torpor, and imitation to stagnation. So many doors of the psyche open onto this space of inertial gloom we might conclude that it lurks not at the edge but at the center of the human condition. Here, in this dark courtyard of the self, all action ceases, creating an ideal environment for "melancholy, dejection, despair, and self-murder."[9] Even love, the most outward of raptures, carries the self back to a state of internal dissolution.[10] Suicide, it seems, is the inevitable fate awaiting anyone who takes pleasure in the world as it is.

For the conservative theorist, passages like these pose something of a challenge. Here is the inventor of the conservative tradition articulating a vision of the self dramatically at odds with the self of conservative thought. The conservative self, as he has come to be known, prefers "the familiar to the unknown . . . the tried to the untried, fact to mystery, the actual to the possible, the limited to the unbounded, the near to the distant, the sufficient to the superabundant, the convenient to the perfect, present laughter to utopian bliss."[11] He is partial to things as they are not because he thinks they are just or good but because they are familiar. He knows them and is attached to them. He wishes neither to lose them nor to have them taken away. Enjoying what he has, rather than acquiring something better, is his highest good. But should the self of *The Sublime and the Beautiful* be assured of his attachments and familiars, he'd quickly find himself confronting the specter of his own extinction, more than likely at his own hand.

Perhaps it is this lethal ennui, lurking just beneath the surface of conservative discourse, that explains the failure of the conservative politician to follow the lead of the conservative theorist. Far from embracing the cause of quiet enjoyments and secure attachments, the conservative politician has consistently opted for an activism of the not-yet and the will-be. Ronald Reagan's First Inaugural Address was a paean to the power of dreams: not small dreams but big, heroic dreams, of progress and betterment, and not dreams for their own sake but dreams as a necessary and vital prod to action. Three months later, in an address before Congress, Reagan drove the point home with a quote from Carl Sandburg: "Nothing happens unless first a dream." And nothing happening—or too few things happening or things not happening quickly enough—is what the conservative in politics dislikes. Reagan could scarcely contain his impatience with the dithering and temporizing of politicians: "The old and comfortable way is to shave a little here and add a little there. Well, that's not acceptable anymore." Old and comfortable was the indictment, no "half-measures" the verdict.[12]

Reagan was hardly the first conservative to act for the sake of the invisible and the ideal as against the material and the real. In his acceptance speech to the 1964 Republican National Convention, Barry Goldwater could find no more potent charge to level at the welfare state than that it had made a great "nation becalmed." Thanks to the New Deal, the United States had lost its "brisk pace" and was now "plodding along." Calm, slow, and plodding are usually welcomed by the conservative theorist as signs of present bliss. But to the conservative politician, they are evils. He must declare war against them, rallying his armies against the listless and the languid with talk of "causes," "struggle," "enthusiasm," and "devotion."[13]

That crusading zeal is hardly peculiar to American conservatism. It is found in Europe as well, even in England, the land that made moderation the moniker of conservatism. "Whoever won a battle," scoffed Margaret Thatcher, "under the banner 'I stand for Consensus'?"[14] And then there is Winston Churchill, traveling to Cuba in 1895 to report on the Spanish war against Cuban independence.[15] Ruminating on the disappointments of his generation—latecomers to the Empire, they were deprived of the opportunity for imperial conquest (as opposed to administration)—he arrives in Havana. This is what he has to say (looking back on the experience in 1930):

> The minds of this generation, exhausted, brutalized, mutilated and bored by War, may not understand the delicious yet tremulous sensations with which a young British Officer bred in the long peace approached for the first time an actual theatre of operations. When first in the dim light of early morning I saw the shores of Cuba rise and define themselves from dark-blue horizons, I felt as if I sailed with Long John Silver and first gazed on Treasure Island. Here was a place where real things were going on. Here was a scene of vital action. Here was a place where anything might happen. Here was a place where something would certainly happen. Here I might leave my bones. These musings were dispersed by the advance of breakfast . . . [16]

Whatever the relationship between theory and practice in the conservative tradition, it is clear from *The Sublime and the Beautiful* that if the self is to survive and flourish it must be aroused by an experience more vital and bracing than pleasure or enjoyment. Pleasure and enjoyment act like beauty, "relaxing the solids of the whole system."[17] That system, however, must be made taut and tense. The mind must be quickened, the body exerted. Otherwise, the system will soften and atrophy, and ultimately die.

What most arouses this heightened state of being is the confrontation with non-being. Life and health are pleasurable and enjoyable, and that is what is wrong with them: "they make no such impression" on the self because "we were not made to acquiesce in life and health." Pain and danger, by contrast, are "emissaries" of death, the "king of terrors." They are sources of the sublime, which is "the strongest"—most powerful, most affecting—"emotion which the mind is capable of feeling."[18] Pain and danger, in other words, are generating and generative experiences of the self.

Pain and danger are generative and generating because they have the contradictory effect of minimizing and maximizing our sense of self. When sensing pain or danger,[19] our mind "is so entirely filled with its object, that it cannot entertain any other." The "motions" of our soul "are suspended," as harm and the ideas it arouses "rush in upon the mind."

In the face of these ideas, "the mind is hurried out of itself." While we experience the sublime, we feel ourselves evacuated, overwhelmed by an external object of tremendous power and threat. Everything that gave us a sense of internal being and vitality, of being alive, ceases to exist. The external is all, we are nothing. God is a good example, and the ultimate expression, of the sublime: "Whilst we contemplate so vast an object, under the arm, as it were, of almighty power, and invested upon every side with omnipresence, we shrink into the minuteness of our own nature, and are, in a manner, annihilated before him."[20]

Paradoxically, we also feel our existence to an extent we never have felt it before. Seized by terror, our "attention" is roused and our "faculties" are "driven forward, as it were, on their guard." We are pulled out of ourselves. We are cognizant of the immediate terrain and our presence upon it. Before, we barely noticed ourselves or our surroundings. Now we spill out of ourselves, inhabiting not only our bodies and minds but the space around us. We feel "a sort of swelling"—a sense that we are greater, our perimeter extends further—that "is extremely grateful to the human mind." But this "swelling," Burke is quick to remind us, "is never more perceived, nor operates with more force, than when without danger we are conversant with terrible objects."[21]

In the face of the sublime, the self is annihilated, occupied, crushed, and overwhelmed. In the face of the sublime, the self is heightened, aggrandized, and magnified. Whether it is possible to occupy such opposing, almost irreconcilable, poles of experience at the same time, it is precisely that contradiction, the oscillation between wild extremes, that generates a strong and strenuous sense of self. As Burke writes elsewhere, intense light resembles intense darkness not only because it blinds the eye and thus approximates darkness but also because both are extremes. And extremes, particularly opposing extremes, are sublime because sublimity "in all things abhors mediocrity."[22] It is the extremity of opposing sensations, the savage swing from being to nothingness, that makes for the most intense experience of selfhood.

The question for us, which Burke neither poses nor answers, is: what kind of political form entails this simultaneity of—or oscillation between—self-aggrandizement and self-annihilation? One possibility is hierarchy, with its twin requirements of submission and domination; the other is violence, particularly warfare, with its rigid injunction to kill or be killed. Perhaps not coincidentally, both are of great significance to conservatism as a theoretical tradition and historical practice.

The Limits of Rule

Rousseau and John Adams are not usually thought of as ideological bed-fellows, but on one point they were agreed: social hierarchies persist because they ensure that everyone, save those at the very bottom and very top, enjoys the opportunity to rule and be ruled in turn. Not, to be sure, in the Aristotelian sense of self-government, but in the feudal sense of reciprocal governance: each person dominates someone below him in exchange for submitting to someone above him. "Citizens only allow themselves to be oppressed to the degree that they are carried away by blind ambition," writes Rousseau. "Since they pay more attention to what is below them than to what is above, domination becomes dearer to them than independence, and they consent to wear chains so that they may in turn give them to others. It is very difficult to reduce to obedience anyone who does not seek to command."[23] The aspirant and the authoritarian are not opposing types: the will to rise precedes the will to bow. More than thirty years later, Adams would write that every man longs "to be observed, considered, esteemed, praised, beloved, and admired."[24] To be praised, one must be seen, and the best way to be seen is to elevate oneself above one's circle. Even the American democrat, Adams reasoned, would rather rule over an inferior than dispossess a superior. His passion is for supremacy, not equality, and so long as he is assured an audience of lessers, he will be content with his lowly status:

> Not only the poorest mechanic, but the man who lives upon common charity, nay the common beggars in the streets . . . court a set of admirers, and plume themselves on that superiority which they have, or fancy they have, over some others. . . . When a wretch could no longer attract the notice of a man, woman or child, he must be respectable in the eyes of his dog. "Who will love me then?" was the pathetic reply of one, who starved himself to feed his mastiff, to a charitable passenger who advised him to kill or sell the animal.[25]

One can see in these descriptions of social hierarchy lineaments of the sublime: annihilated from above, aggrandized from below, the self is magnified and miniaturized by its involvement in the practice of rule. But here's the catch: once we actually are assured of our power over another being, says Burke, it loses its capacity to harm or threaten us. It loses its sublimity. "Strip" a creature "of its ability to hurt," and "you spoil it of every thing sublime."[26] Lions, tigers, panthers, and rhinoceroses are sublime not because they are magnificent specimens of strength but because they can and will kill us. Oxen, horses, and dogs are also strong but lack the instinct to kill or have had that instinct suppressed. They can be made to serve us and in the case of dogs even love us. Because such creatures, however strong, cannot threaten or harm us, they are incapable of sublimity. They are objects of contempt, contempt being "the attendant on a strength that is subservient and innoxious."[27]

> We have continually about us animals of a strength that is considerable, but not pernicious. Amongst these we never look for the sublime: it comes upon us in the gloomy forest, and in the howling wilderness. . . . Whenever strength is only useful, and employed for our benefit or our pleasure, then it is never sublime; for nothing can act agreeably to us, that does not act in conformity to our will; but to act agreeably to our will, it must be subject to us; and therefore can never be the cause of a grand and commanding conception.[28]

At least one-half, then, of the experience of social hierarchy—not the experience of being ruled, which carries the possibility of being destroyed, humiliated, threatened, or harmed by one's superior, but the experience of ruling another—is incompatible with, and indeed weakens, the sublime. Confirmed of our power, we are lulled into the same ease and comfort, undergo the same inward melting, we experience while in the throes of pleasure. The assurance of rule is as debilitating as the passion of love.

Burke's intimations about the perils of long-established rule reflect a surprising strain within conservatism: a persistent, if unacknowledged, discomfort with power that has ripened and matured, authority that has grown comfortable and secure. Beginning with Burke himself, conservatives have expressed a deep unease about ruling classes so assured of their place in the sun that they lose their capacity to rule: their will to power dissipates; the muscles and intelligence of their command attenuate.

In his *Reflections on the Revolution in France*, Burke famously describes Marie Antoinette as a "delightful vision . . . glittering like the morning star, full of life, and splendor, and joy." He takes her beauty as a symbol of the loveliness of the Old Regime, where feudal manners and mores "made power gentle" and "by a bland assimilation, incorporated into politics the sentiments which beautify and soften private society."[29] Ever since he wrote those lines, Burke has been mocked for his sentimentality. But readers of *The Sublime and the Beautiful* know that beauty for Burke is never a sign of power's vitality; it is always a sign of its decadence and decline. And, indeed, as Burke goes onto note in the *Reflections*, one of France's problems over the last several decades has been the beauty of the

Old Regime and the sublimity of the Revolution. The landed interest, the cornerstone of the Old Regime, is "sluggish, inert, and timid." It cannot defend itself "from the invasions of ability," with ability standing in for the new men of power that the Revolution brings forth. The monied interest, also allied with the Revolution, is stronger than the landed interest because it is "more ready for any adventure" and "more disposed to new enterprises of any kind."[30] The Old Regime is beautiful, static, and weak; the Revolution is ugly, dynamic, and strong. "It is a dreadful truth," Burke admits in the second of his *Letters on a Regicide Peace*, "but it is a truth that cannot be concealed; in ability, in dexterity, in the distinctness of their views, the Jacobins are our superiors."[31]

Joseph de Maistre was less tactful than Burke in his condemnations of the Old Regime—perhaps because he took its failings more personally. Long before the Revolution, he claims, the leadership of the Old Regime had been confused and bewildered. Naturally, it was unable to comprehend, much less resist, the onslaught unleashed against it. Impotence, physical and cognitive, was—and remains—its great sin. The aristocracy cannot understand; it cannot act. Some portion of the nobility may be well meaning, but it cannot see its projects through. It is foppish and foolish. It has virtue but not *virtú*. It "fails ridiculously in everything it undertakes." The clergy has been corrupted by wealth and luxury. The monarchy consistently has shown that it lacks the will "to punish" that is the hallmark of every real sovereign.[32] Faced with such decadence, the inevitable outgrowth of decades in power, Maistre concludes that it is a good thing that the counterrevolution has not yet triumphed (he is writing in 1797); the Old Regime needs several more years in the wilderness if it is to shed the corrupting influences of its once beautiful life:

> The restoration of the throne would mean a sudden relaxation of the driving force of the state. The black magic working at the moment would disappear like mist before the sun. Kindness, clemency, justice, all the gentle and peaceful virtues, would suddenly reappear and would bring with them a general meekness of character, a certain cheerfulness entirely opposed to the rigours of the revolutionary regime.[33]

A century later, a similar case will be made by Georges Sorel against the *belle époque*. Sorel is not usually seen as an emblematic figure of the right—then again, even Burke's conservatism remains a subject of dispute[34]—and, indeed, his greatest work, *Reflections on Violence*, is often thought of as a contribution, albeit minor, to the Marxist tradition. Yet, Sorel's beginnings were conservative and his endings proto-fascist, and even in his Marxist phase, his primary worry is decadence and vitality rather than exploitation and justice. The criticisms he lodges against the French ruling classes at the end of the nineteenth century are not dissimilar to those made by Burke and Maistre at the end of the eighteenth. He even makes the comparison explicit: the French bourgeoisie, Sorel writes, "has become almost as stupid as the nobility of the eighteenth century." They are "an ultra-civilized aristocracy that demands to be left in peace." Once, the bourgeoisie was a race of warriors. "Bold captains," they were "creators of new industries" and "discovers of unknown lands." They "directed gigantic enterprises," inspired by that "conquering, insatiable and pitiless spirit" that laid railroads, subdued continents, and made a world economy. Today, they are timid and cowardly, refusing to take the most elemental steps to defend their own interests against unions, socialists, and the left. Rather than unleash violence against striking workers, they surrender to the workers' threat of violence. They lack the ardor, the fire in the belly, of their ancestors. It is difficult not to conclude that "the bourgeoisie is condemned to death and that its disappearance is only a matter of time."[35]

Carl Schmitt formalized Sorel's contempt of the weaknesses of the ruling classes into an entire theory of politics. According to Schmitt, the bourgeois was as he was—risk-averse, selfish, uninterested in bravery or violent death, desirous of peace and security—because capitalism was his calling and liberalism his niche. Neither provided him with a good reason for dying for the state. In fact, both gave him good reasons, indeed an entire vocabulary, not to die for the state. Interest, freedom, profit, rights, property, individualism, and other such words had created one of the most autistic ruling classes in history, a class that enjoyed privilege but believed that it did not have to defend that privilege. After all, the premise of liberal democracy was that economics and culture were separate from politics: one could pursue profit, at someone else's expense, and think freely, no matter how subversively, without disrupting the balance of power. It just so happened, however, that the bourgeoisie was confronting an enemy that very much understood the connections between ideas, money, and power, that economic arrangements and intellectual arguments were the stuff of political combat. Marxists got the friend-enemy distinction, which is constitutive of politics; the bourgeoisie did not.[36] The spirit of Hegel used to reside in Berlin; it has long since "wandered to Moscow."[37]

Sorel identified one exception to this rule of capitalist decadence: the robber barons of the United States. In the Carnegies and the Goulds of

American industry, Sorel thought he saw "the indomitable energy, the audacity based on an accurate appreciation of strength, the cold calculation of interests, which are the qualities of great generals and great capitalists." Unlike the pampered bourgeoisie of France and Britain, the millionaires of Pittsburgh and Pittston "lead to the end of their lives a galley-slave existence without ever thinking of leading a nobleman's life, as the Rothschilds do."[38]

Sorel's spiritual counterpart across the Atlantic was not so sanguine about American industrialists and financiers. (Burkean anxiety about the ruling classes, it turns out, is common to the European and American conservative.) The capitalist, Teddy Roosevelt declared, sees his country as a "till," always weighing the "the honor of the nation and the glory of the flag" against a "temporary interruption of money-making." He is not "'willing to lay down his life for little things'" like the defense of the nation. He cares "only whether shares rise or fall in value."[39] He shows no interest in great affairs of state, domestic or international, unless they impinge upon his own. It was no accident, Roosevelt claimed, perhaps with a nod to Carnegie, that such men opposed the great expedition that was the Spanish-American War.[40] Complacent and comfortable, assured of their riches by the success of the labor wars of previous decades and the election of 1896, these simply are not men who can be counted upon to defend the nation or even themselves. "We may some day have bitter cause," Roosevelt declared, "to realize that a rich nation which is slothful, timid, or unwieldy is an easy prey" for other, more martial peoples. The danger facing a ruling class—and nation—that has grown "skilled in commerce and finance" is that it "loses the hard fighting virtues."[41]

Roosevelt was hardly the first—or last—American conservative to worry about ruling classes gone soft and hierarchies over-ripe with power. Throughout the 1830s, as the abolitionists began pressing their cause, John C. Calhoun drove himself into a rage over the easy living and willed cluelessness of his comrades on the plantation. They had grown lazy, fat, and complacent, so roundly enjoying the privileges of their position that they could not see the coming catastrophe. Or, if they could, they couldn't do anything to fend it off, their political and ideological muscles having atrophied long ago. Calhoun's fury reached a peak in 1837, when in a speech on the Senate floor, he urged Congress not to receive an abolitionist petition. "All we want is concert," he pleaded with his fellow southerners, to "unite with zeal and energy in repelling approaching dangers." But, he went on, "I dare not hope that any thing I can say will arouse the South to a due sense of danger. I fear it is beyond the power of the mortal voice

to awaken it [the master class] in time from the fatal security into which
it has fallen."[42]

Published more than a century later, the very first paragraph of Barry
Goldwater's *The Conscience of a Conservative* directs its fire not at liberals
or Democrats or even the welfare state; it is aimed at the moral timidity of
what would come to be called the Republican Establishment.

> I have been much concerned that so many people today with Conservative in-
> stincts feel compelled to apologize for them. Or if not to apologize directly, to
> qualify their commitment in a way that amounts to breast-beating. "Repub-
> lican candidates," Vice President Nixon has said, "should be economic con-
> servatives, but conservatives with a heart." President Eisenhower announced
> during his first term, "I am conservative when it comes to economic prob-
> lems but liberal when it comes to human problems." . . . These formulations
> are tantamount to an admission that Conservatism is a narrow, mechanistic
> *economic* theory that may work very well as a bookkeeper's guide, but cannot
> be relied upon as a comprehensive political philosophy.[43]

And throughout the 1990s—to jump ahead by another three decades—
one could hear Roosevelt's heirs on the right direct his venom about the
American capitalist at the masters of the universe on Wall Street and
geeky entrepreneurs of Silicon Valley.[44]

If the ruling class is to be vigorous and robust, the conservative has
concluded, it must be tested, exercised, and challenged. Not just their
bodies, but their minds, even souls. Not unlike Milton—"I cannot praise
a fugitive and cloistered virtue, unexercised and unbreathed, that never
sallies out and sees her adversary, but slinks out of the race where that im-
mortal garland is to be run for, not without dust and heat. Assuredly we
bring not innocence into the world, we bring impurity and much rather:
that which purifies us is trial, and trial is by what is contrary"[45]—Burke
believes that adversity and difficulty, the confrontation with affliction and
suffering, make for stronger, more virtuous beings.

> The great virtues turn principally on dangers, punishments, and troubles,
> and are exercised rather in preventing mischiefs, than in dispensing fa-
> vours; and are therefore not lovely, though highly venerable. The subordi-
> nate turn on reliefs, gratifications, and indulgences; and are therefore more
> lovely, though inferior in dignity. Those persons who creep into the hearts of
> most people, who are chosen as the companions of their softer hours, and
> their reliefs from care and anxiety, are never persons of shining qualities,
> nor strong virtues.[46]

(Perhaps we see here the origins of the conservative preference for the
warfare over the welfare state, but that is another topic for another day.)
But where Milton and other like-minded republicans believe that impurity

and corruption await the complacent and the comfortable, Burke espies the more terrifying specter of dissipation, degeneration, and death. If the powerful are to remain powerful—if they are to remain alive at all—their power, indeed the credibility of their own existence, must be continuously challenged, threatened, and defended.

The Virtues of Violence

One of the more arresting—though I hope by now intelligible—features of conservative discourse is the fascination, indeed appreciation, one finds there for the conservative's enemies, particularly their use of violence against him and his allies. Maistre's most rapturous comments in his *Considerations on France* are reserved for the Jacobins, whose brutal will and penchant for violence—their "black magic"—he plainly envies. Thanks to their efforts, France has been purified and restored to its rightful pride of place among the family of nations. "The revolutionary government hardened the soul of France by tempering it in blood." They have rallied the people against foreign invaders, a "prodigy" that "only the infernal genius of Robespierre could accomplish." Unlike the monarchy, the Revolution has the will to punish. Had the Old Regime been prematurely returned to power, Maistre wonders, "would the sacred sword of justice have fallen relentlessly like Robespierre's guillotine?" And through the miracle of the Terror, the Revolution has forged the very sword upon which it finally impales itself.[47]

From the perspective of the Burkean sublime, however, Maistre's argument only goes so far. The Revolution rejuvenates the Old Regime by forcing it from power and purifying the people through violence. It delivers a clarifying shock to the system. But Maistre never contemplates, or at least discusses, the revivifying effect that wresting power back from the Revolution might have on the leaders of the Old Regime. And indeed, once he gets around to describing how he thinks the counterrevolution will occur, it turns out to be a stunningly anticlimactic affair, with scarcely a shot fired at all. "How Will the Counter-Revolution Happen if it Comes?" Maistre asks. "Four or five persons, perhaps, will give France a king." Not exactly the stuff of a virile, transformed ruling class, battling its way back to power.[48]

Maistre may never have contemplated the restorative possibilities of hand-to-hand combat between the Old Regime and the Revolution, but Sorel does. And while his allegiances in the war between the rulers and the ruled of the late nineteenth century are more ambiguous than Maistre's,

his account of the effect of the latter's violence upon the former is decid-
edly not. The French bourgeoisie has lost its fighting spirit, Sorel claims,
but that spirit is alive and well among the workers. Their battlefield is the
workplace, their weapon is the general strike, and their aim is the over-
throw of the state. It is the last that most impresses Sorel, for it signals
just how unconcerned the workers are about "the material profits of conquest." Not only do they not seek higher wages and other improvements
in their well-being; they have set their sights on the most improbable of
goals: overthrowing the state by a general strike. It is that improbability,
the distance between their means and ends, that makes proletarian violence so glorious. They are like Homeric warriors, absorbed in the gran-
deur of the battle and ultimately indifferent to the aims of the war: who
really has ever overthrown a state by a general strike? Theirs is a violence
for its own sake, without much concern for costs, benefits, and the calcu-
lations in between.[49] As Ernst Jünger put it a generation later, it "is not
what we fight for but how we fight."[50]

But what grips Sorel is not the proletariat but the rejuvenating effects
it might have on the bourgeoisie. Can the violence of the general strike
"give back to the bourgeoisie an ardour which is extinguished?" Certainly
it might reawaken the bourgeoisie to its own interests and the threats its
withdrawal from politics has posed to those interests. More tantalizing to
Sorel, however, is the possibility that worker violence will "restore to [the
bourgeoisie] the warlike qualities it formerly possessed," forcing the "capitalist class to remain ardent in the industrial struggle." Through the struggle against the proletariat, in other words, the bourgeoisie may recover its
ferocity and ardor. And ardor is everything. From ardor alone—from that
splendid indifference to reason and self-interest—an entire civilization,
drowning in materialism and complacency, will be reawakened. A ruling
class, threatened by violence from the ruled, roused to its own taste and
talent for violence: that is the promise of the civil war in France.[51]

For the conservative, no matter how modulated or moderate, that has
always been the promise of civil war, in France and elsewhere. For between
the easy cases of a Catholic reactionary like Maistre and a proto-fascist like
Sorel stands the more difficult but ultimately more revealing example of
Tocqueville. His drift from the moderation of the July Monarchy to the
revanchism of the 1848 counterrevolution demonstrates how easily and
inexorably the Burkean conservative will swing from the beautiful to the
sublime, how easily and inexorably the music of prudence and moderation gives way to the march of violence and vitriol.[52]

Publicly presenting himself as the consummate realist, discriminating and judicious with little patience for enthusiasm of any sort, Tocqueville was anything but. A closet Werther, he confessed to his brother that he shared their father's "devouring impatience," his "need for lively and recurring sensations." Reason, he said, "has always been for me like a cage," behind which he would "gnash [his] teeth." He longed for "the sight of combat." Looking back on the French Revolution, which he missed (he was born in 1805), he lamented the end of the Terror, claiming that "men thus crushed can not only no longer attain great virtues, but they seem to have become almost incapable of great crimes." Even Napoleon, scourge of conservatives, moderates, and liberals everywhere, earned his admiration as the "most extraordinary being who has appeared in the world for many centuries." Who, by contrast, could find inspiration in the parliamentary politics of the July Monarchy, that "little democratic and bourgeois pot of soup"?

Yet once he set upon a career in politics, it was into that little bourgeois pot of soup that Tocqueville jumped. Predictably, it was not to his taste. Tocqueville may have mouthed the words of moderation, compromise, and the rule of law, but they did not move him. Without the threat of revolutionary violence, politics was simply not the grand drama he imagined it had been between 1789 and 1815. "Our fathers observed such extraordinary things that compared with them all of our works seem commonplace." The politics of moderation and compromise produced moderation and compromise; it did not produce politics, at least not as Tocqueville understood the term. During the 1830s and 1840s, "what was most wanting . . . was political life itself." There was "no battlefield for contending parties to meet upon." Politics had been "deprived" of "all originality, of all reality, and therefore of all genuine passions."

Then came 1848. Tocqueville didn't support the Revolution. Indeed, he was among its most vociferous opponents. He voted for the full suspension of civil liberties, which he happily announced was done "with even more energy than had been done under the Monarchy." He welcomed talk of a dictatorship—to protect the very regime he had spent the better part of two decades bemoaning. And he loved it all: the violence, the counterviolence, the battle. Defending moderation against radicalism, Tocqueville was given a chance to use radical means for moderate ends, and it's fairly clear which of the two most stirred him.

> Let me say, then, that when I came to search carefully into the depths of my own heart, I discovered, with some surprise, a certain sense of relief, a sort

of gladness mingled with all the griefs and fears to which the Revolution had given rise. I suffered from this terrible event for my country, but clearly not for myself; on the contrary, I seemed to breathe more freely than before the catastrophe. I had always felt myself stifled in the atmosphere of the parliamentary world which had just been destroyed: I had found it full of disappointments, both where others and where I myself was concerned.

A self-styled poet of the tentative, the subtle, and the complex, Tocqueville burned with illumination upon waking up to a world divided into two camps. Timid parliaments sowed a gray confusion; civil war forced upon the nation a bracing clarity of black and white. "There was no field left for uncertainty of mind: on this side lay the salvation of the country; on that, its destruction. . . . The road seemed dangerous, it is true, but my mind is so constructed that it is less afraid of danger than of doubt." For this member of the ruling class, sublimity welling up from the violence of the lower orders offered an opportunity to escape the stifling beauty of the higher orders.

The Waiting Disappointments

Francis Fukuyama is perhaps the most thoughtful of recent conservatives to have pursued this line of argument about violence. Unlike Maistre, however, or Tocqueville and Sorel—all of whom wrote in the midst of battle, when the outcome was unclear—Fukuyama writes, in 1992, from the vantage of victory. In the long civil war of the short twentieth century, the capitalist classes have won against their Marxist opponents. And it is not a pretty sight, at least not for Fukuyama. For the revolutionary was one of the few thymotic men of the twentieth century. Thymotic man is like Sorel's worker: he who risks his life for the sake of an improbable principle, who is unconcerned with his own material interests and cares only for his honor, glory, and the values for which he fights. After a strange but brief homage to the Bloods and the Crips as thymotic men, Fukuyama looks back fondly to men of purpose and power like Lenin, Trotsky, and Stalin, "striving for something purer and higher" and possessed of "greater than usual hardness, vision, ruthlessness, and intelligence." By virtue of their refusal to accommodate themselves to the reality of their times, they were the "most free and therefore the most human of beings." But somehow or other, these men and their successors lost the civil war of the twentieth century, almost inexplicably to the forces of "Economic Man." For Economic Man is "the true bourgeois." Such a man would never be "willing to walk in front of a tank or confront a line of soldiers" for any cause, even his own. Yet he is the victor, and far from rejuvenating him or restoring him to his primal powers, the war seems only to have secured him an early retirement on a comfortable pension. Conservative that he is, Fukuyama can only chafe at his triumph and "the life of rational consumption" that he has brought about, a life that is "in the end, *boring*."[53]

Far from being exceptional, Fukuyama's disappointment about the actual—as opposed to anticipated or fantasized—effect of violence on a dissipated ruling class is emblematic. "The aims of battle and the fruits of conquest are never the same," Forster observed in *A Passage to India*. "The latter have their value and only the saint rejects them, but their hint of immortality vanishes as soon as they are held in the hand."[54] Deep within the conservative discourse lurks an element of anticlimax that cannot be contained. While the conservative turns to violence as a way of liberating himself—or the ruling classes—from the deadening ennui and softening atrophy that comes with power, virtually every encounter in conservative discourse with actual violence entails disillusion and deflation.

Recall Teddy Roosevelt, brooding on the materialism and weakness of America's capitalist classes. Where, he wondered, could one find an example of the "strenuous life"—the thrill of difficulty and danger, the strife that made for progress—in contemporary America? Perhaps in the foreign wars and conquests America had undertaken at the end of the century. Yet even here, Roosevelt encountered frustration. Though his reports from the Spanish-American War were filled with bravery and bravado, a careful reading of his adventures in Cuba suggests that his exploits there were a fiasco. Each of the famous charges Roosevelt led up or down a hill was an anticlimax. The first culminated with him seeing just two Spanish soldiers shot by one of his men: "These were the only Spaniards I actually saw fall to aimed shots by any one of my men," he wrote, "with the exception of two guerillas in trees." The second found him leading an army that neither heard nor followed him. So it was with a certain amount of grim appreciation that he recited the dyspeptic comments of one of the army's leaders in Cuba, a certain General Wheeler, who "had been through too much heavy fighting in the Civil War to regard the present fight as very serious."[55]

In the bloody occupations that followed the Spanish-American War, however, Roosevelt thought he saw the true bliss it was in that dawn to be alive. Roosevelt was sure that America's occupation of the Philippines and elsewhere were as close to a replay of the Civil War, that noble crusade of unsullied virtue, as he and his countrymen were ever likely to see. "We of this generation do not have to face a task such as that our fathers faced," he declared in 1899, "and woe to us if we fail to perform them! . . . We cannot avoid the responsibilities that confront us in Hawaii, Cuba, Porto [sic] Rico, and the Philippines." Here—in the islands of the Caribbean and the Pacific—was the confluence of blood and purpose he had been searching for his entire life. The task of imperial uplift, of educating the natives in "the cause of civilization," was arduous and violent, imposing a mission upon America it would take years, God willing, to fulfill. If it succeeded—and even if it failed—it would create a genuine ruling class in America, hardened and made strenuous by battle, nobler and less grubby-minded than Carnegie's minions.[56]

It was a beautiful dream. But it too could not bear the weight of reality. Though Roosevelt hoped the men who ruled the Philippines would be "chosen for signal capacity and integrity," running "the provinces on behalf of the entire nation from which they come, and for the sake of the entire people to which they go," he worried that America's colonial occupiers would come from the same class of selfish financiers and industrialists that had driven Roosevelt abroad in the first place. And so his paeans to imperialism ended on a sour note, of warning, even doom. "If we permit our public service in the Philippines to become the prey of the spoils politicians, if we fail to keep it up to the highest standard, we shall be guilty of an act, not only of wickedness, but of weak and short-sighted folly, and we shall have begun to tread the path which was trod by Spain to her own bitter humiliation."[57]

But if his dream ended badly, Roosevelt at least had the advantage of being able to say that he always suspected it would. The same could not be said of the Fascists of Italy, whose self-deception about their wresting of power from the left persisted for decades, testifying to an inability to confront their own disappointment. For years, the Fascists celebrated their 1922 March on Rome as the violent and glorious triumph of will over adversity. October 28, the day of the Blackshirts' arrival in Rome, became a national holiday and the first day of the Fascist New Year upon the introduction of the new calendar in 1927. The story of Mussolini's arrival in particular—wearing the proverbial black shirt—was repeated with awe. "Sire," he supposedly said to King Victor Emmanuel III at their meeting, "forgive my attire. I come from the battlefields." In actual fact, Mussolini had traveled by train overnight from Milan—where he had been conspicuously attending the theater—snoozing comfortably in the sleeping car.

The only reason he even made it into Rome was that a timid establish-ment, led by King Victor Emmanuel III, telephoned him in Milan with a request that he form a government. Barely a shot was fired, on either side.[58] Maistre could not have written it better.

More recently, we can see a similar phenomenon at play in the war on terror. Though many view the war on terror, the Bush administration, and neoconservatism as departures from proper conservatism—the most recent and influential statement of this thesis being Sam Tanenhaus's *The Death of Conservatism*[59]—the neocon project of imperial adventur-ism traces the conservative arc of violence from beginning to end. I have written elsewhere about how the neoconservatives saw 9/11 and the war on terror as a chance to escape from the decadent and deadening peace and prosperity of the Clinton years, which they believed had weakened American society. Oozing in comfort, Americans—and more important their leaders—had supposedly lost the will, the desire and ability, to gov-ern the world. "I think it would be natural for the United States," said Irving Kristol in 2000, "to play a far more dominant role in world affairs. Not what we're doing now but to command and to give orders as to what is to be done." But with public discussion moderated by businessmen and accountants—"There's the Republican Party tying itself into knots. Over what? Prescriptions for elderly people? Who gives a damn? I think it's disgusting that . . . presidential politics of the most important coun-try in the world should revolve around prescriptions for elderly people. Future historians will find this very hard to believe. It's not Athens. It's not Rome. It's not anything"—Kristol thought it unlikely that the United States would take its rightful place as the successor to empires past. Then 9/11 happened, and suddenly it seemed as if it could.[60]

That dream, of course, now lies in tatters, but one of its more idiosyn-cratic aspects is worth noting, for it presents an interesting wrinkle in the long saga of conservative violence. According to many conservatives, and not just the neocons, one of the recent sources of American deca-dence, traceable back to the Warren Court and the rights revolutions of the 1960s, is the liberal obsession with the rule of law. This obsession, in the eyes of the conservative, takes many forms: the insistence on due process in criminal procedure; a partiality to litigation over legislation; an emphasis on diplomacy and international law over war; attempts to re-strain executive power through judicial and legislative oversight. However unrelated these symptoms may seem, conservatives see in them a single disease: a culture of rules and laws slowly disabling and devitalizing the blond beast of prey that is American power. These are signs of a Nietzschean unhealthiness, and 9/11 was its inevitable result.

If another 9/11 is to be prevented, that culture must to be repudiated and reversed. As the reporting of Seymour Hersh and Jane Mayer makes clear, the war on terror—with its push for torture, for overturning the Geneva Conventions, for refusing the restrictions of international law, for illegal surveillance, and for seeing terrorism through the lens of war rather than crime and punishment—reflects as much, if not more, these sensibilities and sensitivities as it does the actual facts of 9/11 and the need to prevent another 9/11.[61] "She's soft—too soft," says now retired Lieutenant General Jerry Boykin about the United States, pre- and post-9/11. The way to make her hard is not merely to undertake difficult and strenuous military action but also to violate the rules—and the culture of rules—that made her soft in the first place. The United States must learn how to "live on the edge," says former NSA director Michael Hayden. "There's nothing we won't do, nothing we won't try," former CIA director George Tenet helpfully adds.[62]

The great irony—and disappointment, from the point of view of the conservative—of the war on terror is that far from emancipating the blonde beast of prey, the war has made law—and lawyers—far more critical than one might imagine. As Mayer reports, the push for torture, unbridled executive power, overthrowing the Geneva Conventions, and so on came not from the CIA or the military; it came from lawyers in the White House and the Justice Department like David Addington and John Yoo. Far from being Machiavellian virtuosos of transgressive violence, Addington and Yoo are fanatics about the law and insist on justifying their violence through the law. Lawyers, moreover, consistently oversee the actual practice of torture. As Tenet wrote in his memoir, "Despite what Hollywood might have you believe, in situations like this [the capture, interrogation, and torture of Al Qaeda logistics chief Abu Zubayda] you don't call in the tough guys; you call in the lawyers." Every slap on the face, every punch in the gut, every shake of the body—and much, much worse—must first be approved by higher-ups in the various intelligence agencies, inevitably in consultation with their attorneys. Mayer compares the practice of torture to a game of "Mother, May I?" As one interrogator puts it, "Before you could lay a hand on him [the torture victim], you had to send a cable saying, 'He's uncooperative. Request permission to do X.' And permission would come, saying 'You're allowed to slap him one time in the belly with an open hand.' . . ."[63]

Rather than free the blonde beast to roam and prey as he wishes, the lifting of the ban on torture and suspension of the Geneva Conventions have made him, or at least the lawyers who hold his leash, more anxious. How far can he go? What can he do? Every act of violence, as this exchange between two Pentagon lawyers reveals, becomes a law school seminar:

> What did "deprivation of light and auditory stimuli" mean? Could a prisoner be locked in a completely dark cell? If so, could he be kept there for a month? Longer? Until he went blind? What, precisely, did the authority to exploit phobias permit? Could a detainee be held in a coffin? What about using dogs? Rats? How far could an interrogator push this? Until a man went insane?[64]

Then there is the question of whether or not it is possible to combine approved techniques of torture. May an interrogator withhold food from the prisoner and turn down the temperature of his cell at the same time? Does the multiplying effect of pains doubled and tripled and quadrupled cross a never-defined line?[65] As Orwell taught us, the possibilities for cruelty and violence are as limitless as the imagination that dreams them up. But the armies and agencies of today's violence are vast bureaucracies, and vast bureaucracies need rules. Eliminating those rules does not Prometheus unbind; it just makes lawyers that much more important.

"No yielding. No equivocation. No lawyering this thing to death." That was George W. Bush's vow after 9/11 and his description of how the war on terror would be conducted. Like so many of Bush's other declarations, it has turned out to be an empty promise. This thing was lawyered to death. But, and this is the critical point, far from minimizing state violence—which was the great fear of the neocons—lawyering has proven to be perfectly compatible with that violence. In a war already swollen with disappointment and disillusion, this realization—the fact that the rule of law can authorize the most sublime adventures of violence and death—must be, for the conservative, the greatest disillusion of all.

Had they been closer readers of Burke, the neoconservatives—like Fukuyama, Roosevelt, Sorel, Schmitt, Tocqueville, Maistre, Treitschke, and so many more on the American and European right—could have seen it coming. Burke certainly did. Even as he wrote of the sublime effects of pain and danger, he was careful to insist that should those pains and dangers "press too nearly" or "too close"—that is, should they become realities rather than fantasies, should they become "conversant about the present destruction of the person"—their sublimity would disappear. They would cease to be "delightful" and restorative and become simply terrible.[66] Burke's point was not that nobody, in the end, really wants to die or that nobody enjoys unwelcome, excruciating pain. It was that sublimity of whatever kind and source depends upon obscurity: get too close to anything, whether an object or experience, see and feel its full extent, and it loses its mystery and aura. It becomes familiar. A "great clearness" of the sort that comes from direct experience "is in some sort an enemy to all enthusiasms whatsoever."[67] "It is our ignorance of things that causes all our admiration, and chiefly excites our passions. Knowledge and acquaintance make the most striking causes affect but little."[68] "A clear idea," Burke concludes, "is therefore another name for a little idea."[69] Get to know anything, including violence, too well, and it loses whatever attribute—rejuvenation, transgression, excitement, awe—you ascribed to it when it was just an idea.

Earlier than most, Burke understood that if it was to retain its sublimity, violence had to remain a possibility, an object of fantasy—a horror movie, a video game, an essay on war. For the actuality (as opposed to representation) of violence was at odds with the requirements of sublimity. Real, as opposed to imagined, violence entailed objects getting too close, bodies pressing too near, flesh upon flesh. Violence stripped the body of its veils, and made its antagonists familiar to each other in a way that they had never been before. It dispelled illusion and mystery, making things drab and dreary. That is why, in his discussion in the *Reflections* of the revolutionaries' abduction of Marie Antoinette, Burke takes such pains to emphasize her "almost naked" body and turns so effortlessly to the language of clothing—"the decent drapery of life," the "wardrobe of the moral imagination," "antiquated fashion," and so on—to describe the event.[70] The disaster of the revolutionaries' violence, for Burke, was not its cruelty; it was the un-asked-for enlightenment.

Since 9/11, many have complained, and rightly so, about the failure of conservatives—or their sons and daughters—to fight the war on terror themselves. For many on the left, that failure is symptomatic of the class injustice of contemporary America, and it is. But there is an additional element to the story. So long as the war on terror remains an idea—a hot topic on the blogs, a provocative op-ed, an episode of 24—it is sublime. As soon as it becomes a reality, it can be as cheerless and tedious as a discussion of the tax code or a trip to the DMV.

NOTES

1. Andrew Sullivan, *The Conservative Soul: Fundamentalism, Freedom, and the Future of the Right* (New York: Harper Perennial, 2006), 276–77.

2. Francis Fukuyama, *The End of History and the Last Man* (New York: Harper Collins, 1992), xxiii, 147, 150–51, 255–56, 318, 329.

3. In his 1962 address at West Point, MacArthur states, "Only the dead have seen the end of war," and he attributes this statement to Plato. No scholar has ever found such a statement in Plato, but it (and the Plato attribution) does appear on a wall in London's Imperial War Museum and in Ridley Scott's 2001 film *Black Hawk Down*. The most likely source of the statement is George Santayana, in his *Soliloquies in England* (New York: Scribner's, 1924), 102. See Bernard Suzanne's excellent and thorough discussion at plato-dialogues.org/faq/faq008.htm#note1.

4. *Selections from Treitschke's Lectures on Politics*, trans. Adam L. Gowans (New York: Frederick A. Stokes, 1914), 24–25.

5. Edmund Burke, *A Philosophical Enquiry into the Origin of Our Ideas of the Sublime and the Beautiful*, ed. David Womersley (New York: Penguin, 1998, 2004), 79.

6. Ibid., 82.

7. Ibid., 88.

8. Ibid., 96.

9. Ibid., 164.

10. Ibid., 177–78.

11. Michael Oakeshott, "On Being Conservative," in *Rationalism in Politics and Other Essays* (Indianapolis: Liberty Press, 1962), 408. Also see Walter Bagehot, "Intellectual Conservatism," in *The Portable Conservative Reader*, ed. Russell Kirk (New York: Penguin, 1982), 239–41; Russell Kirk, "What Is Conservatism?" in *The Essential Russell Kirk*, ed. George A. Panichas (Wilmington: ISI Books, 2007), 7; Roger Scruton, *The Meaning of Conservatism* (London: Macmillan, 1980, 1984), 21–22, 40–43; Robert Nisbet, *Conservatism* (Minneapolis: University of Minnesota Press, 1986), 26–27.

12. Ronald Reagan, First Inaugural Address and address before a Joint Session of the Congress, in *Conservatism in America since 1930*, ed. Gregory L. Schneider (New York: New York University Press, 2003), 343, 344, 351, 352.

13. Barry Goldwater, acceptance speech at 1964 Republican National Convention, in *Conservatism in America*, 238–39.

14. Hugo Young, *One of Us* (London: Macmillan, 1989, 1991), 224.

15. William Manchester, *The Last Lion: Winston Spencer Churchill. Visions of Glory 1874–1932* (Boston: Little, Brown, 1982), 222–31.

16. Winston Churchill, *My Early Life: 1874–1904* (New York: Scribner, 1996), 74–87.

17. Burke, *Sublime and the Beautiful*, 177.

18. Ibid., 86.

19. I do not deal just yet with Burke's stipulation that this sensation of pain or danger should arise from objects at some distance or remove from the person. I discuss this stipulation at the very end of the essay.

20. Ibid., 101, 106, 108, 111.

21. Ibid., 96, 123.

22. Ibid., 121.

23. Jean-Jacques Rousseau, *Discourse on the Origin and Foundations of Inequality Among Men*, in *Rousseau's Political Writings*, ed. Alan Ritter and Julia Conaway Bondanella (New York: Norton, 1988), 54.

24. John Adams, *Discourses on Davila*, in *The Political Writings of John Adams* (Indianapolis: Hackett, 2003), 176.

25. Ibid., 183–84.

26. Burke, *Sublime and the Beautiful*, 108.

27. Ibid., 109.

28. Ibid..

29. Burke, *Reflections on the Revolution in France*, ed. J. C. D. Clark (Stanford: Stanford University Press, 2001), 239.

30. Ibid., 207–8, 275.

31. Burke, *Letters on a Regicide Peace*, ed. E. J. Payne (Indianapolis: Liberty Fund, 1999), 157.

32. Joseph de Maistre, *Considerations on France*, trans. and ed. Richard A. Lebrun (New York: Cambridge University Press, 1974, 1994), 4, 9–10, 13–14, 16–18, 100.

33. Ibid., 17. For other examples, see Jean-Louis Darcel, "The Roads of Exile, 1792–1817," and Darcel, "Joseph de Maistre and the House of Savoy: Some Aspects of His Career," in *Joseph de Maistre's Life, Thought, and Influence: Selected Studies*, ed. Richard A. Lebrun (Montreal: McGill-Queen's University Press, 2001), 16, 19–20, 52.

34. Cf. David Bromwich, "Introduction," in Edmund Burke, *On Empire, Liberty, and Reform: Speeches and Letters*, ed. David Bromwich (New Haven: Yale University Press, 2000), 10.

35. Georges Sorel, *Reflections on Violence*, ed. Jeremy Jennings (New York: Cambridge University Press, 1999), 61–63, 72, 75–76.

36. Carl Schmitt, *The Concept of the Political*, trans. George Schwab (New Brunswick: Rutgers University Press, 1976), 22, 48, 62–63, 65, 71–72, 74, 78.

37. Ibid., 63.

38. Sorel, Reflections, 75.

39. Theodore Roosevelt, address to Naval War College, June, 2, 1897, in *Theodore Roosevelt: An American Mind. Selected Writings*, ed. Mario R. DiNunzio (New York: Penguin, 1994), 175–76, 179.

40. Roosevelt, address to Hamilton Club of Chicago, April, 10, 1899 ("The Strenuous Life"), and *An Autobiography*, in ibid., 186, 194.

41. Roosevelt, address to Naval War College, 174.

42. John C. Calhoun, "Speech on the Reception of Abolitionist Petitions," in *Union and Liberty: The Political Philosophy of John C. Calhoun*, ed. Ross M. Lence (Indianapolis: Liberty Fund, 1992), 476.

43. Barry Goldwater, *The Conscience of a Conservative* (Princeton: Princeton University Press, 1960, 2007), 1.

44. Fukuyama, *End of History*, 315–18, 329; Corey Robin, "Remembrance of Empires Past: 9/11 and the End of the Cold War," in *Cold War Triumphalism: The Misuse of History after the Fall of Communism*, ed. Ellen Schrecker (New York: New Press, 2004), 274–97.

45. John Milton, *Aeropagitica*, in *Complete Poems and Major Prose*, ed. Merritt Y. Hughes (New York: Macmillan, 1957), 728.

46. Burke, *Sublime and the Beautiful*, 145.

47. Maistre, *Considerations*, 14, 16, 18–19. Also see Darcel, "The Apprentice Years of a Counter-Revolutionary: Joseph de Maistre in Lausanne, 1793–1797," in *Joseph de Maistre's Life, Thought, and Influence*, 43–44.

48. Maistre, *Considerations*, 77.

49. Sorel, *Reflections*, 63, 160–61.

50. Cited in William Pfaff, *The Bullet's Song: Romantic Violence and Utopia* (New York: Simon and Schuster, 2004), 97.

51. Sorel, *Reflections*, 76–78, 85.

52. What follows is an abridged account of my discussion in *Fear: The History of a Political Idea* (New York: Oxford University Press, 2004), 88–94. Sources for all quotations cited here can be found there.

53. Fukuyama, *End of History*, 148, 180, 304–5, 312, 314, 328–29.

54. E. M. Forster, *A Passage to India* (New York: Harcourt, 1924), 289.

55. Roosevelt, *The Rough Riders*, in *Theodore Roosevelt*, 30–32, 37. One might also point to Roosevelt's Naval War College address, where several thousand words in praise of manliness and military preparedness come to a climax in a call for United States to build a modern navy that might well never be used. *Theodore Roosevelt*, 178.

56. Roosevelt, "The Strenuous Life," *Theodore Roosevelt*, 185, 188.

57. Roosevelt, Lincoln Club address of 1899, and "The Strenuous Life," *Theodore Roosevelt*, 182, 189.

58. R. J. B. Bosworth, *Mussolini* (New York: Oxford University Press, 2002), 167–69; Robert O. Paxton, *The Anatomy of Fascism* (New York: Knopf, 2004), 87–91.

59. Sam Tanenhaus, *The Death of Conservatism* (New York: Random House, 2009).

60. Robin, "Remembrance of Empires Past," 275, 277–79, 282–86. Also see Robin, "Grand Designs: How 9/11 Unified Conservatives in Pursuit of Empire," *Washington Post* (May 2, 2004), B1; Robin, "Endgame: Conservatives after the Cold War," *Boston Review* (February 2004), 26–30.

61. Seymour Hersh, *Chain of Command: The Road from 9/11 to Abu Ghraib* (New York: Harper Collins, 2004); Jane Mayer, *The Dark Side: The Inside Story of How the War on Terror Turned into a War on American Ideals* (New York: Doubleday, 2008). Also see Corey Robin, "Was he? Had he?" *London Review of Books*, October 19, 2006, 10–12; Corey Robin, "Protocols of Machismo," *London Review of Books*, May 19, 2005, 11–14.

62. Mayer, *Dark Side*, 69, 132, 241.

63. Ibid., 55, 120, 150, 167, 231, 301.

64. Ibid., 223.

65. Ibid..

66. Burke, *Sublime and the Beautiful*, 86, 92, 165.

67. Ibid., 104.

68. Ibid., 105.

69. Ibid., 106.

70. Burke, *Reflections*, 232, 239.

2

Violence without Agency

RUTH A. MILLER

This is not an essay about violence. I want to make that clear from the outset because when the word "violence" appears in academic writing, there is frequently a rush to diagnose and to condemn it, to expose it and those who are complicit in it, to feel, in short, that something must be done. When the word "violence" appears, it is rarely just a word; it is an incitement. If there is a diagnosis happening in this essay, therefore, it is not another diagnosis of violence. Rather, it is a diagnosis of discussions of violence. The questions driving this essay are not where is the violence, who has committed this violence, and how can we denounce it? These questions have already been tirelessly dissected. Instead, I ask why it is that discussions of violence have remained trapped in this world of righteous indignation and thoughtless redress.[1]

Why do even the most careful and critical descriptions of violence, and even those most wary of models of autonomous sovereign subjectivity, seem so often reducible to descriptions of victims, of perpetrators, and of methods of helping or punishing them?

My working hypothesis is that this difficulty in describing violence, this difficulty posed by a simple seeming question—"what does it mean to say that someone performs an act of violence?"—is the result of an enduring link in scholarly discussion between agency on the one hand and the performance of violence on the other. Over the following pages, I explore the possibility that delinking agency from the performance of violence might broaden conversations about violence, might open up new dimensions for thinking about the violent act, and might, above all, rescue these conversations from their current residence in the realm of caricature.[2] I should emphasize that this essay is therefore a speculative one. In the same way that my interest is not in finding, diagnosing, and condemning violence, nor is it in describing some pre-existing argument, attacking it, and claiming victory for an alternative interpretation. Although I devote time to describing some of the ways in which the invocation of agency seems to short circuit[3] discussions of the violent act, my goal is nonetheless a modest one: I do not argue that agency is bad (as bad, even, as violence); instead I explore what happens when agency disappears from discussions of performing violence.

It is for this reason that I have chosen to focus in the latter half of this essay on the women's suffrage movement in the United States as a case study for thinking about violence without agency. Conversations about the violent aspects of various women's suffrage movements are an excellent example of conversations that have become flattened via repetitive recourse to the idea of agency. Whether suffragists are held up as early feminists worthy of admiration, or as participants in colonial, imperial, or racist political discourses, the given is that these women were relentless in their appropriation of agency.[4] Becoming successful feminist agents themselves, or undermining the possibility of agency for others, suffragists have been described as violent precisely to the extent that they have been described as possessing agency. My point in this part of the essay is not that such interpretations of the suffrage movement are incorrect. I do, however, raise the possibility that there are alternative interpretations of the suffragists' performance of violence that are not expressible in a vocabulary of agency. Indeed, by removing agency from the picture, I believe that it is possible to describe the simultaneity of the suffragists' physical and linguistic violence in effective—and perhaps more effective—ways.

Put broadly, abandoning agency provides additional insight into the peculiarly physical nature of linguistic violence and the peculiarly linguistic nature of physical violence. That linguistic existence tends toward violent physicality and physical existence toward violent speech is certainly not a new theme in theories of existence and politics. Thomas Hobbes plays on it, for example, when he opposes the sovereign's physical passions to the subject's disloyal speech (and comes down on the side of the former);[5] Carl Schmitt does so when he critiques liberal discussion for turning bloody battles into parliamentary debates (and when he valorizes the non-liberal decision as above all a physical effect);[6] Catharine MacKinnon likewise does so when she analyzes pornographic speech as a form of physical battering.[7] As Corey Robin notes in his contribution to this volume, Edmund Burke situates the sublime at precisely the meeting point of linguistic and physical assault. The assumption underlying this essay is that these formulations and others like them can best be described when agency disappears. The oddity of opposing, matching, mismatching, and juxtaposing linguistic and physical violence is odd, that is, only when discussions of violence are reduced to discussions of agency, identity, and redress. When agency disappears, so too do the arbitrary distinctions among these categories. Violence, in other words, is not in itself impossible to describe; the vocabulary of agency has made violence indescribable.

Some Problems with Agency

Both the complexity of agency and its potential to limit, narrow, or flatten conversation have become increasingly recognized in scholarly writing. To mention only one influential example of this work, Talal Asad has argued that invocations of agency have been in part responsible for the uncritical acceptance of "secularism" as both a coherent political category and a modern good.[8] Although he does not go so far as to suggest that agency be eliminated altogether from discussions of secularism, he does emphasize that even in the most critical writing on subjectivity,[9] "agency is built on the idea of blame and pain. A world of apparent accidents is rendered into a world of essences by attributing to a person moral/legal responsibility on whose basis guilt and innocence (and therefore punishment or exoneration) are determined."[10] More specifically, he notes the "lack of adequate attention to the limits of the human body as a site of agency" that appears in "the anthropological literature on the subject."[11]

Agency is thus in part responsible for reducing a complex and multidimensional issue—in this case secularism rather than violence—into a story of nothing more than condemnation, indignation, and redress. As a result, Asad states, we might take measures to prevent agency from reducing secularism to this caricature, and to prevent it from eliminating any chance of describing it in its complexity. The first of these measures is to recognize that "agents need not necessarily coincide with individual biological bodies and the consciousness that is said to go with them."[12] A second is to realize that "the idea of representation underlying agency is rooted in a paradox: that who or what is represented is both absent and present at the same time (re-presented). Theoretical representation, when the actor's body makes present someone who is absent, exemplifies in a different way the same paradox."[13] Finally, a third measure becomes clear in Asad's reading of Oedipus' self-mutilation, in which he makes the case that "acts *can* have an ethical significance without necessarily having to be interpreted in terms of 'answerability.'"[14] Indeed, "Oedipus' self-inflicted pain" can be thought of "as itself the passionate performance of an embodied ethical sensibility. Oedipus suffers not because he is guilty but because he is virtuous."[15]

Again, Asad does not conclude that secularism might therefore be more effectively described without any invocation of agency at all. His critique of agency, however, is very much in keeping with the critique that underlies this essay: first, agency need not coincide with any one, conscious, biological body;[16] second, agency relies on a theory of representation that posits simultaneous physical presence and physical absence; and third, agency erases the possibility of unanswerable acts that are no more and no less than performances, of acts whose ethical character operates outside the world of guilt and redress. When I go a step further and ask what might happen if agency were removed from the picture, I therefore keep Asad's position in mind. Indeed, it is my assertion that discarding agency allows for two distinct new ways of thinking about the performance of violence, each of which is suggested by Asad's analysis. The first addresses the performance of violence as a simultaneously linguistic and physical performance, and as a performance that assumes physical presence as well as physical absence; the second addresses the unanswerability of the violent act—the extent to which the violent act allows for neither a linguistic nor a physical response.[17]

Some Problems with Agency and Violence

Before describing these alternative approaches to the performance of violence, however, I explain in more detail how invocations of agency have limited existing conversations. After all, despite the fact that scholars have begun questioning agency—and especially agency linked solely to self-conscious human beings—as an effective analytical framework, to say that someone performs an act of violence remains more often than not to say something about agency.[18] My starting point in this section is thus, once again, not violence per se, but rather discussions of violence, and more particularly discussions of performative speech and violence. I take performative speech as the foundation for my argument both because of the long-running association between violent speech and violent acts in political writing, and also because, as Asad notes, agency itself—and the theory of representation on which it rests—assumes a collapse of linguistic existence and physical existence. In this section, therefore, I first provide a few examples of agency at work in writing on performative speech; I then discuss how this writing insists on the simultaneity of linguistic and physical violence even while disallowing any description of this simultaneity; and finally, I explain how this writing likewise presupposes the unanswerability of the violent act while nonetheless making a description of this unaswerability impossible.

With that in mind, most interpretations of performative speech include at least a reference to J. L. Austin's *How to Do Things with Words*. The question of agency remains relatively muted in this work, but the distinction that Austin makes between the "perlocutionary act"—that is, speech that produces a future effect—and the "illocutionary act"—that is, the "speech act" proper,[19] or speech that is, in and of itself, an effect—is at least implicitly reliant on some notion of agency.[20] Likewise, Austin's repeated return to the "dangerous" aspects of speech,[21] or to the problematic physicality of the speech act,[22] indicates a relatively coherent narrative of the sovereign agent at work.

As Judith Butler has pointed out in her reading of Austin, however, when sovereign subjectivity gets linked to theories of performative speech, it almost immediately becomes suspect. One of the more paradoxical aspects of Austin's work from the legal perspective, for instance, is that the illocutionary act—the speech *act* itself—is arguably the type of speaking least relevant to the will, intention, or desire of the subject. Whereas the perlocutionary act can to some extent be articulated in a linear story of a subject who, first, intends to speak, second, inaugurates speech, and third, produces certain desired effects as a result of this speech, the illocutionary act can be understood only within a discursive field, absent any linearity, and certainly absent any sovereign will.[23] The illocutionary act is necessarily an act of repetition,[24] an act that can only construct and situate a subject within an already existing linguistic realm.[25] In order for speech to *be* an act, therefore, intention and will—individual agency—must disappear.

One of the most effective concrete examples that Butler provides of this disintegration of the agency of the sovereign subject appears in her challenge to Catharine MacKinnon's work on pornography. When MacKinnon develops and extends the theory of the speech act, or speech-as-conduct, to the realm of pornography, Butler argues, she does two things. First, she creates a space outside of U.S. First Amendment protections for political and legal response to this conduct. Second, and undermining the first, she eliminates the possibility of intentionality in the production of the pornography—the possibility, in legal language, of determining *mens rea*.[26] In order for pornography to be the bad conduct, the illocutionary *act,* that MacKinnon wants it to be, it must also be an act of repetition. The person or institution that produces the pornography thus cannot be the initiator of the bad conduct, cannot be possessed of an intent to cause harm, but must rather be one of many voices within a pre-existing discursive field.

Understanding pornography as a speech act, therefore, does open up an enormous—and, according to Butler, authoritarian—realm of political or legal redress. More to the point as far as MacKinnon's own project is concerned (if less important to Butler's critique): extending the reach of speech-as-conduct to the sphere of pornography also destroys any chance of determining liability.[27] The sovereign individual possessed of agency is destabilized when brought to bear on speech acts as acts of violence. Sovereign subjects—those who spend their time speaking truth to power—as well as liable subjects—those who must be assigned criminal responsibility—are both impossible figures when shifted into the realm of speech-as-conduct.

Butler's interpretation of MacKinnon's argument thus highlights the flattening function of agency in discussions of violence. By operating in a framework of the sovereign subject's individual agency, MacKinnon does two things: she first insists on the simultaneity of linguistic and physical violence *and in the process* eliminates the possibility of any coherent legal narrative of this simultaneity. Agency in this way plays the dual role in MacKinnon's work that Asad sees it playing in discussions of secularism—it raises the specter of physical and linguistic pain and suffering while eliminating any effective description of this pain and suffering. It is not just that irrelevant and/or parodic forms of condemnation and indignation are the most satisfying responses to the violent nature of pornography, therefore—it is that, in this rhetorical field, they are the *only* responses available.

Although these short-circuiting effects of agency are more overt in writing that valorizes sovereign subjects possessed of individual autonomy, I want to make the case that even in the more critical scholarship that explores the multidimensional aspects of agency these same effects occur. In order to make this case, I turn to Butler's own theorization of speech and violence in her book *Excitable Speech,* and argue that—although nuanced—it too disallows any description of the performance of violence, beyond the realm of guilt, innocence, and redress.[28] *Excitable Speech* begins with the point that agency operates at the heart of any analysis of violent speech. Indeed, Butler's argument in the book rests on the notion that the violent speech act assigns agency both to the speaking subject and to language—that the speaking subject as well as the words themselves are understood to "wound."[29]

Although the injurious potential of speech can best be understood by "untethering the speech act from the sovereign subject," and by "more fully acknowledging the way in which the subject is constituted in language, how what it creates is also what it derives from elsewhere,"[30] therefore, agency by no means disappears from the picture. Rather, agency is re-articulated in a more complex, and careful, vocabulary. The subject, for example,

> is neither a sovereign agent with a purely instrumental relation to language, nor a mere effect whose agency is purely complicit with prior operations of power. The vulnerability to the Other constituted by that prior address is never overcome in the assumption of agency (one reason that "agency" is not the same as mastery).[31]

An "injury" is therefore, according to this analysis, "performed by the very act of interpellation, the one that rules out the possibility of the subject's autogenesis (and gives rise to that very fantasy)"; as a result it becomes even more necessary to "realize how inevitable is our dependency on the ways we are addressed in order to exercise any agency at all."[32]

Butler in this way challenges the idea that agency can be relevant only to self-conscious or purely active subjects, subjects with mastery over an inert or passive language, or subjects who both initiate and direct speech. Indeed, like Asad, she insists that agency need not be tied even to a singular body possessed of consciousness. For her, the subject is a fragile figure, a figure constituted by language, and a figure whose agency is as vulnerable to the activity of language as language is vulnerable to the activity of the subject. It is, moreover, precisely this fraught relationship between subject and speech, mediated through agency, that collapses physical and linguistic violence. Butler argues, for instance, that the fact that "linguistic injury . . . is, as it were, forced to draw its vocabulary from physical injury"[33] suggests an interaction that is far more than metaphorical. To the extent that the body is constituted by language, and to the extent that "it is by being interpellated within the terms of language that a certain social existence of the body first becomes possible,"[34] speech necessarily puts physical existence at stake. As she states in the conclusion to the book, "one need only consider . . . how the words enter the limbs, craft the gesture, bend the spine,"[35] to understand the simultaneity of physical and linguistic violence.

Although this reading of the role that agency plays in the performance of violence is convincing, it nonetheless makes indescribable physically violent speech *in and of itself*. It derails any conversation about the physical *and* linguistic performance of violence. Even while it presents the violence of language in an emphatically physical manner, it also, by invoking agency, demands the separation of the linguistic from the physical. Put another way, the idea underlying Butler's theorization of agency—that the subject is the instrument of language as much as language is the instrument of the subject—does not eliminate the problem of instrumentality writ large. Indeed, a separation of cause and effect, of subject and object, and of the linguistic and the physical remains necessary precisely in order to rescue agency as a viable concept:

> the gap that separates the speech act from its future effects has its auspicious implications: it begins a theory of linguistic agency that provides an alternative to the relentless search for legal remedy. The interval between instances of utterance not only makes the repetition and resignification of the utterance possible, but shows how words might, through time, become disjoined from their power to injure and recontextualized in more affirmative modes.[36]

Butler's argument thus disallows an analysis of illocutionary speech, or speech that is simultaneously act and effect, simultaneously linguistic and physical,[37] because it is only in perlocutionary speech—speech that produces later effects—that agency can be found. Whereas she provides an indispensable account of the physical and bodily *effects* of speech, therefore—speech constitutes bodily experience or speech destroys intentionality—she does not get at the physicality of the speech act itself. As agency enters the picture, it becomes impossible to conceptualize the *simultaneity* of physical and linguistic violence, or the ways in which the speech act packs its physical punch.

Moreover, this vocabulary of agency also eliminates the possibility of thinking about the violent act as pure performance—as, in Asad's language, something unanswerable. Insisting as it does on the instrumentality of language, Butler's argument, like MacKinnon's, both poses the question of unanswerable violence *and* blocks any narrative of this performance. It is true in that in this formulation the existence of the subject who can speak, the existence of the subject who can be wounded, and the force of the injurious speech itself are all reliant on a pre-existing field of discourse—on a history of violent language that "exceeds in all directions the history of the speaking subject."[38] It is likewise true that the word-that-wounds is not a unitary event, but rather a repetition or a citation of a series of prior linguistic injuries.[39] At the same time, though, once agency becomes the framing concept, the only linguistic operation open to these subjects is speaking *to* other subjects, and then waiting for a response. There is no performance absent an object and an indirect object. There is no performance absent a response.

Interpellation, for example, goes in only one direction—the call that brings the subject into existence comes from outside of the subject; and as much as this subject may then internalize some injurious repetition of the call, this too comes from elsewhere, from someone else. When Butler argues, for instance, that "the speaker who utters the racial slur is . . . citing that slur, making linguistic community with a history of speakers,"[40] she is reinforcing both the instrumentality of language and its necessary answerability. What is important is not the speech itself, but the way in which this speech forges community among some subjects and excludes others. What is important is how the subject uses speech and how people respond to that usage. By emphasizing agency and instrumentality, Butler in fact suggests that speech that assumes an answer is the only type of speech that matters. Any other type of speech is quite literally "impossible,"[41] and thereby in and of itself unspeakable.

Moreover, what makes it unspeakable is not just that it threatens the "dissolution of the subject," that it calls "the viability of the subject into question," or that it leads to "a sense that one is 'falling apart.'" What makes it unspeakable is that "if the subject speaks impossibly, speaks in ways that cannot be regarded as speech or as the speech of a subject, then that speech is discounted."[42] The questions of who will be doing this discounting and why discounted speech is so unthinkable (or unspeakable) are—perhaps paradoxically—left unanswered.

And they are left unanswered, I suggest, because when agency is linked to the performance of violence, the only sort of speech that can be described is speech that relies on a separation of subject and object, of cause and effect, of linguistic existence and physical existence, and of statement and response. When agency is linked to the performance of violence, one of the most prevalent and violent forms of contemporary speech—the monologue that invites no response[43]—is left out of the picture. I would in fact go a step further, and argue that when agency is linked to the performance of violence, the result is a dangerously incomplete understanding of the violent potential of speech and act.

In concluding this section, however, let me be clear: I am not arguing that whereas some theories of speech and violence optimistically position the sovereign subject as the cause of speech, and other theories of speech and violence optimistically position the discursive subject as simultaneously cause and effect of speech, I pessimistically position the subject as "mere effect" of speech. Rather, I am trying to re-think the optimism and pessimism that underlie both of these positions. I suggest, in other words, that any theory of the performance of violence that rests on a separation of speech and subject, or on an instrumental relationship between (optimistic, active) cause and (pessimistic, passive) effect—on, in short, a desire for agency—leads to flattened and caricatured discussions of this violence. There indeed seems to be very little reason, outside of this pre-existing optimism or pessimism, to insist that agency has anything at all to do with the performance of the violent act. The return to agency as something not only necessary, but desirable, thus to me points not so much to a subversion of pre-existing oppressive discursive structures but rather to a nostalgia for the lost mastery of the sovereign individual in a world of not playful—but relentless and aggressive—repetition.

By discarding agency, therefore, it becomes possible to address the complexity and multi-dimensional nature of performance, and the performance of violence, without the repeated return to guilt and innocence, condemnation and valorization. It becomes possible to think about multiple, simultaneous, moments of interpellation—to think about subjects called into existence not just by the external voice of the law,[44] or by some coherent pre-existing identity discourse,[45] but by constant, clamorous imaginary voices that destroy any boundary between the internal and the external. It becomes possible to think about performances of violence that mock cause and effect and that are brutally physical. And finally, it becomes possible to think about violence as a template for modern and contemporary democratic engagement writ large.

Abandoning Agency

What, then, might a theory of violence absent agency look like? In this section, I provide a few possible starting points for thinking about the performance of violence outside of the framework of agency, and hence for addressing, first, the simultaneity of the physical and linguistic in these performances and, second, their unanswerability. I begin with one of Austin's more straightforward examples of performative illocutionary speech—namely the raised voice of the law. Regardless of whether the voice of the law is articulated by a judge saying "I find, pronounce, deem you to be guilty"[46] or by a sign that reads "notice is hereby given that trespassers will be prosecuted,"[47] Austin argues, this is a voice that collapses completely the act of saying and the act of doing. Now it is true that the physical violence of this speech seems to lie more in its effects than in its performance—the sentencing leads eventually to incarceration or the notice of prosecution leads to arrest. In fact, however, the physical effects of legal speech are secondary to the physicality of the legal speech act itself—and this physicality becomes conceivable only when agency exits the discussion.

In one of Michel Foucault's analyses of the apparent malfunctioning of law, for instance—presented in his series of lectures, *Abnormal*—the physicality of the legal speech act as an act of violence becomes apparent. In these lectures, Foucault argues that although "the monstrous" can be considered "a breach of the law,"

> the monster does not bring about a legal response from the law. It could be said that the monster's power and its capacity to create anxiety are due to the fact that it violates the law while leaving it with nothing to say. It traps the law while breaching it.[48]

A few pages later, he continues that monstrosity

> is that kind of natural irregularity that calls law into question and disables it. Law must either question its own foundations, or its practice, or fall silent, or abdicate, or appeal to another reference system, or again invent a casuistry. Essentially, the monster is the casuistry that is necessarily introduced into law by the confusion of nature.[49]

Foucault thus links the physicality of violent speech precisely to its unanswerability. And indeed, although he is to some extent operating in a cause and effect framework, predicated on agency, this linkage becomes intelligible only when he complicates cause and effect to such an extent that they become meaningless. Foucault is explicitly not, for instance, describing a classical sovereign relationship in which the monster does something and the law responds. Nor, however, is he describing a straightforward discursive relationship in which the monster is constituted by law (or the law's silence) and the law (or the law's silence) is then re-constituted by the monster. There is simply no space in this scenario for any sort of initiating speech or any sort of response. Rather the problem of the monster's physical existence becomes identical to the problem of the law's linguistic existence. They are the same thing. The monster's physical existence *is* the law's linguistic non-existence and the law's linguistic existence *is* the monster's physical nonexistence.

In this variation on legal speech, therefore, to say that someone performs an act of violence is to say precisely that the problem of someone's linguistic and physical existence is the problem of the law's linguistic and physical existence. And it becomes possible to say this only because there is no cause and effect, no agency. There is no calling or conjuring into existence and no subversive repetition of the call. Nor is there any intent or *mens rea*. Rather, both the performance of the act and the (legal) narrative of this performance express—unlike in MacKinnon's analysis—the absolute simultaneity of physical and linguistic violence. If agency *were* brought into play, the linguistic and the physical would be dissociated from one another. In turn, the performance of the violent act would no longer be violent, would no longer be physical, and would no longer be a performance, absent response. Put another way, as Mary Atwell argues in her contribution to this volume, it was only as a "monster" that Aileen Wuornos could be the subject of three distinct types of violence: linguistic, subjective, and systemic; I would go a step further and posit that it is only by removing agency from the discussion of Wuornos that the interconnectedness of these types of violence can be made clear.

Another starting point for theorizing the performance of violence in the absence of agency can be found in a later series of Foucault's lectures, on *parrhesia,* speaking freely, or as he puts it in the title of the series, *Fearless Speech.* I should note right away that although I take Foucault's discussion of *parrhesia* as a useful example of performance without agency, I depart from his analysis in two respects. First, whereas Foucault argues that *parrhesia* is distinct from Austin's "performative utterance"—a "speech activity," he says, rather than a "speech act"[50]—I suggest that the two are very much related, and that the illocutionary speech act can be understood as precisely the "activity" that Foucault is describing.[51] Second, whereas Foucault argues that *"parrhesia,* in this Greek sense, can no longer occur in our modern epistemological framework,"[52] I locate variations on *parrhesia* in the modern political realm. Indeed, one effective way of getting at the multi-dimensional nature of the performance of violence is to address it as very much a type of modern *parrhesia.*

A key characteristic of *parrhesia,* in fact, is that its relentless physicality is grounded first and foremost in the overlap of speaker and speech—in the demolition of the subject/object and cause/effect frameworks demanded by agency. In *parrhesia,* Foucault states, the speaker "is the subject of the opinion to which he refers."[53] This seems like a relatively simple relation-ship—or, if not, then a sort of hyperbolic variation on the sovereign subject brought about by the fantasy of autogenesis that Butler describes. But by understanding the freely spoken subject as both the subject who speaks and the subject who is spoken—and spoken not by anyone else but "himself"—Foucault has articulated a theory of speech that avoids the problem of instrumentality and the short circuiting of discussion. These are not active subjects who produce passive speech. Nor are these subjects formed by discourse who in turn manipulate discourse. Rather these are subjects who *are*, physically, speech.[54]

Indeed, as Foucault continues, when engaging in *parrhesia* "you risk death to tell the truth instead of reposing in the security of a life where the truth goes unspoken;" or, more bluntly, *parrhesia* sets up a constant, if always potential, dichotomy between being "a truth-teller" on the one hand and being "living" on the other.[55] When you are engaging in *parrhesia*, that is, linguistic and physical existence cannot be unrelated. At the same time, though, this is not an attack on the body through the instrument of speech; nor is this a social experience of the body formed through discourse; rather it is, once more, the problem of linguistic experience made identical to the problem of physical existence. The question of whether you exist linguistically is exactly the same as the question of whether you exist physically. The two cannot be delinked. Both the "bad" and "good" forms of *parrhesia*—"chattering"[56] or "having a mouth like a running spring"[57] in the first case, and existing as nothing more nor less than the one who speaks the truth in the second[58]—get at precisely this simultaneity of physical and linguistic being. Neither can have anything to do with agency because there is no space between speaker and speech. Both understand physical existence as the thing that is speech.[59]

Now it is from this point that Foucault develops his argument that *parrhesia* is not possible in the modern world, where there must be a distinction between subject and object, or between cause and effect—where there must be agency—for speaking the truth to be possible. Again, though, I want to suggest that this discussion of *parrhesia* can nonetheless be brought to bear on the modern speech act and its physical violence. Indeed, Foucault's theorization of subjects who are their own speech, of linguistic existence that problematizes physical existence, and of truth that is a physical activity rather than the product of dialogue—rather than the result of repetitive call and response—can serve as a starting point for rethinking the performance of violence. More particularly, it can move conversations about violence away from the realm of intent, instrumentality, will, and indignation, of victim-perpetrator relationships and the politics on which these relationships are founded.

Voters without Agency

I move now to one concrete example of how removing agency from the picture might help descriptions of the performance of violence.[60] The late nineteenth- and early twentieth-century women's suffrage movement has, again, been a movement very much associated with theories of agency. Especially to the extent that suffragists were violent, they were understood to be agents; to the extent that their violence was damaging or inappropriate, it was so in that it undermined the agency of others. An alternative narrative of the suffrage movement is also possible, however—one that does not distill the movement's violence into another lesson about agency, indignation, condemnation, and redress. In this narrative, speaking and writing about women's suffrage plays up the simultaneous problems of linguistic, physical, and now political existence. In this narrative, both pro-suffrage and anti-suffrage advocates understand talking about suffrage, as well as women's votes themselves, to be examples of contemporary *parrhesia*—examples of performative speech that elicits no answer or response. And finally, in this narrative, women's votes, as well as speech about women's votes, become acts of emphatically physical assault—a transformation possible only when agency is withdrawn from the discussion.

I begin, therefore, with an 1867 *New York Times* article written by Horace Greeley, a progressive newspaper publisher and prominent nineteenth-century anti-suffrage advocate. In this article, Greeley gave voice to what would become a running theme in the anti-suffrage literature—the silent desire on the part of women not to vote:

> I hold that this consent may be, and often is, tacitly given, but that it is none the less conclusive on that account. I sought information from different quarters on the main point, and all practically agreed in the conclusion that the women of our State do not choose to vote.[61]

Less than a decade later, advocates of women's suffrage took up the theme of silence and desire for their own purposes. In an effort to reinforce their argument that women voters would purify politics, they used Wyoming—where women had started voting in state but not federal elections in 1869—as a recurrent example of the wholesome potential of a female electorate. "No noisy discussion would arise around the polls," they argued, "because invariably, when a woman came up, all such conversation would cease. . . . [T]he people went to the polls and voted as quietly as they go to church."[62] Finally, in 1910, the liberal social reformer and minister Lyman Abbott once again re-appropriated the silence trope as a means of excluding women from the electorate. Starting with the general moral point that "to set class against class is bad, to set race against race is worse, to set religion against religion is even more perilous; but to set sex against sex is a degradation so deep that political polemics can no further go," he then narrowed his argument to the question of law: "all lawyers know that the prejudice of all juries and of many judges is in favor of woman in any case in which a woman is involved. . . . [W]hat cannot be accomplished by legislation cannot be accomplished by suffrage."[63]

I have started with these passages because each implicitly or explicitly equates the problem of women's political existence with silence, or with the problem of linguistic existence. Moreover, each understands silence to be a fundamental underpinning of democratic politics more generally. By insisting on women's tacit desire not to vote, for example, Greeley takes nineteenth-century social contract theory, along with its valorization of consent, in a radical direction. The passage is not simply a repetition of the misogynist notion that women are, or should be, politically nonexistent, and thus are, or should be, silent. Rather, it explodes such linear cause/effect relationships—leaving no framework at all within which a cause, speech, might produce an effect, political existence. And in place of such relationships, Greeley develops a theory that makes political existence precisely the same thing as linguistic nonexistence—or, more broadly, that makes the problem of political existence *into* the problem of linguistic existence. What Greeley describes, in other words, is a total simultaneity between subject and silence or subject and speech. Moreover, as soon as any space is opened up between a subject and speech—as soon as, for instance, a woman speaks, votes, or produces a linguistic effect—political existence, consent, and desire cease to have any narrative coherence.

Once more, however, it was not only opponents of women's suffrage who understood the problem of linguistic existence to be identical to the problem of political existence—and indeed, my point in this section is emphatically not that when women overcame the misogynist demands for their silence, and raised their voices in protest, they achieved a more effective form of political engagement. Rather, again, regardless of whether the conversations surrounding suffrage supported women voting or attacked it, all stressed the political—and then eventually physical—violence that rested in this speech. When women's suffrage advocates celebrated the decorum of the Wyoming elections as a triumph for their cause, they were essentially arguing that women's votes and women's voices represented an end to speech—represented the breaking off of the offensive, meaningless nonsense that everyone knew speech at the polls to be.

When a woman entered political space, suffrage advocates argued, all discussion would cease. Instead of raising their voices in debate, citizens would recognize that such *effects* of speech were unimportant—that persuasion or the exchange of views, that the perlocutionary result, was a secondary and pointless characteristic of talking. They would recognize, in other words, that the importance of speech was identical to the existence of speech—in the same way that importance of religious belief was identical to the existence of this belief. The ideal was thus precisely the creation of a political sphere into which "political polemics [could] no further go"—a sphere in which law silenced would indeed, as Abbott suggested, become as monstrously meaningful as voices raised.

Again, though, this idealization of silence does not mean that there was no possibility of speech at all in these scenarios. The freely spoken citizen who engaged in *parrhesia* continued to be invoked, even as this invocation acknowledged the monstrous aspects of such engagement. The writing of another prominent anti-suffrage advocate, the historian Francis Parkman, for example, repeatedly described both the annihilating capacity of what was nonetheless necessary speech and the problematic simultaneity of linguistic, physical, and political existence. Throughout his books and essays on women's suffrage, Parkman repeatedly expressed his hope for, and fear of, monstrous, parrhesiastic political speech. In his article "The Woman Question Again," for instance, he links the unsuitability of women voting directly to their sentimental desire *to* vote, arguing that women,

> have a feeling that because [voting] is unpleasant, it must be right. Many a woman is moved by this feeling who would be unmoved by temptation in the shape of ease or pleasure. Simply because her nature revolts from politics, she cannot entirely rid herself of an idea that it is her duty to take part in them.[64]

He then moves on to the delicate balance that must, or ought to, exist between political truth or political principles on the one hand and the performance of these principles on the other:

Government should be guided by principles; but they should be sane and not crazy, sober and not drunk. They should walk on solid ground and not roam the clouds hanging to a bag of gas. Rights may be real or unreal. Principles may be true or false; but even the best and truest cannot safely be pushed too far, or in the wrong direction. The principle of truth itself may be cornered into absurdity.[65]

Finally, he concludes the article with a variation on the well-traveled idea that women's speech allows for no response:

We have replied to our critics, but must decline further debate. We do not like to be on terms of adverse discussion with women . . . and we willingly leave them the last word if they want it. Whatever we may have to say on the subject in the future will not be said in the way of controversy.[66]

According to Parkman, therefore, what is at stake in the question of women's suffrage is both the problematic physicality of linguistic existence—for women, pain, pleasure, and speech are the same thing—and the potential collapse of constative political speech (speech that can be true or false) into performative or illocutionary political speech (speech that can be absurd or not, unhappy or not).[67] For Parkman, that is, women's speech is a physical act that both tends toward the collapse of all speech into illocutionary performative speech and that denies any response or answer. Women's speech, in short, is parrhesiastic speech.

Again, though, Parkman's arguments are no different from those mobilized by women's suffrage advocates in the late nineteenth and early twentieth centuries—especially as these advocates sought explicitly to turn their speech acts into acts of bodily harm. In her 1916 Presidential Address to the National American Woman Suffrage Association, for example, Carrie Chapman Catt emphasized that the movement had reached a "crisis"—arguing indeed that even if it had not, "it is better to imagine a crisis where none exists than to fail to recognize one when it comes." She then encouraged suffragists to "take the crisis into victory" by "compel[ling] this array of lawmakers to see woman suffrage, to think woman suffrage, to talk woman suffrage every minute of every day until they heed our plea."[68] For Catt, that is, the precipitation of the crisis required a compulsive barrage of speech—speech that allowed for no distinction between speaker and listener, between body and language—such that lawmakers as well as suffragists *could* see, think, and talk nothing else. Here, the physically performative nature of women's speech, of speech that allowed for no response, and of speech of the sort that Parkman so feared, was deliberately mobilized as a physical threat.

This take on political speech, however, was, once more, nothing new. Some years earlier, a review of *History of Woman Suffrage* by Elizabeth Cady Stanton, Susan B. Anthony, and Matilda Johnson Gage played at length with the idea that excessive, compulsive, physically violent speech was a particular attribute of the suffrage movement. After discussing the book's lack of organization and general disarray, the reviewer concludes, "if the history of temperance, the missionary, and other similar movements were written in this way and on this scale, there are no libraries large enough to hold the books, and human life would need to be indefinitely extended to enable anybody to read them."[69] In the reviewer's dystopian fantasy, that is, the logical conclusion to the violent speech act is reached. In this scenario, the physicality of speech would both explode space and extend life, biopolitically, toward some horrifying indefinite limit. Not only does such speech allow for no response, but it physically batters both speaker and listener.

The women's suffrage movement can thus in at least one sense be characterized by the *challenge* it poses to the ostensible connection among speech, violence, and agency—by its eradication of the space between subject and speech, by its positing of speech as a constant, compulsive, and physical activity, and above all by its valorization of performances of violence precisely according to the unanswerability of these performances, to their denial of any response. As Parkman stated, he was addressing the "woman question" *again*. Once more, however, these conversations were by no means reiterating some sort of traditional, pre-modern, misogynist theme. Instead, they were getting at an essential quality of modern political existence linked to an essential quality of the performance of violence. Neither Parkman nor the reviewer, for instance, disqualifies women from voting because women are incapable of political engagement. Their arguments are more complicated than that. Women instead cannot vote because women are already too political—a point that Catt recognizes and makes use of. Women represent the horrifyingly physical endpoint to democratic engagement, they represent what it truly means to perform an act of violence, and therefore they must not vote, must not engage in what has been idealized as a purely rational, purely linguistic, cause/effect procedure.

When Parkman says that there is such a thing as taking truth too far, the key to his statement is not just that excess is undesirable. It is that this excessive truth and these excessive political principles, first, are inappropriately physical, second, collapse the constative and performative into one, and third, lead to silence, to the end of "controversy," to the end of any purely linguistic cause and effect relationship. He never argues that these truths are not in fact *true*. The reason that women cannot vote is indeed never that they are apolitical or cannot grasp political concepts. It is that they show the political speech act to be the inherently and physically violent act that it is. It is that women remove political truth from the realm of instrumentality. In a word, Parkman disqualifies women from the vote because their political speech is a form of *parrhesia*. And, like Foucault, Parkman recognizes that *parrhesia* is dangerous or "impossible"[70] when transferred to a modern political sphere that valorizes agency above all else.

When Catt thus calls on suffrage advocates to take the crisis into victory and to make their voices heard, her call is not to persuasion or discussion, not to speech that produces or repeats effects, but to an overwhelming physical assault. The primary difference between Catt and Parkman is therefore not how they theorize political speech. Each is addressing a type of *parrhesia*. The difference is that whereas Parkman describes *parrhesia* as something terrifying both politically and physically, Catt describes it as inevitable and also desirable.

In concluding, I repeat: this is not an essay about violence. Rather, it is an essay about discussions of violence, and why these discussions so frequently ignore violence in order to focus on guilt and innocence, condemnation and survival. It is an essay that asks why it is so hard to answer the question, "what do we mean when we say that someone performs an act of violence?" Again, to say that someone performs an act of violence is frequently to say something about agency. Perhaps, though, what is being said about agency is that agency is irrelevant to the performance of the violent act. As central as agency has been to the rhetoric of violence, that is—performing it, combating it, providing redress for it, preventing it—when it is mobilized as a means of understanding the violent *act,* it seems to provoke, in the words of Austin (and Felman citing Austin), a "misfire."[71] There is an attempt to engage violence linguistically, but the context is all wrong.

When agency enters the picture, it indeed opens up a space between subject and speech such that classical sovereign ideas (and ideals) of cause and effect, or of master and tool, become impossible to avoid. And let me reiterate: these ideas and ideals are questionable not just because they seem to undermine the political goals of critical scholarly engagement;

more so, and more important, they make impossible any narrative of the performance of violence in and of itself. They raise the specters of linguistic violence as physical violence, and the unanswerability of the violent act, but then short circuit any descriptions of these situations. What the elimination of agency does, therefore, is close up this space of instrumentality, and in turn raise the possibility of an interpretation of violence that does not automatically invoke perpetrators and their victims.

What the elimination of agency also does, however, is disallow any redress for, response to, or subversive repetition of the violent act. But this disallowance of redress or repetition—this move away from the active—is not necessarily a pessimistic move. By getting away from agency, we can start to think more clearly about what exactly it is that disturbs us about violence in general. And it is for this reason that I have focused my discussion on the seemingly narrow or marginal question of the violent speech of nineteenth- and twentieth-century suffragists in the United States. Although I am certainly not arguing that the political speech of these women is actually more parrhesiastic (or violent) than other types of political speech, their speech has nonetheless been held up repeatedly as an example of speech that is also an act of bodily harm. Both late nineteenth-century anti-suffrage advocates and late twentieth-century identity theorists discussed this linguistic/physical violence at length—the first condemning unhappy suffragists for presuming to speak for or about happy anti-suffragists,[72] and the second condemning privileged white women for presuming to speak for or about oppressed nonwhite women.[73] In both cases, what seemed to be at stake was the question of agency—who was allowed to use speech as an instrument on whose behalf.

Agency, however, can also be seen as quite marginal to the fear and disgust with which women's political speech has been met. Indeed, if agency and instrumentality—presuming to speak for or about someone else—were the sole problem, then any impetus toward representation, any democratic engagement at all, undertaken by anyone, would be equally reprehensible. There is thus arguably something more going on in these responses to the women's suffrage movement—something physical and something visceral. And this something can be teased out only when agency ceases to play the dominant role that it has in descriptions of the violent act. My point, again, is not therefore that agency is wrong, bad, or useless. My goal has instead been to explore what it might mean to talk about violence in the absence of agency. It has been to suggest that although agency provides an excellent framework for thinking about the performance of violence, it is at the same time only one of many frameworks.

NOTES

1. Bruno Latour, drawing on Luc Boltanski and Laurent Thévenot, has identified this mode of criticism as a symptom of the modern, and has likewise questioned its usefulness: "Luc Boltanski and Laurent Thévenot have done away with modern denunciation. . . . [Before] it was only a matter of choosing a cause of indignation and opposing false denunciation with as much passion as possible. To unmask: that was our sacred trust, the task of us moderns. . . . [W]ho is not still foaming slightly at the mouth with that particular rabies? . . . [Boltanski and Thévenot] do not denounce others. They do not unmask anyone. They show how we all go about accusing one another. . . . [I]nstead of practicing a critical sociology, the authors quietly begin a sociology of criticism." Bruno Latour, *We Have Never Been Modern*, trans. Catherine Porter (Cambridge: Harvard University Press, 1993), 44.

2. See, for instance, "Come and see the violence inherent in the system! Help! Help! I'm being repressed!" Terry Gilliam and Terry Jones, *Monty Python and the Holy Grail* (10 May 1975).

3. I borrow this term as well from Bruno Latour, who argues that much of the current discussion surrounding the sciences seeks (like the discussion surrounding violence) "by no means to *describe* the sciences . . . but to *short circuit* any and all questions as to the nature of the complex bonds between the sciences and societies." Bruno Latour, *Politics of Nature: How to Bring the Sciences into Democracy*, trans. Catherine Porter (Cambridge: Harvard University Press, 2004), 13 (italics in original).

4. See the discussion of the women's suffrage movement in England, for example, in Inderpal Grewal, *Home and Harem: Nation, Gender, Empire, and Cultures of Travel* (Durham: Duke University Press, 1996), 67–69.

5. Thomas Hobbes, *Leviathan* (New York: Simon and Schuster, 1962), 193.

6. Carl Schmitt, *Political Theology: Four Chapters on the Concept of Sovereignty*, trans. George Schwab (Chicago: University of Chicago Press, 2005), 63.

7. Catharine A. MacKinnon, *Feminism Unmodified: Discourses on Life and Law* (Cambridge: Harvard University Press, 1987, 129.

8. "Why agency? Because the secular depends on particular conceptions of *action* and *passion*." Talal Asad, *Formations of the Secular: Christianity, Islam, Modernity* (Stanford: Stanford University Press, 2003), 67 (italics in original).

9. "The assumption here is that power—and so too pain—is external to and repressive of the agent, that it 'subjects' him or her, and that nevertheless the agent as 'active subject' has both the desire to oppose power and the responsibility to become more powerful so that disempowerment—suffering—can be overcome" (ibid., 71).

10. Ibid., 74.

11. "The anthropological literature on the subject seems to me marked by a lack of adequate attention to the limits of the human body as a site of agency—and in particular by an inadequate sensitivity to the different ways that an agent engages with pain and suffering" (ibid., 68).

12. Ibid., 74.

13. Ibid., 75.

14. Ibid., 94.

15. Ibid., 95.

16. In this sense, Asad echoes or reinforces much of the recent writing, frequently referred to as "posthumanist," that situates agency not only with humans, but with systems, networks, or environments. See, for instance, in addition to the work of Latour, the work of N. Katherine Hayles, especially *My Mother Was a Computer: Digital Subjects and Literary Texts* (Chicago: University of Chicago Press, 2005) or, more recently, Jane Bennett, *Vibrant Matter: A Political Ecology of Things* (Durham: Duke University Press, 2010).

17. An unsympathetic reader might point out here that although the second interpretation is in keeping with Asad's discussion of agency—in which the invocation of agency disallows a discussion of the unaswerability of the performance of violence—the first departs from his argument by replacing his *reformulation* of agency with an *elimination* of agency. What I hope will become clear over the following pages is that the elimination of agency is in some ways *one* logical conclusion to Asad's reformulation.

18. Sometimes this is an agency articulated in a vocabulary of sovereign subjectivity—where the statement that a person has done violence leads to questions about whether that person intended to do violence, whether there was a choice involved in the act, whether the effect of the violence was foreseeable, whether, in short, the performance was initiated by an individual possessed of rational free will. Sometimes, though, this is an agency articulated in a more critical vocabulary—where to say that someone performs an act of violence is to ask whether the performance of the violent act constructed an intelligible subject within a given discursive field, whether this performance subverted or reinforced existing discursive structures, whether the repetition of this performance contested or supported similar structures, or whether the performance of the act produced an effective "scene of [culturally intelligible] agency," in which subjects might simultaneously be constituted and act. As Judith Butler has argued with regard to performance in general (if not the performance of violence specifically), "construction is not opposed to agency; it is the necessary scene of agency, the very terms in which agency is articulated and becomes culturally intelligible. . . . [T]he critical task is . . . to locate strategies of subversive repetition enabled by those constructions, to affirm the local possibilities of intervention through participation in precisely the practices of repetition that constitute identity and, therefore, present the immanent possibility of contesting them" (Butler, *Gender Trouble* [New York: Routledge, 1990], 201). In both of these scenarios the performance of—and narratives of the performance of—violence are inextricably linked to agency. In the first, agency makes violence possible because violence is an act of sovereign choice and will. In the second, agency makes violence possible because it is only through repetition and resignification that an act can become intelligible as violence at all. And in both, violence also makes agency possible, either by excluding alternative modes of choice and will, or by calling the active subject into being in the first place. There is, however, something of a paradox at the heart of this association between violence and agency. Even as agency appears in narratives of violence, the foundations upon which it rests—rational intentionality on the one hand and intelligible subjectivity on the other—start to disintegrate. Even as it is valorized as the thing that redirects discourse, that nullifies linguistic violence (as Butler, for instance, argues that it does in her analysis of Toni Morrison's point that "oppressive language . . . *is* violence": Judith Butler, *Excitable Speech: A Politics of the Performative* [New York: Routledge, 1997], 9), it becomes dissociated from any kind of coherent subject formation. If nothing else, agency occupies a far more problematic place in discussions of violence than its repeated invocation would suggest.

19. As it was further developed by John Searle, *Speech Acts: An Essay in the Philosophy of Language* (Cambridge: Cambridge University Press, 1969), 54–72.

20. J. L. Austin, *How to Do Things with Words* (Cambridge: Harvard University Press, 1975), 109–14.

21. He notes, for instance, the danger of arguing that, say, the act of marriage, betting, judicial sentencing, etc. are "only words": "But probably the real reason why such remarks sound dangerous lies in another obvious fact, which is this. The uttering of the words is, indeed, usually a, or even *the*, leading incident in the performance of the act (of betting or whatnot), the performance of which is also the object of the utterance, but it is far from being usually, even if it is ever, the *sole* thing necessary if the act is to be deemed to have been performed" (ibid., 8).

22. Ibid., 133–40.

23. "In this sense, an 'act' is not a momentary happening, but a certain nexus of temporal horizons, the condensation of an iterability that exceeds the moment it occasions." Butler, *Excitable Speech*, 14.

24. As Austin argues (120–21), one of the important characteristics of the illocutionary act is that it is a "*conventional*" act (italics in original). Or, as Butler puts it, "But how does one go about delimiting the kind of 'convention' that illocutionary utterances presume? Such utterances do what they say on the occasion of the saying; they are not only conventional, but in Austin's words, 'ritual or ceremonial.' As utterances, they work to the extent that they are given in the form of a ritual, that is, repeated in time, and hence, maintain a sphere of operation that is not restricted to the moment of the utterance itself." Butler, *Excitable Speech*, 3.

25. Butler, *Excitable Speech*, 150–51.

26. "The legal effort to curb injurious speech tends to isolate the 'speaker' as the culpable agent, as if the speaker were at the origin of such speech. The responsibility of the speaker is thus misconstrued. The speaker assumes responsibility precisely through the citational character of speech. The speaker renews the linguistic tokens of a community, reissuing and reinvigorating such speech. Responsibility is thus linked with speech as repetition, not as origination" (ibid., 39). "The constraints of legal language emerge to put an end to this particular historical anxiety, for the law requires that we resituate power in the language of injury, that we accord injury the status of an act and trace that act to the specific conduct of a subject. Thus, the law requires and facilitates a conceptualization of injury in relation to a culpable subject, resurrecting 'the subject' . . . in response to the demand to seek accountability for injury" (78).

27. Ibid., 78.

28. I should note that my reading relies on a complete (working) distinction between perlocutionary speech and illocutionary speech—a distinction that is in some ways arbitrary. My purpose in maintaining this distinction, however, is once again to pursue just one possible avenue of inquiry. By assuming this distinction, for the sake of this argument, it becomes possible to examine more clearly some of the problems with agency in discussions of violence.

29. "When we claim to have been injured by language, what kind of claim do we make? We ascribe an agency to language, a power to injure, and position ourselves as the objects of its injurious trajectory. We claim that language acts, and acts against us, and the claim we make is a further instance of language, one which seeks to arrest the force of the prior instance. Thus, we exercise the force of language even as we seek to counter its force, caught up in a bind that no act of censorship can undo" (ibid., 1).

30. Ibid., 15.

31. Ibid., 26–27.

32. This passage continues with an effective critique of calls such as MacKinnon's to regulate or curtail violent speech: "It is therefore impossible to regulate fully the potentially injurious effect of language without destroying something fundamental about lan-

guage and, more specifically, about the subject's constitution in language. On the other hand, a critical perspective on the kinds of language that govern the regulation and constitution of subjects becomes all the more imperative once we realize how inevitable is our dependency on the ways we are addressed in order to exercise any agency at all" (ibid.).

33. "there is no language specific to the problem of linguistic injury, which is, as it were, forced to draw its vocabulary from physical injury. In this sense, it appears that the metaphorical connection between physical and linguistic vulnerability is essential to the description of linguistic vulnerability itself" (ibid., 4).

34. Ibid., 5.

35. Ibid., 159.

36. Ibid., 15.

37. As Austin argues (by way of scare quotes), "The illocutionary act 'takes effect' in certain ways, as distinguished from producing consequences in the sense of bringing about states of affairs in the 'normal' way, i.e. changes in the natural course of events. . . . [S]o here are three ways, securing uptake, taking effect, and inviting a response, in which illocutionary acts are bound up with effects; and these are all distinct from the producing of effects which is characteristic of the perlocutionary act." Austin, 117–18. I address the question of "producing a response" below.

38. "That linguistic domain over which the subject has no control is exercised by the speaking subject. Autonomy in speech, to the extent that it exists, is conditioned by a radical and originary dependency on language whose historicity exceeds in all directions the history of the speaking subject. And this excessive historicity and structure makes possible the subject's linguistic survival as well as, potentially, that subject's linguistic death." Butler, *Excitable Speech*, 28.

39. Ibid., 52.

40. Ibid.

41. Ibid., 136.

42. "Acting one's place in language continues the subject's viability, where that viability is held in place by a threat both produced and defended against, the threat of a certain dissolution of the subject. If the subject speaks impossibly, speaks in ways that cannot be regarded as speech or as the speech of a subject, then that speech is discounted and the viability of the subject called into question. The consequences of such an irruption of the unspeakable may range from a sense that one is 'falling apart' to the intervention of the state to secure criminal or psychiatric incarceration" (ibid., 136).

43. Austin (117–18) highlights the fragility of the response in the illocutionary situation when he notes that it is "by convention" that "many illocutionary acts invite . . . a response or sequel," but that the line between convention and lack of convention is difficult to define, and that the responses themselves blur the distinction between illocutionary and perlocutionary speech.

44. As in Butler's discussion of Louis Althusser's description of interpellation: "this account appears to imply that social existence, existence as a subject, can be purchased only through a guilty embrace of the law, where guilt guarantees the intervention of the law and, hence, the continuation of the subject's existence. If the subject can only assure his/ her existence in terms of the law, and the law requires subjection for subjectivation, then, perversely, one may (always already) yield to the law in order to continue to assure one's own existence. The yielding to the law might then be read as the compelled consequence of a narcissistic attachment to one's continuing existence." Judith Butler, *The Psychic Life of Power: Theories in Subjection* (Stanford: Stanford University Press, 1997), 112–13.

45. Required for "hate speech" to operate effectively *as* hate speech.

46. Austin, 62.

47. Ibid., 57.

48. Michel Foucault, *Abnormal: Lectures at the Collège de France, 1974–1975*, trans. Graham Burchell (New York: Picador, 2005), 56.

49. Ibid., 64.

50. Michel Foucault, *Fearless Speech*, ed. Joseph Pearson (Los Angeles: Semiotext(e), 2001), 12–13.

51. Butler (*Excitable Speech*, 14) makes a similar point when she notes that "an 'act' is not a momentary happening, but a certain nexus of temporal horizons, the condensation of an iterability that exceeds the moment it occasions."

52. Foucault, *Fearless Speech*, 14.

53. Ibid., 12.

54. To some extent this interpretation of subject and speech is similar to Benveniste's as it is presented (and then critiqued) by Shoshana Felman: "'The act is thus identical with the utterance of the act. The signified is identical to the referent.' The (performative) utterance is the mirror image of the (performative) statement. This reasoning is not without relevance, and yet, it draws false implications from Austin's thought. The performative is indeed self-referential, but for Austin this does not mean that it refers to an exhaustive specularity or to a perfect symmetry between statement and enunciation. On the contrary, it is from *asymmetry* that Austin's thought proceeds, from the *excess* of utterance with respect to the statement, from the 'force of utterance' as a—referential—residue of statement and meaning." Shoshana Felman, *The Scandal of the Speaking Body: Don Juan with J. L. Austin, or Seduction in Two Languages*, trans. Catherine Porter (Stanford: Stanford University Press, 2003), 53. In other ways, I follow Felman's lead in addressing the (physical) excess of the speech act.

55. Foucault, *Fearless Speech*, 17.

56. Ibid., 13.

57. Ibid., 63.

58. I should note here that there is a difference between being the one who speaks the truth and being one who chooses to speak the truth. The latter type—possessed of agency and choice—is very alien to the realm of *parrhesia*. If, that is, you know the truth and "choose" not to speak it, then you are not in fact a parrhesiastic subject. The point of *parrhesia* is precisely that knowing the truth and speaking the truth are the same thing—choice or desire does not enter the picture.

59. Indeed, it is arguably for this reason that Foucault is so insistent on *parrhesia* being an ongoing "activity" rather than a singular "act." An activity is physical, constant, detached from cause and effect. An act, on the contrary, is unitary, coherent, and hints almost necessarily at intent, will, and satisfied desire. Felman likewise points out the contradiction between satisfaction and the speech act: "Thus Austin, like Don Juan, reveals the erotic scandal of linguistic philosophy—the incongruous interdependence of the failed operations of sex and language. Failure, to be sure, pervades every performance, including even that of theory, which in turn becomes erotic for being nothing but a failed act, or an act of failing. . . . [F]ar from achieving the satisfaction of theoretical 'felicity,' the Austinian performance is itself exposed to misfire. . . " (Felman, 79).

60. At the same time, I do not address what may seem like the most obvious coming together of the physical and the linguistic in early twentieth-century suffrage history—the militant suffragette movement's mobilization of women's bodies against women's political exclusion. My reasons for doing so are, first, that implicit in this tentative theory of violence without agency is the idea that performances of violence, although encompassing embodied human subjects, become intelligible only when evaluated beyond embodied human activity and according to their systemic, posthuman operations. Second, I tend to agree with Laura E. Nym Mayhall that the overriding scholarly focus on suffragists' bodies has detracted from conversations about the broader implications of the suf-

frage movement. See Laura E. Nym Mayhall, *The Militant Suffrage Movement: Citizenship and Resistance in Britain, 1860–1930* (New York: Oxford University Press, 2003). See also Laura E. Nym Mayhall, "Defining Militancy: Radical Protest, the Constitutional Idiom, and Women's Suffrage in Britain, 1908–1909," *Journal of British Studies* 39, no. 3 (July 2000): 340–71, 341–42, 344.

61. Horace Greeley, "Mr. Greeley on Female Suffrage," *New York Times,* October 3, 1867, 4.

62. J. W. Kingman, "Woman Jurors in Wyoming," *Christian Union* 7 (6) (February 5, 1873): 106.

63. Lyman Abbott, "Answer to the Arguments in Support of Woman Suffrage," *Annals of the American Academy of Political and Social Science* 35 (May 1910): 28–32, 28–29.

64. Francis Parkman, "The Woman Question Again," *North American Review* 130, no. 278 (January 1880): 16–30, 24.

65. Ibid., 29.

66. Ibid., 30.

67. For the problematic aspects of the collapse of constative and performative speech, see Felman, 14.

68. Terry Croy and Carrie Chapman Catt, "The Crisis: A Complete Critical Edition of Carrie Chapman Catt's 1916 Presidential Address to the National American Woman Suffrage Association," *Rhetoric Society Quarterly* 28, no. 3 (Summer 1998): 49–73, 51–52, 62.

69. "History of Woman Suffrage" *New York Evangelist* 52, no. 23 (June 23, 1884): 1.

70. In Butler's sense of the term.

71. Austin, 25. Felman, 29.

72. For instance, Thomas Wentworth Higginson, "Unsolved Problems in Women's Suffrage," *Forum,* January 1887, 439–50.

73. For instance, Philip N. Cohen, "Nationalism and Suffrage: Gender Struggle in Nation-Building America," *Signs* 21, no. 3 (Spring 1996): 707–27.

3
Performing Monstrous Violence
Aileen Wuornos, Murder, Abuse, and Exploitation

Mary Welek Atwell

Aileen Wuornos, labeled a "monster" and "the first female serial killer" provides an outstanding case study of the process whereby the doer is constituted through the deed.[1] Wuornos performed acts of violence—she admitted to killing seven men. Those acts of violence came to constitute her public identity as a serial killer and a "monster." Meanwhile, others performed acts of violence on the body and the psyche of Aileen Wuornos. She was abused by family members and others during her childhood. As a prostitute, she was assaulted by clients, and as a convicted murderer, she was killed by the state of Florida. Thus Wuornos also represents victim characteristics through a sustained set of acts performed by other individuals and through the systemic violence of a society in which she was exploited and marginalized. In the story of Aileen Wuornos, there is an analogy with Judith Butler's discussion of gender not as integral but as shifting, as a reiterated social performance.[2] So it is with the offender/victim nexus. Status as a victim or as an offender is related not to a fundamental identity but to the performance of acts deemed criminal.[3] As James Clifford argues, identity is not simply a matter of historical or legal record but rather a collection of ambiguous images, "a nexus of relations actively engaging a subject."[4] Wuornos provides a case study that highlights the gaps between the performance of violent acts and the master status of "serial killer," a status defined by the perception of others.[5] Her story illustrates the limitations of any single label and the inadequacy of the legal process and the popular culture to cope with the ambiguity of identity.

But public perception often conflates acts with essence. This essay will examine first of all, the chronology of Wuornos's life and the process whereby the violence incorporated into her personal history was transformed into the public perception of a large, ugly, frightening creature, an inhumanely cruel or wicked person, a "monster," malignantly responsible for her own fate and the tragedies of others. It will further examine the violent context in which Wuornos's story evolved, the "background" systemic violence of the larger society and the specific violence of the criminal justice system.[6] Finally, I will consider the portrayal of Wuornos in the media, particularly the documentary and feature films that purported to reveal a version of her biography.

At the time of her 2002 execution, press coverage noted that Aileen Wuornos had been the subject of three books, two allegedly documentary made-for-TV movies, and an opera. The next year, Charlize Theron, made up as a startling look-alike for Wuornos, earned an Oscar for her role in *Monster*.[7] Wuornos's life became a spectacle in which violence featured almost as a character and viewers were invited to gawk and gloat. The "true crime" books and to a large extent, the film productions, emphasized the sensational aspects of the case. None hesitated to label Wuornos a "serial killer." Other sobriquets quickly attached to her were "damsel of death" and, most provocatively, "monster." Why was there such fascination with this story? What veins of interest in violence were tapped by the media and the justice system which dissected the life and death of Aileen Wuornos? One might say that the Wuornos story is a conflict between different ways of "encoding violence." For those who prosecuted Wuornos, her violent acts were instrumental, intended for a purpose, and that purpose was power and money. For her defenders, Wuornos's violence should be seen as expressive, as an emotional response to abuse, violence, and exploitation.[8]

Chronology

This discussion begins with an account of the events leading up to Wuornos's arrest, her subsequent trials, her death sentences, and her execution. Between December 1989 and November 1990, police found the bodies of six men along Florida highways.[9] A seventh man's car was found, although his body was never located. All of the men were middle aged. All had been robbed. The recovered bodies had been shot with a .22 caliber handgun. Three of the men were undressed—one totally nude, one wearing only a baseball cap, and one in a pair of tube sox, all in humiliating poses. Police linked the murders, and the media latched onto the idea of a "serial killer." Investigators developed composite pictures of two women seen near one of the abandoned cars. One suspect was tall and blond, the other shorter and dark-haired. Receipts found in several of the cars led the police to question convenience store clerks who remembered two women matching the sketches making purchases. Within three weeks of releasing the composites to the public, by mid-December 1990, the authorities had received over 900 leads. At least four phone calls identified the shorter dark woman as Tyria Moore and the taller as Aileen Wuornos.

Wuornos and Moore had been involved in a four-year relationship, beginning as lovers and apparently remaining as roommates. Moore left Wuornos and moved to Pennsylvania around the time the two were identified by the authorities. Wuornos's life became extremely disorganized without her partner. She had pawned or given Moore everything valuable taken from the victims. All her possessions fit into one suitcase and a few boxes in a storage locker. Homeless, Wuornos spent her last night of freedom on an abandoned car seat outside the Last Resort, a biker bar. Police arrested her there on the morning of January 9, 1991. A key on a chain around her neck opened a storage space at Jack's Mini-Warehouse. A few items of personal property belonging to the murder victims, apparently too worthless to pawn, were found there. The case of "the damsel of death" had been solved.

As Nick Broomfield points out in his documentary film, *Aileen Wuornos: The Selling of a Serial Killer,* the label "serial killer," affixed to Wuornos before her arrest, colored everything that would happen later. Once that term was used, it may be argued that both the media and the state tried to fit Aileen Wuornos into the existing definition, despite the difficulty of forcing her into that pigeonhole. To qualify as a serial killer according to the FBI's definition, one must murder three or more people over a period of more than thirty days. The motive is usually power or psychological gratification, and a sexual element is often involved.[10] The vast majority of serial killers are male; most are highly intelligent. They often come from dysfunctional families and have been victims of abuse or neglect.[11] But the term is only a label, although a label laden with resonance. It will become clear that Aileen Wuornos, at most, fit only a few elements of the serial killer profile, yet it may be argued that the differences between her and the profile, the very novelty of her sex—the first *female* serial killer—subjected her to greater exploitation on the part of many within the justice system as well in the popular media. The novelty made her and her story a more valuable commodity.[12] She fit David Garland's description of "the criminology of the other," which involves demonizing the offender, acting out popular fears and resentments, and promoting support for state punishment."[13]

Perhaps it was the advantage of identifying a single villain in the case

that led Florida authorities not to charge Tyria Moore as an accessory but
to engage her cooperation in getting a confession from Aileen Wuornos.[14]
It was also alleged that Moore had entered into a profitable contract, along
with two detectives, to sell her story for a television movie. The two detectives were later removed from their positions.[15] In any case, Moore was
invaluable in extricating a confession from Wuornos. After eleven telephone conversations taped by police in which Moore alternately cried and
pretended to fear arrest, she convinced Wuornos to take full blame for the
crimes. The defense would later claim that Moore "exploited" the relationship and Wuornos's "tremendous love" for her to get a rambling, virtually
incoherent three-hour statement from Wuornos.[16]

The confession was recorded on audio and videotape and released to
the press before the trial. It was later published as a sort of monograph,
Monster: My True Story.[17] Wuornos admitted to seven killings, but claimed
all were in self defense. "When they started getting rough with me, I went
. . . I just opened up and fired at them. Then I thought to myself, Why are
you giving me such hell for when I just . . . I'm trying to make my money
. . . and you're giving me a hassle."[18] Although a public defender was
present, Wuornos ignored his advice to refuse to answer the questions.
Instead, in her effort to protect Moore from any blame, she bragged about
being with "a hundred thousand guys," all of whom were unharmed unless they threatened her. Oddly, Wuornos did not seem to know the details
of the murders and when she did mention them, she mixed them up. She
claimed to be drunk at the time of the events and did not even know the
victims' names. Nonetheless, she claimed to be telling the truth. "I mean I
can't be any truthfuller."[19] However, one cannot read her confession without realizing that Wuornos did not or could not recall the specifics of the
crimes. Her tendency to conflate the murders might be seen as proof that
she was a sociopath who had no respect for human life, as the state and
most of the media would portray her. Or her confusion of the details of the
episodes might provide evidence to support her claim of self-defense if
each threatening encounter triggered some type of Post-Traumatic Stress
Disorder, where she struck out in what she perceived as protecting herself.[20]

Wuornos's confession provides an instance of contested interpretations
of performing violence. Were Wuornos's violent actions cold-blooded killing or self-defense? Is self-defense limited to the terms spelled out in the
law or is the response governed by the perception of the person threatened (even if that perception is inaccurate)?[21]

The cold-blooded killer version carried the day when Wuornos was tried for the capital murder of the first victim, Richard Mallory. As Austin Sarat states, it is the "bad" violence by the defendant that prosecutors choose to portray vividly at trial. Such a version of events allows both the violence of the state in the criminal justice process and the history of violence in the defendant's life to be minimized.[22] Instead it encourages a focus on individual responsibility rather than on the circumstances that breed violence. By blaming the killer, defining her as a "monster," rather than as a person who did violent deeds, it is possible to obscure the moral ambiguity in the violence perpetrated by the state.[23] Slavoj Zizek makes a similar point. He identifies three levels of violence: the violence of language; the systemic violence caused by the "smooth functioning of the political and economic systems, which is invisible but helps to explain outbursts that oppose it"; and the subjective violence performed by individuals. In his view, the focus on the subjective violence distracts from the true site of trouble, the system (capitalist, patriarchal) that automatically excludes dispensible individuals.[24] This is surely true in the legal proceedings against Aileen Wuornos.

Chimene Keitner notes that themes of lesbianism, man-hating, deceitfulness, greed, deviance, and manipulativeness featured in Wuornos's trial and that both the prosecution and the defense tried to win over the jury using sex-role stereotypes.[25] The prosecutor's opening statement portrayed Wuornos as a predator, motivated by greed and a desire to subjugate men, even confounding prostitution with domination. "She was no longer satisfied with $10, $20, $40. She wanted it all. And she had to take it. And she did. And she used a gun to take it. And she shot him to keep it . . . Aileen Carol Wuornos liked control. She had been exercising control for years over men. Tremendous power that she had through prostitution. She had devised a plan now and carried it out to have the ultimate control."[26] As the murder victim in this case was a man who paid for sex, he could not be portrayed simply as an innocent. Instead it seems the state had to make the defendant even worse, to encapsulate the violence she performed in the most unfeminine motives of power, control, and greed. And quite possibly the prosecutor hoped the jury would consider that her crime was aggravated because it was a subversion of the natural order of male dominance.

The state also reiterated the stereotype that a prostitute could not be raped. Instead, the prosecutor insisted that Wuornos *chose* to earn her living by prostitution because she "loved the guys, she loved the money, she loved the penis."[27] By claiming that Wuornos was the aggressor, physically and sexually, the prosecutor could deny that she acted in self-defense. Rather, her behavior was doubly deviant, both violent and immersed in unhealthy sexuality.

According to her defense attorney, Wuornos's behavior should not have been labeled aggression. On the contrary, she was repeatedly victimized. "Existence for Lee was getting to be very dangerous . . . Time after time she was raped. Time after time she was beaten up and she wasn't paid."[28] For Wuornos to earn the jury's empathy, her acts had to be seen as reasonable despite her lifestyle. She was "not like us" (i.e., she was a prostitute who killed several men), but it was not her fault. She "did what anyone would do, she defended herself."[29] In other words, if Wuornos's work in prostitution was outside the mainstream, her act of killing Mallory was built on the universal human instinct for self-preservation. She was both "like us" and "not like us." Clearly in the trial, both the prosecution and the defense were arguing that the context in which the violence was performed determined its legitimacy. Both employed what Josephine Gattuso Hendin calls the "strategic use of the narrative of violent action." She contends that the narrative becomes more important than "the actions that occasion the need for the strategy in the first place."[30]

Clifford also describes the stories constructed in the adversarial context of the courtroom. One side (in this case the prosecution) may rely on the formal historical record, the other side may invoke human memories, with all their natural gaps.[31] This became apparent when Wuornos took the stand during the guilt phase of the trial. This time her version of the encounter with Mallory differed significantly from her confession. In court, she described how she and Mallory had driven to an isolated place where they drank beer and vodka for hours, and where Wuornos became "drunk royal."[32] When she demanded payment before sex, Mallory wrapped a cord around her neck and threatened to kill her, "like the other sluts I've done." She described how he tied her hands to the steering wheel and raped her vaginally and anally. After cleaning himself off with rubbing alcohol, Mallory squirted it into Wuornos's vagina and rectum. Fearing Mallory would rape her again when he untied her, Wuornos described how she grabbed the gun from her purse and shot him.[33] Unlike the garbled version of events in her confession, the story Wuornos told in court was detailed and specific. By clouding the distinction between victim and killer, it cast her actions in an entirely different light from the image of the serial killer monster.

The district attorney took the opportunity to expose the contradictions between Wuornos's testimony and her earlier confession, which had contained none of the gruesome details. Wuornos explained that in her confession her main objective had been to protect Tyria Moore. At trial, she implicated her former partner, stating that Moore knew Mallory had been killed in self-defense, but had lied about it to cash in on book and movie deals. However, the longer Wuornos remained on the witness stand, the more rambling and incoherent she became. Her frustration was especially obvious when the prosecutor attempted to bring up the other murders.[34] Wuornos's testimony may be an example of what Zizek sees as a distinction between "truth" and "truthfulness." Truth is what people think of as facts and statistics. Truthfulness is more elusive. Factual deficiencies may be a way of demonstrating the reality of a trauma. The very inconsistency in a description of a traumatic experience may be a measure of its truthfulness.[35] Of course in court, it is the "truth" that is supposed to prevail over truthfulness. As Clifford notes, the adversarial system requires a "yes" or "no," not a "yes but . . ." or "it depends."[36]

Florida law allowed testimony about "collateral offenses" even though a defendant had not been convicted of them, if it could be shown that there was a plan or pattern of criminal conduct. This was the state's strategy in portraying Wuornos as a serial killer, even though she was on trial only for the murder of Richard Mallory. The "similar crimes evidence" would challenge her claim that she killed Mallory in self-defense. Instead the prosecution wanted to show that Wuornos had a "common scheme or plan to use her status as a prostitute to lure and trap men in isolated areas" to rob and kill them. Of the six-day trial, the state devoted four days to testimony about the other murders. The defense claimed that the later killings did not prove that Mallory's murder was part of a plan. Just as logically, it could have been self-defense and the incident that provoked the others when Wuornos found herself in similar situations.[37] This was a particularly strong argument, as between the trial and the appeal a reporter for *Dateline NBC* uncovered information that Mallory had earlier served a ten-year sentence for violent rape. Neither the prosecution nor the defense had introduced that evidence at Wuornos's trial, yet the reporter found it merely by checking the FBI's data base.[38] It is quite possible that Mallory's criminal history would have added some credibility to Wuornos's claim of rape and self-defense, but the appellate courts found it insufficient to reverse either the conviction or the sentence. In addition, the Florida Supreme Court upheld the introduction of the collateral offenses. They found that the crimes showed a "pattern of similarities" and the "relevance outweighed prejudice."[39]

After the jury found Aileen Wuornos guilty of the first-degree murder and armed robbery of Richard Mallory, the trial entered the penalty phase, which permitted the state to argue that she deserved to be executed and the defense to claim there were mitigating factors to consider before sentencing her. Before hearing such testimony, the jury most likely was influenced by her outburst when the verdict was announced. "I'm innocent. I was raped. I hope you are raped, you sons of bitches and scumbags of America."[40] Her yelling and cursing in the courtroom might also be seen as Wuornos's verbal reaction to the violence of the state against her. Robert Cover notes one perspective on such verbal explosions as a response to violence, that at a deeper level they shatter the façade that all the violence is on the defendant's side and all the civility is on the state's side.[41]

The major issue in the sentencing phase was Wuornos's mental health. Both defense and prosecution psychologists testified that she suffered from borderline personality disorder and antisocial personality disorder. Among the three doctors called by the defense, one stated that she was "one of the most primitive people I've seen outside an institution," who spent most of her time dealing with the basic needs for food, shelter, clothing, and security. With a ninth-grade education and mental, emotional, and physical disabilities, prostitution seemed her only way to survive. Because of earlier abuse and earlier rapes, Wuornos reasonably perceived Mallory as a threat and acted accordingly.[42] Meanwhile, the prosecution psychologist claimed that Wuornos's personality disorders and impaired capacity at the time of the crime were not "substantial" factors. In his closing statement, the district attorney characterized Wuornos's violent acts as her own totally free choice. He minimized the violence committed against her. "The question is whether she knew what she was doing and chose to do it in spite of its wrongness . . . Aileen Wuornos at the time of the killing knew right from wrong."[43] Maximizing the "bad violence" committed by the defendant and her individual responsibility, he stated, "By an act of her will, he was no more."[44]

The language of the defense attorney was hardly more respectful of Wuornos's human dignity. According to public defender Tricia Jenkins, Wuornos "dealt with her experience with the insight of a damaged, primitive child. In her mind, she thought she was in danger, she was threatened. It was the only thing she knew how to do."[45]

Had the jury been limited to considering the Mallory case, they might have accepted Wuornos's claim of self defense. But, given the picture drawn by the state, the multiple murders committed in the commission of robbery, jurors saw the violent character the prosecution wanted them to see—the serial killer who committed murder that was cold, calculated, and premeditated, without moral or legal justification.[46] They sentenced Aileen Wuornos to death for the murder of Richard Mallory. Instead of the usual "May God have mercy on your soul," the judge in Wuornos's case pronounced, "May God have mercy on your corpse."[47] In contrast to the prosecutor's claim, "by an act of her will he was no more," the judge did have the power to end Wuornos's life—not by an act of will, but by an interpretive act. As Cover explains, a judge's verbal act in pronouncing sentence authorizes and legitimizes the violent deed of execution, although the actual killing will be carried out through the cooperative specialized behaviors of wardens, guards, police officers, and others.[48]

Between March 1992 and February 1993, Wuornos pleaded guilty to the five additional murders of Charles Humphreys, Troy Burress, David Spears, Charles Carskaddon, and Walter Antonio. She had given up her public defender and hired Steve Glazer, who represented her in exchange for the rights to sell her story to documentary filmmaker Nick Broomfield. Admitting at the fifth and final plea hearing that he was incompetent to argue the case in court, Glazer told the judge, "Ms. Wuornos understands that I do not have the capital experience necessary to take the case to trial . . . And if this case were to go to trial, I would immediately ask to withdraw because I could not possibly defend her the way she needs to be defended." To this admission the judge merely replied, "Well, all right. I understand."[49]

Many capital defendants have had notoriously bad lawyers. Inadequate assistance of counsel is a common theme in death penalty appeals, and the stories of sleeping or drunk lawyers are familiar to all observers of the process. Wuornos's appellate attorneys raised the issue of Glazer's incompetence, lining his own pockets while he advised his client to take five guilty pleas. In one appeal, Wuornos argued that she was the victim of Glazer's failures. "What happens, though, in a case like this where a defendant has counsel who apparently does nothing to apprise his client of her defenses, but simply acceded to her wish to plead guilty?" Making an overt point that her attorney was depriving his client of her life, the ultimate act of violence, her appeal asked, "Was Glazer merely a Dr. Kevorkian of the law, who did what he could to facilitate Wuornos' desire to end her life? The law should condemn lawyers who cannot give reasonable advice to their clients as Glazer manifestly could not and did not do here. An attorney does more than simply stand by his client while she bumbles through a plea hearing. Glazer's incompetence fairly shouts from this record."[50] Wuornos had certainly bumbled through, stating for example at the Carskaddon hearing, "I understand everything, and as far as I'm concerned, I'm tired of the re-electorial [sic] scandals of trying to take these cases to court. And I've got three death sentences already that I'm not going to get appealed. I got one that may be appealed, very good appeal, and this one is silly, and I just don't . . . I know everything. Guilty."[51]

It is clear from the Broomfield documentary, *Aileen Wuornos: The Selling of a Serial Killer,* that Glazer was looking for a financial payoff from peddling his client's story. He demanded $20,000 from Broomfield.[52] Broomfield also includes footage of Glazer smoking marijuana on the way to meet with Wuornos at the prison. Whether he imagined himself as a media star or whether he simply wanted to make a few thousand dollars, it is clear that Glazer would have a better story to sell if he was representing "the first female serial killer" than if he represented a down-and-out woman who suffered from mental illness. The more death sentences Wuornos racked up, the more sensational her story. Lack of experience in the law, a mind befogged by drugs, and greed for personal gain constitute Glazer's behavior toward his client. In the conventional telling of the story, he committed no violence, yet surely he bore some personal responsibility for killing Aileen Wuornos. Cover discusses how the social organization of violence associated with the death penalty provides a setting where no single individual (incompetent attorney, judge, juror, prison guard, executioner) generates the outcome. Instead the blame for the violence is diffused among a variety of people, effectively absolving each of them from responsibility. Such diffusion of accountability stands in contrast to the simple blame associated with the defendant.[53]

Wuornos was executed by the state of Florida on October 9, 2002. After her first round of appeals failed, she insisted upon abandoning the appellate process. When someone sentenced to death becomes a "volunteer" and drops further appeals, the state must determine her competency to proceed. Once again, the mental state of Aileen Wuornos became the terrain where her future would be decided. While on death row, she complained that the prison staff were mistreating and even torturing her by poisoning her food and infiltrating her thoughts. Such charges might be a sign of her deteriorating mental state, or they might be, as an FBI analyst found, proof of her sanity.[54] According to that psychologist, it was normal for prisoners to complain about food and about correctional officers. Crackling sounds from the public address could account for Wuornos's claim that her thoughts were being controlled. He also cited another reason why Wuornos would abandon her appeals—she did not like to go to court because of the clothes, the uncomfortable shackles, and the possibility of being hit with a "jolt" if she became unruly.[55] This testimony merits further analysis as it reveals the multiple layers of violence to which the state could subject a death row prisoner, in this case, Aileen Wuornos.[56]

There is also the possibility that, in volunteering for execution, Wuornos seized the opportunity to make the one decision available to her. Wuornos was, according to her statement, willing to face execution, to undergo the ultimate violence, having the state take her life. To get to the death chamber, she had to prove that she was sane enough to abandon all efforts to prolong her life. If she was sane, what about her claims that she was being tortured by the prison authorities who allegedly interfered with her food, harassed her, and threatened to rape her? What of the brutality she experienced in prison? If she had fantasized those charges against her captors, she must arguably be too mentally ill to be put to death. As her last attorney argued, either she was delusional and should not be executed or her complaints had merit in which case her death wish is also more comprehensible. But, unsurprisingly, her grievances were dismissed as imaginary even while she was found competent to be put to death.

The mental health standard for execution is extraordinarily low. The convicted must only seem to express an understanding of why they are being put to death. They need not even understand the finality of the process.[57] Wuornos apparently met that minimal threshold. The district attorney who had prosecuted her put his stamp of approval on Wuornos's sanity. "She knew exactly what she was doing," he stated confidently. Governor Jeb Bush agreed to proceed with the execution.[58]

Whether the woman sent to the death chamber on October 9, 2002, was mentally sound is much less certain when one notes the observation of filmmaker Nick Broomfield and writer Christopher Berry-Dee, who said her mind had disintegrated. She was "all but insane."[59] Likewise in the last interview with Broomfield shown in the movie, *Aileen Wuornos: The Life and Death of a Serial Killer,* she spoke not only of conspiracies against her by the guards and police but also of being beamed up to another planet in a space vehicle. During the course of that interview, Wuornos became visibly less and less coherent. Broomfield asked afterward, "What would you have to do to fail a psychological test?"[60] It is also possible to infer the quality of her mental state from the instructions Wuornos left with Dawn Botkins, a childhood friend who may have been the only disinterested person communicating with Wuornos in the last days of her life. Aileen wrote imagining her funeral. "Please have a smile put on my face. Hair loose and lying relaxed around pillow and shoulders. Also I'd like a cross in my hands, like a small wooden one also a Bible tucked between my arm and rib cage, as my hands are folded holding the cross. Please put a single rose alongside my arm. Coffin—my taste is brown wood one, with light red or white satin exterior design." She suggested that Dawn have a cookout with music or another "ceremony deal" in her memory.[61] In Wuornos's mind, there would apparently be friends mourning her passing and remembering her life. It was a scene totally at odds with the morbid curiosity and inhumanity that surrounded her actual death by lethal injection.

Is the violence performed by the state less legitimate when the person subject to that violence is mentally ill? What is accomplished by doing what Broomfield described as "executing a person who's mad"?[62] Wuornos's last words cast doubts on the argument that her death was necessary to protect the community from a cold-blooded predator. "I'd just like to say I'm sailing with the rock, and I'll be back like Independence Day, with Jesus June 6. Like the movie, big mother ship and all, I'll be back."[63] After hearing that incoherent statement, some observers watched Wuornos die with ghoulish interest in the details of the seventeen minutes between the injections and her death. According to a TV reporter she turned toward the witnesses, made a bizarre face, "a kind of smile," then rolled her eyes and turned away. Then she "shut her eyes and her head jerked backwards . . . her mouth seemed to drop open, her eyes opened to slits, and it appeared she was gone."[64] Even as the state was ending her life, the focus of observers was not on the administration of the deadly poisons into her system, but on the facial expressions of the "monster" brought low by the power of the state of Florida, with invaluable assistance from the media for whom this woman had been a goldmine.

The Context

The fascination with Aileen Wuornos the "serial killer" and "monster" came not only from the criminal justice system but also from the news and entertainment media. But if the focus began with the prostitute-lesbian-murderer, it left out the backstory, the violence Wuornos experienced in her earlier life and the failures of social institutions to protect her from that brutality.

Born in Michigan, she was the daughter of a father convicted of child rape and kidnapping and a mother who deserted Aileen when she was an infant.[65] The maternal grandparents became Aileen and her brother's default guardians. They led the two siblings to believe they were their real parents and that an aunt and uncle were actually another brother and sister. Aileen became aware of her mother's abandonment when she was about twelve years old, a time when she came into increasing conflict with her grandparents, both of whom were alcoholics. Her grandfather was at the very least physically and verbally abusive to Aileen; her grandmother was powerless and helpless. In her home, Wuornos saw no models for healthy relationships. A woman could either become the victim of a brutal man or take the offensive.

Various accounts from Wuornos herself and others describe how her grandfather beat her regularly, how he killed her pet kitten, and how she was neglected when others in the family received gifts at Christmas. Around the time Aileen learned of her true parenthood, she began to have problems in school. School officials administered tranquilizers and suggested that she be taken for counseling—an idea her "parents" never followed. She was also diagnosed with hearing and vision problems. Those too were left untreated. Broomfield's film shows the neighborhood where Wuornos was raised. It is not a shantytown, but a working-class area with neat homes and lawns. It was not abject poverty that prevented her putative caregivers from attending to the child's needs.

Wuornos also claimed that her grandfather, her uncle, and her real brother had sexually abused her. Whether or not all of those allegations were true, the girl was definitely raped at the age of thirteen. She claimed it was an older friend of the family who offered her a ride home. Instead he drove her into the woods, threatened her with violence, and raped her. Wuornos became pregnant as a result of the rape and although she hid her condition as long as possible, she was eventually sent to the Florence Crittenden Unwed Mothers' Home where she gave birth—alone—to a child she never saw. Her grandparents made no effort to charge the man who had committed statutory rape against their granddaughter. Instead, they blamed her and offered her no support or assistance with her trauma even though the caseworker at the Crittenden Home told them she was immature, impulsive, and had no conception of the future. Her aunt stated that with the rape and its aftermath, Aileen became very angry and began to hate men.[66] Things only became worse when her grandmother died the next year. Blaming the pregnancy for his wife's death (actually it was from cirrhosis of the liver), the grandfather threw Aileen out of the house. She lived rough—in abandoned cars, in the woods, occasionally sleeping on a friend's sofa. Not one adult nor a single person in the helping professions came forward to help the fifteen-year-old. Yet as her former neighbors told Broomfield, everyone knew she was homeless. Boys thought of her as a "cigarette slut" who would have sex for a small payment or a few cigarettes. She drank a lot and experimented with drugs. Aileen Wuornos left "home" at sixteen and went on the road, eventually landing in Florida. There she met Tyria Moore in a gay bar and the two became lovers. Soon, in her effort to make money to support the two of them, Wuornos ended up in a car with Richard Mallory.

Psychologists Stacey L. Shipley and Bruce A. Arrigo have analyzed the connections between Wuornos's early experiences and her later mental illness. Among other things, they note that her early life was filled with "terror, rejection, and pain," and that she suffered from self-hatred and saw her body only as a commodity. They point out that as the men who were her customers further dehumanized her, she responded with anger and hatred. She had so little self-esteem that even the slightest insult could enrage her.[67] Shipley and Arrigo further argue that Wuornos's young life predisposed her to psychopathic antisocial personality disorder (ASPD).

Several observations flow from this diagnosis. On the one hand, all the factors that were symptoms of a psychosis could also be seen by jurors and other laypersons as reasons to condemn her behavior. As psychiatrist Dorothy Otnow Lewis argues, the offenders with the most severe mental illness often generate the least sympathy from the public or the legal system.[68] The violence performed in the throes of mental disease is likely to be treated by the criminal justice system as if it were violence performed based on totally free and rational choice, particularly if the violence is "heinous, atrocious, or cruel."

Second, although the psychological analysis can describe a link between childhood abuse and neglect and adult violence, for women in particular the line between victimization and offending is a blurry one. Such a woman wounded by those who were supposed to be her caregivers or her intimates lives with a chronic injury that may be turned outward, especially when traditional methods of self-medication through drugs or alcohol do not suffice.[69]

Both the psychological approach and the victim/offender nexus focus on the effects of violence by and on individuals. Neither approach looks at the larger social responsibility for violence. One could argue that Wuornos's story illustrates the systemic nature of violence identified by Zizek. In her youth, she experienced the violence of a criminal justice system that failed to punish her rapist and a social service process that punished her instead. More significantly, with few resources she tried to support herself in a patriarchal society where men bought women's bodies in exchange for money and where those women were blamed for the transaction. Further it is a system where those same sex workers were deprived of legal protection when they were subjected to violence at the hands of their customers. In such a social structure, Wuornos was marginalized and expendable. It is even further evidence of patriarchy that Wuornos's victims were relieved of moral responsibility for engaging in sexual commerce. They continued to enjoy the protection and even the adulation of the law that denied a prostitute could fight back in self-defense. The ultimate expression of the patriarchal structure in which the Wuornos case unfolded came from District Attorney John Tanner. He voiced concern that testimony in the Wuornos case might have damaged the reputations of her grandfather and of Richard Mallory (who had a prior conviction for violent rape). Tanner expressed pleasure that by sentencing Wuornos to death, the court had vindicated the good names of Mallory and her grandfather.[70] The patriarchal structure, with its permissiveness toward violence against women, remained unscathed.[71]

Why the Fascination with Aileen Wuornos?

What was it about the Aileen Wuornos story that led to an almost frantic interest on the part of journalists and filmmakers? If she was, as alleged, the first female serial killer, why was that so fascinating? The notion of a female outlaw is, on the one hand, inherently destabilizing. Outlaws in popular culture often serve the purpose of reinforcing the security of the law. In the traditional Western movie plot, outlaws are ultimately brought "inside" by the forces of law and order. But as Elizabeth Spelman and Martha Minow discuss in their analysis of *Thelma and Louise,* depending in part on their race, class, gender, or sexual orientation, outlaws can also be cast in the heroic role of rectifying injustice. Of course for the revenge to be successful, the "victim" of the revenge must be a despicable character. In the case of *Thelma and Louise,* when Thelma was the target of a sexual assault, Louise took matters into her own hands and shot the attacker. When the law does not protect women, heroic female outlaws exact revenge on the perpetrators.[72]

There is ample evidence that the legal system does not protect women, especially prostitutes, from violence, including sexual assault. Nor does the legal framework for claims of self-defense with its model of male hand-to-hand combat provide a realistic context for the violence women experience.[73] So in the film narrative *Thelma and Louise* and in the real saga of Aileen Wuornos, the public was treated to the spectacle of outlaw women. Spelman and Minow contend that outlaw women who take the law into their own hands in response to being humiliated and brutalized can provide a catharsis for others who recognize at least a partial vicarious identification with the avenger.[74] If their analysis is correct, it may provide at least one explanation for the interest in Aileen Wuornos. Although as portrayed in the popular press and in court, she was not in any sense heroic or glamorized as an outlaw, the documentary films by Nick Broomfield and *Monster* (discussed below) could be read that way. It is certainly possible that others who followed her story also felt the appeal of the outlaw image. If so, it was even more critical that the state destroy that version of reality. Andrew McKenna provides further explanation of that imperative. He explains that from the view of the sexual mainstream, gays, lesbians, and feminists "occupy the margins of sexually and socially differentiated roles."[75] One might add that prostitutes are comparably marginal. In McKenna's view, as historically the frontier was the line between "civilization" and "wilderness," in contemporary culture sexual unorthodoxy stands in for whatever is threatening, the modern wilderness. In such a scenario, the popular imagination thrives on "ritual spectacles of expulsion."[76] The need to banish the lesbian-prostitute by identifying her as a monster would justify the ultimate ritual spectacle of expulsion, the death penalty.

Josephine Gattuso Hendin's work addresses violence and women in contemporary culture. She notes that portrayals of violent women "reflect alternative interpretations of structures, power, meaning, and language." Women who engage in violence may be villains, but they demonstrate a "dramatic vortex . . . in which crises of culture and character become one."[77] Because violence by women is exceptional and rare compared to violence by men, Hendin argues that it evokes feelings that "affect self-concepts and relations with others and mobilize reactions from the community at large." In other words, representations of violent women "deform" the traditional male and female roles. In a Judith Butlerian sense, violent women expose a contingent identity, an "oscillation between passivity and empowerment, self-despair and grandiosity," between "self-affirmation and self-doubt."[78] Perhaps that is one reason violent women evoke both great fascination and great fear.

Hendin further explains that narratives of violence by women share communicative and expressive power when the individual experience intersects with the larger culture. Her work here suggests Spelman and Minow's view of the female outlaw avenging a system that permits violence against women. Hendin claims that the stories of female violence in popular culture are "strikingly different from those of male violence."[79] Such is the case with Aileen Wuornos, where both the violence she performed and the violence performed against her are incomprehensible outside a gendered context.

But Hendin maintains that many American portrayals of violent women depict intense personal motivations. They serve as paradigms of mainstream thinking, with an emphasis on individualism, subjective truth, and free will rather than on a larger cultural context.[80] Unlike Spelman and Minow, however, Hendin predicts negative consequences from the use of female violence as a device to communicate cultural contradictions. Rather than a catharsis, Hendin suggests that the emergence of images of "remorseless violent women" denies the real (legal and social) vulnerability of women, justifies male aggression, and "projects a world without sensibility, [one that] sanctions aggression."[81]

She seems to be saying that as long as the real world remains a patriarchal one, where power is unequally distributed, cultural portrayals of violent women may reveal social evils and injustices, they may highlight the fallacies of gendered assumptions, but they may also serve as justification for further repression of women. One might ask whether the media focus on Aileen Wuornos served as a pretext for subjugating other women.

Aileen Wuornos in the Movies

British director Nick Broomfield made two films focused on Aileen Wuornos. The first, *Aileen Wuornos: The Selling of a Serial Killer*, is subtitled, "The 1992 Interviews." Through most of the film, Broomfield carries on a series of negotiations with Steve Glazer, Wuornos's lawyer and self-styled "agent," and Arlene Pralle. The latter added another bizarre twist to an already extraordinary story. Pralle, a born-again Christian, claimed that Jesus had spoken to her and told her to help Aileen Wuornos. She wrote to Wuornos, who was at the time in jail awaiting the Mallory trial. When she was denied access to the defendant during the trial, Pralle decided to adopt the thirty-six-year-old Wuornos. Therefore as her "mother," she could visit and confer with her adopted daughter.[82] Most important, Pralle introduced Wuornos to Glazer, a lawyer who advertised on television as "Dr. Legal" and handled the adoption. Pralle persuaded Wuornos to hire Glazer as her attorney in exchange for access to interviews with her and rights to sell her story. It is absolutely clear from Broomfield's film that Pralle and Glazer were selling Aileen Wuornos. It is almost as clear that they were selling her out.

Among other things, Glazer and Pralle encourage Wuornos to plead no contest to the other murders. Pralle talks about seeking divine forgiveness and "getting right with Jesus." Glazer used other strategies, including playing music for Wuornos such as Phil Ochs's "The Iron Lady," a song about the electric chair. He joked to Broomfield that his advice to his client facing execution was "Don't sit down." Glazer also claimed that he intended to sell the film rights to Wuornos's story to "show the horrors of the electric chair." But the overall impression of Glazer is of a buffoon, albeit a dangerous buffoon. He tells Broomfield that he was the "perfect defender" because other attorneys simply ignored him and put less effort into the prosecution. That might have been true had his incompetence been an act. However, as Glazer admits, he could not handle an actual trial if Wuornos were to plead not guilty.

Glazer and Pralle frame the story, but Broomfield's goal in the film is to talk to Aileen Wuornos herself. The two represent impediments standing between Broomfield and the star, but finally the director and the audience come face to face with the "serial killer." Earlier the movie has featured footage from TV news coverage of Wuornos's trials, but in the final scene she sits calmly across the desk from Broomfield, talking reasonably about her frustrations with the situation she faces. According to Wuornos, she has determined that Glazer and Pralle are using her to make money for themselves, and that Tyria Moore cooperated with "crooked cops" to sell the story to movie studios. She pleads with Broomfield to uncover the truth behind the various schemes to profit from her probable execution. Although Wuornos admits to killing the men, she also maintains that all assaulted and threatened her. She argues that calling her a "serial killer" is only about the number of victims. The term is in conflict with what she calls "the principle," self-defense. The only reason for the "serial killer" term is to promote sales of her story. As one watches the interview, one is faced with two possible interpretations—either Wuornos has a legitimate point and she has been denied justice because others profited from her demise, or she is paranoid and out of touch with reality.

When one knows that, shortly after the interview, three police officers were disciplined for their contacts with film promoters, Wuornos's version of reality becomes more plausible.

Nicole Rafter describes the film as "a paradigm of historical excavation and assemblage, e.g., of the process of uncovering and reconstructing events," much the same process that Clifford discovered in the courtroom. There are multiple versions of "truth" put forth in the movie and multiple views of Aileen Wuornos, from the despairing person who confessed, to the furious one who cursed and swore in the courtroom, to the apparently reasonable woman in the final interview. As Rafter notes, the film "emphasizes the circumstantial and constructed nature of knowledge."[83] No one knows for sure what happened when Aileen Wuornos confronted her victims, nor does anyone know for sure why she acted as she did or why so many people saw her case as an opportunity for personal advantage. What is clear from Broomfield's film is that some of those involved on all sides "devise[d] and revise[d]" their story lines.[84]

At one point, Broomfield seems to interrupt the development of the film to include an interview with a prison guard who shows him the electric chair and describes the execution process. While detailing each feature of the chair and explaining the role of the corrections staff, the guard is completely without emotion. He might be describing how to make potato salad. When the executioner flips the switch, he states, the only reaction from the inmate is "tensing muscles." The scene seems out of place until one contrasts it to the high level of emotion in other episodes. The death of an inmate, the state-activated violence, is carried out with impeccable planning and forethought. It is made to feel clean, rather than being messy and unpredictable like the violence on the outside.

In 2003 after Wuornos was executed, Broomfield made a second documentary, *Aileen: The Life and Death of a Serial Killer*. Broomfield used the term "serial killer" in both films, even while pointing out how the label exploited Aileen Wuornos. Each opens with a TV reporter intoning that Florida was threatened by *two* serial killers who were "murdering with a feminine touch." He clearly implies that the role of Tyria Moore remains unresolved. Using the police confession video and the final interview from the 1992 documentary, Broomfield sets up the final episodes in Wuornos's life before her execution in 2002.

Even more overtly than in *The Selling of a Serial Killer*, the later film makes use of road imagery, perhaps in homage to Wuornos's nomadic life or perhaps as a means to show Broomfield's own journey searching for the truth. It opens with a shot of a back road similar to the settings where the bodies of the victims were found. Later roads take the viewer to the Daytona Beach area where Wuornos lived with Tyria Moore, to the prison where Wuornos awaited her death, to Troy, Michigan, where she grew up, to the Upper Peninsula of Michigan where Wuornos's long-estranged mother lived, and finally back to the prison where she was put to death. No final answers emerge from this film. The explanations for the murders of the seven men and the "truth" about Aileen Wuornos's life remain elusive. None of the roads leads to revelation.

What is most obvious in the second film is the deterioration of Aileen Wuornos's mental health. From the reasonably fit and competent-seeming woman who spoke with Broomfield at the end of the first film and the opening sequences of the second, Wuornos appears to become more and more convinced of massive plots against her—by Moore and the police officers who sold her story, by the prison officials and psychologists who contaminate her food and also contaminate the air going into her cell, by the media who profit from her reputation as a serial killer. Because she is certain of all the plots against her, Wuornos stops talking about self-defense, confesses repeatedly to killing all the men for their possessions, and expresses the desire to speed up her execution. At that point, she does seem to have chosen to exercise the agency to end her life. But she also admits to Broomfield when she thinks the cameras are off that she is lying about her motive, that it was in fact self-defense.

How does one unravel the many strands of narrative about the violence in Aileen Wuornos's life? During *The Life and Death,* Broomfield was able to shoot film of witnesses testifying at one of her appeals. The hearing was meant to determine whether Glazer had provided adequate assistance. Wuornos's appellate attorneys attempted to make the case that Glazer should have uncovered mitigating information about abuse in her childhood and teenaged years. To reveal those stories, a parade of witnesses describes Wuornos's life in appalling terms. One witness tells of having oral sex with the nine-year-old Aileen when she was being prostituted by her brother. Another tells how he had sex with her and then "treated her like dirt," called her an "ugly bitch" and threw rocks at her. Testimony involved descriptions of Wuornos's family life—how her brother had sex with her and how her grandfather, "a bastard," beat her brutally. Wuornos objected to this testimony, angrily denying that it was true. She told Broomfield her family was "straight and clean," but she also admitted that her grandfather threw her out of the house and forced her to live in the woods and support herself by selling sex. Asked about any happy times in her life,

Wuornos could not remember a single one. Yet after the testimony about her miserable youth, Wuornos insisted upon dropping her appeals. She claimed she could no longer stand to be in prison. Perhaps she could no longer stand to live in what seemed a completely hostile world.

Governor Jeb Bush signed Wuornos's death warrant one month before an election in which he was running for a new term. He reiterated his support for the death penalty, and one of his aides expressed the wish that Florida would become more like Texas with more and speedier executions. Wuornos was happy to oblige, "volunteering" for lethal injection by dropping all appeals. The rush to put her to death was barely slowed by the final psychological examination, in which three psychiatrists for the state found her competent after a fifteen-minute consultation.

Wuornos was allowed one last interview with the media, and she chose to meet only with Nick Broomfield. In a room surrounded by fifteen guards, with Wuornos shackled and behind a rope, she again described torture in the prison, the malfeasance of the police, and her hatred for her mother. She concluded by screaming, "You sabotaged my ass, society. You killed a raped woman." She cried out that she had been "used" for book and movie deals. "Thanks a lot for the money you made off me."

After that interview, Brookfield posed the question "What would you have to do to fail the psychological test?" Wuornos does seem completely irrational during the last meeting, yet her assertions that she was sold out and exploited are consistent with her earlier claims. Indeed, isn't the final irony that even at the end, the apparently sympathetic Broomfield was selling her "serial killer" image?

The ultimate chilling sequence of the film visits the "media compound" where dozens of TV cameras and reporters linger outside the prison waiting for confirmation that the serial killer has been injected. One reporter asks who will be happier after the execution, Wuornos or the victims' families? "Happy" seems an odd adjective to describe the response to a state killing. The official spokesman for the department of corrections is less effusive. He seems at pains to assert that the state has gone through all the proper procedures, to legitimize taking Wuornos's life. When she awoke on her last morning, she was given a towel and wash cloth to clean up and provided with a priest whom she "sent packing." Probably attempting to reassure the public, the spokesman states that the execution was "very professional." He then reads Wuornos's last statement. "I'd just like to say I'm sailing with the rock, and I'll be back like Independence Day, with Jesus June 6. Like the movie, big mother ship and all, I'll be back." One could argue that the state had asserted its power to subdue a "monster," or as Broomfield stated, they had "executed a person who's mad."

Although most modern death penalty stories draw little notice, the media attention and the financial dealings surrounding the execution of Aileen Wuornos are reminiscent of the spectacles that accompanied the deaths of Gary Gilmore in 1977 and Karla Faye Tucker in 1998. Norman Mailer in *The Executioner's Song* and Gilmore's brother Mikal in *Shot in the Heart* take on the story of Gary Gilmore's crimes and punishment. Both books were made into films. Because Gilmore was the first person executed after the reinstatement of the death penalty in 1976 his story led to a media feeding frenzy. Journalist Larry Schiller paid more than $100,000 to Gilmore and his family for the raw material that became Mailer's book, material that was worth much more because Gilmore was put to death. Had he been sent to prison for life, his story would have had little market value. Mailer called him a "mediocrity enlarged by history"[85] simply for being the first. As with Wuornos, Gilmore's price was contingent on the framing of his violent life and death.

Karla Faye Tucker also drew an amazing amount of media attention. Her appearances on television at the end of her life were less simple fascination with a vicious killer and more a matter of capitalizing on the story of her transformation from ax murderer to a "glowing," born-again Christian. In Tucker's case, Larry King, the 700 Club, and the news magazines featured a tale of spiritual redemption and titillated audiences with speculation about whether conversion could lead to commutation.

Gilmore, Tucker, and Wuornos all serve as examples of the commercialization of violence, framed both as crime and as punishment.

Monster

Perhaps the most widely seen performance of Aileen Wuornos's violent life and death came in the 2003 film *Monster*. Many reviews commented on Charlize Theron's physical transformation that made a beautiful woman into a large, ungainly, masculine, aggressive bully. More interesting, however, are the differences among the perspectives of the reviewers who view Theron's and Wuornos's performances as they "explain" the main character. The interpretations of Wuornos's violent acts as portrayed in the film range widely.

Stephanie Zacharek in *Salon.com* comments that director Patty Jenkins is "less interested in Wuornos' innocence or guilt than she is in probing the humanity of a person capable of committing such nakedly inhumane acts."[86] Although the film portrays the first killing as self-defense in response to a rape, the subsequent murders lack any such obvious justification. As the explanations for the murders are muddled, Zacharek observes that there is a "sameness to the suffering that defies our perceived right to decide whether or not it's deserved." Yet in this critic's eyes, the film shows Wuornos, whether or not she was victimized, whether or not she was deranged, as responsible for her own actions.[87] But responsibility is not a simple matter of yes or no, although the legal process forces such a choice. A film can provide a more complex and nuanced view, and it may be argued that Jenkins attempts to do that in the voice-overs at the beginning and end of *Monster*. In those voice-overs, Wuornos first tells of her fairy-tale dreams as a child and concludes with repeating a number of bromides: "Everything happens for a reason," "Where there's life there's hope." Finally she says, "Well, they gotta tell you something." Her experience has given the lie to those clichés and shown Wuornos to be not only deceived but violated, rejected, and completely unprepared to pull herself into the social mainstream.

Monster offers several ways of conceptualizing Wuornos's repeated murders. She met and fell in love with "Selby Wall." Finding the only semblance of normality in her horrible life, Wuornos wanted to "take care" of her girlfriend. Possibly Selby's neediness and whining persuaded her to do whatever was necessary to pay their living expenses and perhaps to offer them the means to start a new life. After the first killing, she determined to give up prostitution and to find legitimate work. When in one of the film's harshest sequences, Wuornos is repeatedly rebuffed by potential employers who sneer at her lack of qualifications, she returns to highway hooking. Critics have seen the subsequent killing of clients as "a mix of self-defense, transferred retribution, moral vigilantism, and financial desperation."[88] Do those motives make Wuornos more human or do they make her a monster?

As the story unfolds in *Monster,* it appears that the relationship with Selby influences everything that happens. Unlike the real-life large, very masculine-looking Tyria Moore, Selby as played by Christina Ricci is petite, cute, and often naïve. When she meets Wuornos, she has a broken arm (wing?). The film frequently shoots the tall, mannish Aileen with her arm draped protectively over Selby, her girl. The butch/femme image is unmistakable. Selby becomes whiney and demanding, she pushes Aileen, who loves her too much to refuse, back onto the highways and ultimately into the robbery/murders. Wuornos acts the traditional male role in the movie relationship—the protector and breadwinner. Selby is the nagging "wife." Perhaps that stereotype suited the moviemakers. It provided one clear cause/effect explanation for Wuornos's actions. There are, however, only a few parallels with the reality of Wuornos and Moore's relationship. Moore did depend financially on Wuornos after they became a couple. Wuornos did use some of the spoils of the murders as gifts and treats for Moore. But there are serious doubts about Moore's innocence, both as she may have actually participated in some of the killings and as she tried to sell out her former partner. She was not an immature girl of 18, but a woman of 28. According to Wuornos's first defense attorney, Moore, rather than Aileen, was the one who got into bar fights.[89] In the film, Selby points the finger at Aileen in the courtroom and identifies her as the murderer. Tyria Moore, although never charged, had many more fingers pointing at her.

To a few reviewers of *Monster,* Wuornos's acts have a simple explanation. She was a bad person who made rational choices to act badly. Manohla Dargis in the *Los Angeles Times* finds total harmony between her essence and her acts. She is "inwardly monstrous, as ugly as her ugly deeds," and "a poster girl for deluded feminists who rationalized the crimes with a battered woman defense."[90] For another commentator, Aileen developed a "fixation: picking up johns and shooting them dead. . . . Once her resentment of men is tapped, it flows like poison lava and she can't keep herself from replaying that vengeance, over and over again."[91] He claims that Theron plays "an unredeemable women," a "vicious and paranoid psychopath" characterized by "squalid, blinkered selfishness."[92] Such interpretations of Wuornos—not just as a movie character but as a person—serve to justify the appropriateness of her death sentence.

An interesting review by David Denby in the *New Yorker* looks at both Broomfield's 2003 documentary and *Monster,* comparing the film performances of the real Aileen Wuornos with the fictionalized version. Denby raises questions concerning the difficulty of knowing which of the many versions of her story to believe. He notes that despite her probable insanity, the power of her presentation in the last interview with Broomfield is unnerving. "She's going to die, and she's determined to make her death mean what she wants it to mean, and not what anyone else wants it to." In a sense, all the films, the books and newspapers, and even this essay are attempts to make sense of her death, to find out "what it meant."

Unlike some other commentators, Denby sees in *Monster* a larger context for the person Aileen Wuornos became. "The foulmouthed slattern has been produced by a foul, slatternly society."[93] He finds the movie "thoroughly ambiguous" regarding the question of whether Wuornos is "taking a prostitute's rage to its ultimate conclusion or is she just crazy?" The point of the movie, he says, is "that this monster is both a victim and a predator, unimaginably exploited and unimaginably vicious."[94] Ultimately, Wuornos becomes the canvas on which observers of the movie and observers of her life story try to compose and engrave meanings for violence in the form of abuse, exploitation, meanness, murder, execution. They try repeatedly, and I have followed in that line here, because there are no simple categories of right and wrong, normal and abnormal, just and unjust, victim and offender, sane and insane.

No single word or phrase captures the complexities of Aileen Wuornos. But if one may treat a person as a case study, she offers an excellent challenge in the effort to disentangle the many meanings of violence. Wuornos was abused, neglected, beaten, raped, condemned, belittled, ridiculed, marginalized, scorned, killed, and "sold" in many different ways. There is no possible argument that she was not the target of violence at every level identified by Zizek.[95] At the level of language, one only needs to examine the articles and books written about her case, the films and the reviews. At the level of subjective violence performed by individuals, Wuornos experienced sexual abuse of myriad kinds, physical assault, and deprivation as she was left to fend for herself in the cold at the age of thirteen. And the systemic violence Zizek describes may be located both in the obliviousness to her needs shown by the "helping" institutions and of course in the conduct of the criminal justice system. One might also identify the violence of the economic system toward marginalized persons like Wuornos in the scenes of her job interviews in *Monster*. Those episodes were fictionalized, but they captured eloquently the experience of the "outsider."

Judith Butler would argue that it is the presence of outsiders, those whose behaviors defy categories, that threatens hierarchy. The criminal justice system seems especially ill equipped to deal with such multiplicity of meaning. Perhaps this discomfort helps to explain the attention to the case of Aileen Wuornos. Not only does her story blur the simple categories of victim and offender, that very blurring creates the uneasiness that engrosses our attention.

Explaining her work with death row prisoners, psychologist Dorothy

Otnow Lewis cites a conversation with Paul Tillich. "When you read about witches burned at the stake, do you identify with the witch or with the people looking on?" Tillich asked.[96] Like Lewis, I am certain that I identify with the witch—or with the monster.

NOTES

1. For the many uses of terms like "monster" and "serial killer," see articles collected at www.clarkprosecutor.org

2. See Judith Butler, *Gender Trouble: Feminism and the Subversion of Identity* (New York: Routledge, 1990).

3. See discussion in Veena Das, "Passionate Performance: 26/11, Mumbai," in this volume, where she examines the difficulty of representing the unrepresentable. She notes the lack of clarity in language making it impossible to distinguish perpetrators, witnesses, or victims and the multiple perspectives on what actions mean. See also Paul Steege, "Ordinary Violence on an Extraordinary Stage: Incidents on the Sector Border in Postwar Berlin," in this volume. Steege develops the theme that citizens of Berlin "crafted" or "staged" the division between East and West.

4. James Clifford, *The Predicament of Culture: Twentieth Century Ethnography, Literature, and Art* (Cambridge: Harvard University Press, 1988), 344.

5. According to criminological theory, a master status is most significant in determining a person's social identity as well as how he or she is perceived by others.

6. See discussions of violence in Martha Minow, Michael Ryan, and Austin Sarat, *Narrative Violence and the Law: The Essays of Robert Cover* (Ann Arbor: University of Michigan Press, 1992).

7. Nick Broomfield, *Aileen Wuornos: The Selling of a Serial Killer, The 1992 Interviews* (1992).

8. Definitions of instrumental and expressive violence may be found in Graeme Newman, "Popular Culture and Violence: Decoding the Violence of Popular Movies," in Frankie Y. Bailey and Donna C. Hale, eds. *Popular Culture, Crime, and Justice* (Belmont, Calif.: Wadsworth, 1998), 42.

9. Information about the crimes may be found in Dolores Kennedy, *On a Killing Day* (Chicago: Bonus Books, 1992); Sue Russell, *Lethal Intent* (New York: Pinnacle Books, 2002); Aileen Wuornos with Christopher Berry-Dee, *Monster: My True Story* (London: John Blake Publishing, 2004) at www.clarkprosecutor.org; and Mary Welek Atwell, *Wretched Sisters: Examining Gender and Capital Punishment* (New York: Peter Lang, 2007).

10. Ronald M. Holmes and Stephen T. Holmes, *Contemporary Perspectives on Serial Murder* (Thousand Oaks, Calif.: Sage, 1998); Robert K. Ressler and Thomas Schachtman, *Whoever Fights Monsters: My Twenty Years Tracking Serial Killers for the FBI* (New York: Macmillan, 1993).

11. Harold Schechter and David Everitt, *The A to Z Encyclopedia of Serial Killers* (New York: Simon and Schuster, 2006).

12. See Das, "Passionate Performance: 26/11, Mumbai," for discussion of news as spectacle and commodity.

13. David Garland, *The Culture of Control: Crime and the Social Order in Contemporary*

Society (Chicago: University of Chicago Press, 2001), 137.

14. Moore was located with her sister in Pennsylvania, where she had in her possession several items of property stolen from the victims. Additionally, several witnesses had identified her as one of the two women connected with the crimes.

15. Broomfield features the charges against the detectives in both of his films.

16. Appellant's brief, Wuornos v. State of Florida, 19 Fla Law W.S455 (September 22, 1994).

17. Wuornos and Berry-Dee, *Monster*.

18. Ibid., 152.

19. Ibid., 158.

20. American Civil Liberties Union, American Friends Service Committee, *The Forgotten Population: A Look at Death Row in the United States through the Experiences of Women* (Washington D.C., 2004), 24.

21. See for example, the discussion in Caroline Forrell and Donna Matthews, *A Law of Her Own: The Reasonable Woman as a Measure of Man* (New York: New York University Press, 2001).

22. Austin Sarat, *When the State Kills: Capital Punishment and the American Condition* (Princeton: Princeton University Press, 2001), 122–23.

23. Ibid., 14–15.

24. Slavoj Zizek, *Violence* (New York: Picador, 2008), 1–3, 14.

25. Chimene Keitner, "Victim or Vamp? Images of Violent Women in the Criminal Justice System," *Columbia Journal of Gender and Law* 11 (2002): 59–60.

26. Quoted in Kennedy, *On a Killing Day*, 142–43.

27. Ibid., 210.

28. Ibid., 142–43. Lee was one of Wuornos's nicknames.

29. Keitner, "Victim or Vamp?" 67.

30. Josephine Gattuso Hendin, *Heartbreakers: Women and Violence in Contemporary Culture and Literature* (New York: Palgrave Macmillan, 2004), 41.

31. Clifford, *The Predicament of Culture*, 321.

32. Wuornos v. Florida (September 22, 1994).

33. Ibid., and quoted in Kennedy, *On a Killing Day*, 178–86.

34. Ibid.

35. Zizek, *Violence*, 4.

36. Clifford, *The Predicament of Culture*, 321.

37. Appellant's brief and Wuornos v. Florida (September 22, 1994).

38. "Serial Killers: A Short History," at www.clarkprosecutor.org

39. Appellant's brief and Wuornos v. Florida (September 22, 1994).

40. Kennedy, *On a Killing Day*, 105.

41. Minow et al., *Narrative, Violence, and the Law*, 221.

42. Wuornos v. Florida (September 22, 1994).

43. Kennedy, *On a Killing Day*, 220.

44. Ibid.

45. Ibid.

46. Wuornos v. Florida (September 22, 1994).

47. Kennedy, *On a Killing Day*, 228; Broomfield, *Life and Death of a Serial Killer*.

48. Minow et al., *Narrative, Violence, and the Law*, 219–27.

49. Appellant's brief, Wuornos v. State of Florida, 626 So 2nd 972 (May 9, 1996).

50. Ibid.

51. Wuornos v. State of Florida, 276 So 2nd 966 (September 21, 1995).

52. Broomfield, *Aileen Wuornos: The Selling of a Serial Killer*.

53. Minow et al., *Narrative, Violence, and the Law*, 237.

54. Russell, *Lethal Intent,* 536.

55. Ibid.

56. See Anne Norton, "On the Uses of Dogs: Abu Ghraib and the American Soul," in this volume. Norton links the torture of prisoners at Abu Ghraib to domestic institutions in the United States. She notes that several Abu Ghraib participants had civilian jobs in American prisons.

57. Catherine Wilson, "Aileen Wuornos Says Prison Guards Abusing Her," Associated Press, July 13, 2002. Governor Bill Clinton, at the time a candidate for president, presided over the 1992 execution of Ricky Ray Rector, who was so confused over the finality of execution that he left some of his pie to finish when he returned from the death chamber.

58. Wilson, "Wuornos Says Prison Guards Abusing Her"; Ron Word, "Florida Executes Female Serial Killer," *St. Petersburg Times,* October 9, 2002, at www.clarkprosecutor.org

59. Wuornos and Berry-Dee, *Monster,* xiv–xv.

60. Nick Broomfield, *Aileen Wuornos: The Life and Death of a Serial Killer (2003).*

61. Quoted in Paul Lomartine, "Aileen and Dawn: A Sisterhood Haunted by Memories and Madness," *Palm Beach Post,* February 29, 2004.

62. Broomfield, *Aileen Wuornos: The Life and Death of a Serial Killer.*

63. Word, "Florida Executes Female Serial Killer."

64. "Florida Executed Female Serial Killer, Wuornos Declines Final Meal," at www.clarkprosecutor.org

65. The basic facts of Wuornos's early life may be found in Kennedy, *On a Killing Day;* Russell, *Lethal Intent;* Wuornos and Berry-Dee, *Monster;* and in Stacey L. Shipley and Bruce A. Arrigo, T*he Female Homicide Offender: Serial Murder and the Case of Aileen Wuornos* (Upper Saddle River, N.J.: Pearson Prentice Hall, 2004). A brief summary is included in Kathleen O'Shea, *Women and the Death Penalty in the United States, 1900–1998* (Westport, Conn.: Praeger, 1999). Nick Broomfield's *Life and Death of a Serial Killer* features interviews with several people who tell stories about Wuornos's life as a child and teenager.

66. See Kennedy, *On a Killing Day,* chap. 3, and Shipley and Arrigo, *Female Homicide Offender,* chap. 8.

67. Shipley and Arrigo, *Female Homicide Offender,* 109–15.

68. Dorothy Otnow Lewis, *Guilty by Reason of Insanity* (New York: Fawcett Columbine, 1998), 293.

69. See Atwell, *Wretched Sisters,* chap. 1.

70. Kennedy, *On a Killing Day,* 222.

71. Anne Norton's discussion of the ambiguities of Lynndie England's role at Abu Ghraib in "On the Uses of Dogs," contains startling parallels with facets of Wuornos's story.

72. See Elizabeth Spelman and Martha Minow, "Outlaw Women," in John Denvir, ed., *Legal Reelism: Movies as Legal Texts* (Urbana: University of Illinois Press, 1996), 261–80.

73. See Forrell and Matthews, *A Law of Her Own.*

74. Spelman and Minow, "Outlaw Women," 268.

75. Andrew McKenna, "Public Execution," in Denvir, ed., *Legal Reelism,* 238.

76. Ibid.

77. Hendin, *Heartbreakers,* 56.

78. Ibid., 52–56.

79. Ibid., 26–27.

80. Ibid., 281.

81. Ibid., 291.

82. Kennedy, *On a Killing Day,* and Russell, *Lethal Intent.* Both examine the involvement of Pralle and Steve Glazer with Aileen Wuornos.

83. Nicole Rafter, *Shots in the Mirror: Crime Films and Society,* 2nd ed. (New York: Oxford University Press, 2006), 181–82.

84. Ibid.

85. Norman Mailer, *The Executioner's Song* (Boston: Little, Brown, 1979), 828–31.

86. Stephanie Zacharek, "Monster," Salon.com, December 25, 2003 online at dir.salon.com

87. Ibid.

88. Laura Sinagra, "The Butcher Girl," *Village Voice,* December 23, 2003.

89. "Crazy to Kill," *New Times Broward-Palm Beach,* January 22, 2004.

90. Manohla Dargis, "Charlize Theron makes a startling physical transition as murderer Aileen Wuornos, but 'Monster' lacks depth," *Los Angeles Times,* December 26, 2003.

91. Owen Gleiberman, "Movie Review: Monster," *Entertainment Weekly,* December 19, 2003.

92. Ibid.

93. David Denby, "Killer," *New Yorker,* January 26, 2004.

94. Ibid.

95. Zizek, *Violence,* 14.

96. Lewis, *Guilty by Reason of Insanity,* 9–10.

4

On the Uses of Dogs
Abu Ghraib and the American Soul

ANNE NORTON

This essay examines acts of violence performed by American soldiers against prisoners at Abu Ghraib. The violence is performative in two senses. First, it is theatrical and spectacular. Much of the violence at Abu Ghraib was staged for the camera. Many of the forms, roles, and poses derived from other forms of theatricality, most notably tourism and pornography. The drive to see, to be seen, to see oneself seen, informed the staging of violence and the photographic records of the violence and impelled the circulatory vortex into which the photographs were cast.

As the photographs from Abu Ghraib and accounts of violence at Guantanamo circulated, the performances of violence at these sites were read and readers took on the role of critic and assumed authority over the photographs and other records of violence. Those who had presented themselves as authors of the violence performed were subjected to critical scrutiny not only as authors but in their performances of their chosen roles. The reader and critic are, however, not always in the service of justice.

The drive to see and be seen (perhaps it is the drive to celebrity, the drive to the pornographic) is followed, echoed, by another. There is also, in the taking and circulation of these photographs, in testimony concerning them, in the quiet speech of shamed refusal, another drive: the drive to record, to confess, to bear witness. These artifacts record the cries that were not heard, the refusals that went unspoken, the confessions that were not made. There are echoes in this silent text: of *Eli, Eli, lema sabbachtani, mea culpa, mea culpa, mea maxima culpa*, and *"sajal, ana arabiyya."*[1]

In performing these acts of violence, soldiers performed roles—assigned and assumed, official and informal, obedient and transgressive—and in doing so enacted a series of claims. These acts of violence interpellated a Muslim identity, gave it content, staged it, and forced it on prisoners. The content of these acts of violence provides a map of American anxieties: about Islam and about themselves. The semiotics of these acts of violence stage fantasies of the Muslim. They are informed by histories of the United States. The bodies of the prisoners, silent and speaking, testify to that in the human which is also beyond the human: to the suffering that binds the human, the animal, and the divine.

The Scene

In taking over the prison at Abu Ghraib, the United States took the place of Saddam Hussein. The prison, already a notorious place of abuse, came under new management, but the abuse continued. The tearing down of the Bastille was, as many historians have observed, a largely symbolic act: there were few prisoners held within its walls. The decision to keep Abu Ghraib intact and use it as Saddam Hussein had used it was both a practical and a symbolic act. "Taking the prison" was an act of conquest. It might have been used to mark the difference between Saddam Hussein's regime and the liberating invaders. The occupation forces however, chose to leave the prison intact, and in doing so, they marked themselves as stepping into Saddam's place. They kept the structures of Iraqi imprisonment intact. The abuses at Abu Ghraib argued that the forces of the American occupation had not only taken the place, but assumed the practices of the former tyrannical regime.

The prison at Guantanamo is located on an American naval base at the southeastern end of Cuba. The United States pays rent for the base to the government of Cuba, which does not accept the rent or acknowledge the legitimacy of the base or the lease. The base is often referred to as "a legal black hole." Guantanamo is the material expression of an America which does not wish to be seen as American. Guantanamo is inside and outside American territory, within and without American governance, governed by and exempt from American law. Guantanamo is a limin, a threshold, a gateway, between what is permitted and forbidden to Americans. What happens here marks the boundaries of the whole.

The United States is itself a carceral society, imprisoning a large portion of its own population. The design, building, maintenance, supply, and staffing of the American prison system is a major industry.[2] The role of former prison guards in the abuses at Abu Ghraib should raise questions about the practices of prison guards at home. The abuses at Abu Ghraib tended instead to fix the debate over torture and the conditions of confinement at a foreign site. These were matters of foreign rather than domestic policy, the abuses were done to aliens rather than our own, under exceptional conditions. Perversely, attention to torture at Abu Ghraib tended to construe the acts as errant and exceptional, predicated on conditions of war and the absence of legal constraints. The role of reservists and mercenaries with experience in the prison system was diminished where it was not concealed.

Veiling

The trope of veiling, often employed to cast the Arab world as the abode of concealment and oppression, should draw attention to other strategies of concealment and the governance of sight.[3] The economy of sight is an important strategic field in the Iraq war. Members of the press are subject to restrictions on what they can show; the people are subject to restrictions on what we can see. A veil is drawn over coffins returning to Dover airbase, as well as photographs and videos of the abuse of women prisoners at Abu Ghraib. The use of embedded journalists may make more of the soldier's life visible, but it means that the one embedded sees not simply through the eyes of a journalist, but through the eyes of a comrade. Americans see, albeit partially and belatedly, photos of Abu Ghraib. We do not see the secret prisons whose presence is known. Like Michael Moore, we hover outside Guantanamo, between America and another place, using what lenses we can find to get a glimpse of what is done in our name. (Scholars are not permitted to enter.[4])

Much is concealed from Americans, but we are increasingly subject to surveillance. The Patriot Act, warrantless wiretapping and other federal practices, the installation of security cameras by municipalities, and the much more pervasive use of security cameras by commercial establishments are rarely considered as instances of questionable surveillance. These seem to be seen instead as benign and desirable means of preserving our safety, regulating traffic, and permitting the identification of the occasional criminal. Debate over secrecy and surveillance has not encompassed, much less challenged, these practices. Americans know they are watched, and know that they do not always know who is watching, when, or how they are watched. Americans know there are secret prisons, ghost prisoners, secret files. Americans know that much is hidden from them. Americans, and indeed, a candid world, knew that much of the war in Iraq was concealed. Journalists were limited in where they could, go, whom they could cover, and under what conditions. They have accepted these constraints.

In such an economy, that which is seen seems to testify to openness and transparency. For those who knew that they were not permitted to see coffins returning to Dover airbase, photographs of the inside of an American prison in Iraq seemed to offer unexpected access. For those who knew they were shown what the occupation forces and the administration wished them to see, photographs of torture seemed to rupture the constraints enveloping coverage of American military procedures and practices. In this context, the Abu Ghraib photographs seemed to offer unmediated access to the previously hidden: sudden, unexpected stolen knowledge that had escaped governance.

The photographs of the violence at Abu Ghraib are, however, profoundly mediated. They were circulated as digital media, and through digital media. They were presented, edited, and censored, by the state and commercial networks.[5] Not all the photographs were made public; indeed government officials continue to deprecate showing much of the evidence obtained, notably the videos and photographs showing the abuse of women (this even after some of these photographs had been released outside the United States). The photographs that were shown were cropped and censored in a variety of ways: including editing out the casual presence of the torturer, and attempting to obscure the identity of the victim. The photographs were staged, composed, and performed in accordance with media conventions, notably those for pornography. They did not offer open and unmediated access to the heart of darkness. They put on display performances of violent degradation that were willful, artful, assertions of authority.

The Abu Ghraib photographs testify to the limits placed on—and accepted by—the media. They also testify to the ways in which the practices and conventions of the mass media have undermined structures, practices, and expectations upon which democracy depends. The Enlightenment taught Westerners to look upon the press, and later, on the mass media, as central to democratic politics. Insistence on freedom of the press followed the confident belief that the media would oversee and chasten government and economic power; to make dissenting voices heard. Market expressions of the people's passionate desire to know would spur the media to greater oversight, greater diligence, greater daring. It has not been so. Sheldon Wolin's recent work demonstrates how capitalism has made the media servants not of subscribers, but of owners and advertisers. Rather than being spurred on by the people's desire to know, the media is ever more closely constrained. Oversight diminishes, the media are fed by the political and economic powers they once (perhaps) challenged. Dissenting voices are silenced, not by the state, but by media who act as strict and unlicensed censors: exiling dissident views to the fringes of discourse or silencing them altogether.[6]

The mediation of the Abu Ghraib photographs goes beyond the process that presented them to the world as a witness (at once for and against) the American regime. They carry a complex of references to visual genres.

The Camera Lies

Knowledge of the atrocities at Abu Ghraib came, for most of us, from photographs. These photographs and videos were taken by soldiers, shown to each other and, in some cases, sent home to friends and relatives. They cast atrocities in the idioms of snapshots, home movies, pornography, tourism, and memorabilia. These are the visual conventions of the banality of evil.

Susan Sontag observed, "most of the pictures seem part of a larger confluence of torture and pornography: a young woman leading a naked man around on a leash is classic dominatrix imagery. And you wonder how much of the sexual tortures inflicted on the inmates of Abu Ghraib was inspired by the vast repertory of pornographic imagery available on the Internet—and which ordinary people, by sending out Webcasts of themselves, try to emulate."[7]

The pornographic aspect of the photographs was also recognized and deployed by fundamentalist clerics who had been reproached for their reluctance to condemn torture at Abu Ghraib. Concerned Women for America issued two articles on the abuse which, as a critical Christian noted, "both blame American pornography for the soldiers' actions." Robert Knight, of CWA's Culture and the Family Institute, blamed homosexuals, feminists, and liberals for "systematically aiding and abetting the cultural depravity that produced the Abu Ghraib scandal." The head of the Southern Baptist Convention's Ethics and Religious Liberty Commission, Richard Land, refusing to fix responsibility in the chain of command, declared, "These people's moral compass didn't work for some reason. My guess is because they've been infected with relativism."[8] The construction of the photographs as pornographic enabled fundamentalists to condemn Abu Ghraib without condemning torture and without raising questions about the policies and governance of the army of occupation and the mercenary forces. They were, moreover, able to blame Abu Ghraib on groups whose culpability would otherwise seem most improbable: liberals, feminists, and homosexuals.

Characterizing the photographs as pornographic was also used to diminish the gravity of the damage done, the pain endured. The "classic dominatrix pose" of Lynndie England, the "dog piles" of naked men" drew the gaze inexorably—drawing it away from photographs of the dead, the bleeding, and the maimed.[9] The photographs which conformed to the conventions of pornography foregrounded a perverse pleasure. Defenders of the Bush administration deployed tropes of pornography and pleasure to render torture benign and defensible.

Sontag recognized this effect:

> To "stack naked men" is like a college fraternity prank, said a caller to Rush Limbaugh and the many millions of Americans who listen to his radio show. Had the caller, one wonders, seen the photographs? No matter. The observation—or is it the fantasy?—was on the mark. What may still be capable of shocking some Americans was Limbaugh's response: "Exactly!" he exclaimed. "Exactly my point. This is no different than what happens at the Skull and Bones initiation, and we're going to ruin people's lives over it, and we're going to hamper our military effort, and then we are going to really hammer them because they had a good time."[10]

The comparison to Skull and Bones was a telling one. Skull and Bones is, after all, not quite a fraternity. (It does not seem to be about fraternity—much less liberty and equality—at all.) Skull and Bones is a secret society, and George Bush is a member. Limbaugh's movement from the caller's "fraternity prank" to "the Skull and Bones initiation" is an unconscious shift that places Abu Ghraib where it belongs, with George Bush and the politics of secrecy. Limbaugh's revision of his caller's remark moves the comparison from the ordinary and familiar practices of fraternity hazing to the concealed acts of a secret and secretive elite. In doing so Limbaugh acknowledges, perhaps unconsciously, the force of the old feminist recognition that pornography may be less about pleasure than about power.

The soldiers at Abu Ghraib were not mere consumers of pornography. They were authors, directors, producers. They knew the conventions of the genre, and they violated or accepted them as they pleased. They enacted their authority as simultaneously literary and political. The photographs cast them as authority figures. They are uniformed, they wear signs of rank, they hold weapons, they are outside the cells, above the pyramids of bodies. They show themselves arranging the bodies in pyramids, attacking the prisoners, stitching their wounds. They author the texts that record their authority.

So too with the conventions of tourism. The tourist moves freely in the world. The tourist comes to a chosen destination. The record of presence is a record of freedom; the tourist travels freely through the world, each movement testifying to will and material resources. The photographic conventions of tourism set the freedom of the soldiers against the manifold imprisonment of the Iraqis. The Iraqis are confined in shackles, in cells, in a prison, in a country they cannot leave, whose boundaries they cannot close. The soldiers entered Iraq and move about within it. They control the space of the prison and move in a relaxed, often casual fashion in the photographs. They are volunteers, who entered the military of their own volition. The conventions of tourism affirm this freedom and conceal its limits and fictions.

The record the torturers made of their acts at Abu Ghraib seems to affirm their power and their freedom. The photographs argue for a radical difference between the prisoner and the torturer, the one a dog, the other a master. This does not hold. Nietzsche's Second Essay on the Genealogy of Morals reminds us that the link of violence to power is a perverse one: the enjoyment of pain depends on the recognition of likeness with the one who suffers. If the photographs record some moment of pleasure for the war criminals who staged them, they reaffirm, silently and insistently, a common vulnerability to pain. If the acts seem to mark the prisoners as alien, animal, and other, they also recall aspects of ourselves we have alternately owned and disavowed. If the acts seem to look outward toward the Arab, they also testify, silently and insistently, to an American history.

Empire

There is a history of America that begins with a woman eaten by dogs. Perhaps it is the history of America as a carceral state. Perhaps it is the history of American empire. It is not the only history, even of these events, but it is a history we are called to record. Tzvetan Todorov dedicates the *Conquest of America* to a woman eaten by dogs in the early European invasions.[11] She figures as a sacrifice inaugurating the history of empires in America. This is the history of conquest, slavery, and the reservation, of the Klan and Jim Crow, of immigration restriction and border vigilantes, of ICE raids and detention centers. This is the history of the prison system. This history records the decimation and confinement of the first nations, the Trail of Tears, and the emergence of the reservation system. This history records the Cold War, Hiroshima and My Lai, McCarthyism and a culture of surveillance. In this history, imprisonment follows in the footsteps of empire.

This is the history of the crowded holds of the Middle Passage, of slave quarters and segregation. This is the history of slave-trading and the Klan, of the plantation and the overseer. This is the history of restrictive immigration laws, of housing covenants and border fences, of gated communities and midnight raids. This is the history of the coyote and the Rubashkins. This is the history of red-lining and subprime mortgages, of usury, eviction, and foreclosure. In this history, greed makes use of violence. In this history, aggrandizement leads not to greatness but to shame and diminution. This history testifies against an easy, natural alliance between capitalism and democracy.

Mindful of this history, one is obliged to question accounts that couple the extension of American dominion with the expansion of the American electorate, civil rights, and political liberty. The extension of dominion is accompanied—in intention, process, and effect—with confinement, imprisonment, reservation, and incarceration. Imperial power is accompanied—again in intention, process, and effect—by structures and practices that imprison: the building of walls, the enforcement of borders, the proliferation of prisons and detention centers. The expansion of American territory across the continent, and American dominion overseas is attended by a diminution of freedom at home and abroad.

Causing a human being to huddle in fear before a dog is a particularly powerful way of indicating that the human being is less than that dog, less than an animal, reduced by fear of an animal to animal fear. The act illustrates the effects of the violation of human rights it enacts. The language of rights is not, however, adequate to the act. This is not a violation of a code or status that remains otherwise intact, a defect in a system. The act strikes at humanity altogether. The dog is used to make the prisoner appear as an animal, act as an animal, confront the animal before him and in himself and find himself wanting.[12]

The use of dogs came to Abu Ghraib from Guantanamo, where they had been used to "fear up" prisoners. The use of dogs went, however, beyond the dogs themselves. The interrogation log of Mohammed al Qahtani records for December 20, 2002, Day 28 of his interrogation: "Told detainee a dog is held in higher esteem because dogs know right from wrong and know how to protect innocent people from bad people. Began teaching detainee lessons such as stay, come, and bark, to elevate his social status up to that of a dog." Later, the interrogator writes, "Dog tricks continue . . . told detainee he should bark happy for these people . . . told detainee he should growl."[13] Guantanamo is an uncanny place: a "legal black hole" whose legal and jurisdictional particularities are carefully parsed; a military base in a country Americans are not permitted to visit directly. The site is replete with Kafkaesque bureaucratic perversities, and as Alex Danchev has noted, "In Kafka's world, humiliation takes canine form.[14] The determination to "Gitmoize" Abu Ghraib entailed the introduction of dogs along with increasingly strenuous procedures for "fear up" and "ego down."

The prisoner menaced by the dog is stripped of the attributes of the human. He is naked, he does not stand upright. If he speaks, he is not heard. If he is heard, he is not understood. The confrontation with the dog-made-weapon throws all involved outside language and into the tyrannical.

Classic writings on tyranny saw it as opposed to politics: destroying friendship in an all-pervasive economy of fear. Aristotle saw tyranny as a harsh, perverse continuation of the household. Human beings became fully human only in politics, in the achievement of a common life in language, in which one ruled and was ruled in turn. Monarchy perpetuated the animal economy of the household. Tyranny reduced language to the speech of dictat and obedience, to cries of pain and enforced silences. Tyranny reduced the human to the animal.

Confinement and interrogation take language from the prisoners. The prisoner is to speak when they tell him to speak, cry when they wish him to cry, scream when they wish him to scream. In the end, he must say what they wish him to say. The photograph silences the prisoner still more thoroughly. He cannot be heard at all. He cannot represent himself, he is represented: by the one who casts him as an animal.

This use of dogs reduces the human twice over. It is not only that the human being who cowers before the dog appears (in the absence of respect for rights, in the absence of language, outside politics) as no more than an animal and a weak one at that. There is a double loss, for the human who holds the leash is transformed as well. The mouth of the dog becomes the hand of the master, and the master forfeits humanity in the inhuman act.

This act has particular force in relation to American history and the American soul. The weaponized dog belongs not to the rebellious American colonies who made a nation, but to the imperial colonizers. The weaponized dog belongs not to the America of inalienable rights, but to the refusals and denials of those rights. The act belongs to a time before America, to the "not now" and "never" that whisper against "not yet."

Those who watched the Civil Rights movement unfold remember the uses of dogs against African American marchers. These acts, like those at Guantanamo and Abu Ghraib, were photographed and circulated. We saw photographs in the newspapers that froze the snarl of the German shepherd and enabled us to count every tooth. The photographs caught the forward lunge of the leashed dog. We saw the marchers thrust back as sharply as they had been by the fire hoses. We saw the uniformed man who held the dog and urged it forward. Television captured the sound and movement of the march and the attack. The images circulated. They testified to the strength and courage of the marchers. Conventional certainties decayed. A dog could be a weapon, a policeman could be an enemy. Children so instructed learned to question the license of the uniform. They may have learned to question the distinction between friend and enemy and its relation to the political. They may have learned more.

There is a passage in the *Republic* where Plato takes up the question of the just man. How would one know the just man? Plato proceeds to treat the just man like Job—"he shall be stripped of everything save justice" —and in that naked deprivation the reader is to see what justice is. So it was with the photographs from Alabama. The marchers, stripped of the protections of the state, held their rights still. They became rights and right incarnate, and the rights they stood for stood or fell with them.

Seeing dogs used against the unarmed evokes powerful and disturbing memories, reminding Americans of past abuses, past errors, past failings as a nation. The use of dogs at Abu Ghraib recalls the use of dogs in Alabama. The photographs raise questions about the actions and the legitimacy of those who, like those earlier dog-handlers, wore the uniform of the state and acted in its name. They place the prisoners in the position of the Civil Rights marchers. The man who is "stripped of everything," who stands naked before the power of the state, still holds the rights that power denies him. The rights he holds in himself—civil, human, natural—stand or fall with him.

Americans once found their soul in those who affirmed, "we shall overcome, someday." The Civil Rights marchers kept open the possibility of an America that was not yet. The men who held the leashes in Alabama wore the uniforms of the state but not the nation. They were provincials, and because of this their act could be read, easily and precisely, as the act of a part against the whole. The role of the federal troops at Little Rock, and the discourse of states' rights concurred in underscoring this particularity. The act came to belong to a place (the South), a time (the past), and an order (Jim Crow and the Confederacy) at odds with the nation in the present, the nation as a whole, the nation's history. The long-standing segregation of American sins—in the South, in the past, in the defeated Confederacy—was not honest, but it was plausible. Even to a more cynical eye, it had the virtue of permitting the nation to acknowledge, even to own, the acts it came to disown and disavow. The acts belonged to our past, our South, and so they were our sins which we might (on the whole) hope to overcome.

Susan Sontag also saw the American past in the photographs from Abu Ghraib. "If there is something comparable to what these pictures show it would be some of the photographs of black victims of lynching taken between the 1880's and 1930's, which show Americans grinning beneath the naked mutilated body of a black man or woman hanging behind them from a tree."[15] What was noteworthy, for Sontag, was the willingness of those photographed with the bodies of the tortured dead to own their acts; to stand unashamed before those to whom they sent the photographs: their families, their friends, and perhaps a larger, more abstract audience.

I am not wholly persuaded of Sontag's claim. The photographs of lynchings are (like those of Abu Ghraib) bound with a history of secret violence. Lynchings were, at best, thought to be of dubious legality—even by those who performed them. The politics of lynching was a politics of particularity. Those who engaged in it advanced an identity predicated on exclusions. It was white supremacist, Protestant, connected in most cases to a postwar mythology of the defeated Confederacy, and refusing integration into the Union. Trophies of lynching circulated secretly, among those committed to the secret societies that advanced white supremacist claims. Secrecy is tied, here as elsewhere, to an antidemocratic politics of hierarchy and exclusion.

At Abu Ghraib the hand that held the leash wore the nation's uniform. The process of disavowal thus took the form of exculpating the state. These were the acts of individuals—in several cases, of Lynndie England, a poor, uneducated woman from West Virginia, a marginal person from a provincial backwater. The acts were made possible by personal pathologies: she did it with her lover, for her lover, because of her lover. The gaze was directed not at the political but at the personal. The narrative was a sordid story of innocence corrupted or trust betrayed: love—not discipline, not policy, not politics—gone wrong.

The Arab, the Human

The use of dogs was frequently described as a strategy meant to exploit a distinctively Arab dislike, and fear, of dogs, in documents including Combined Joint Task Force 180 "Interrogation Techniques" (January 24, 2003), Joint Task Force 170 "Counter-Resistance Strategies" (October 11, 2002) and Combined Joint Task Force-7 "Interrogation and Counter-Resistance Policy" (September 14, 2003).[16]

Strategies of sexual humiliation were explained in this way as well. "The notion that Arabs are particularly vulnerable to sexual humiliation became a talking point among pro-war Washington conservatives in the months before the March, 2003, invasion of Iraq," Seymour Hersh wrote in the *New Yorker*. He continues, "One book that was frequently cited was 'The Arab Mind,' a study of Arab culture and psychology, first published in 1973, by Raphael Patai . . . The book includes a 25-page chapter on Arabs and sex, depicting sex as a taboo vested with shame and repression."[17]

The use of dogs was said to exploit Arab fear and dislike of dogs; the use of female soldiers and interrogators was said to strike at Arab and Muslim vulnerability to sexual humiliation. Each implied a corollary Western superiority. Arab and Muslim vulnerability to sexual humiliation was a consequence of sexism and sexual repression. Arab and Muslim dislike of dogs was—to a population imbued with an Anglo-American canine romanticism (Byron, *Beautiful Joe, Old Yeller*, Cesar Millan, *Marley and Me*)—both alien and unloving. Yet who would not be afraid of a strange dog, snarling inches from one's face and held by an enemy? Who would not be humiliated by being forced to strip naked before strangers and enemies? Who (man or woman) would not cringe at being asked to simulate sexual acts, or find the idea of being smeared with menstrual blood repugnant?

Accounts of the atrocities at Abu Ghraib, by those who participated in and those who reported on them transformed a common human vulnerability into a vulnerability peculiar to one culture and a site of the power of Western over Arab culture. This discursive sleight of hand is the dark reversal of cultural sensitivity.

Lynndie England and the Man on the Leash

Western women, enlisted in the project of liberating—or simply defeating—the Muslim world became tangled in a particularly perverse enterprise in which a project of universal liberation is made the occasion of a double subjection. Consider the case of Lynndie England. England's smiling face figures in a number of the photographs from Abu Ghraib. We know her from the photograph of the man on a leash. We recognize her giving a cheerful thumbs-up over the dog pile, and pointing cheerily at the genitals of various prisoners. We have not seen, though we may have heard of, the photographs that show her having sex.

England became an icon for abuse: the abuse she did and the abuse she endured. The ambivalence of her role, abuser and abused, captures a familiar strategy in the architecture of power and oppression, and alters it, subtly and effectively.

The logic of lynching once supported white supremacy, male power. White women were instructed to fear black men, to fear rape, robbery, and assault from them; black men were taught to seek safety and security from white men. At Abu Ghraib women were once again made the lynchpin of a system of oppression, once again enrolled in a strategy of collaboration. This time, however, the strategy turned not on the fiction of women's weakness, but on the fiction of women's strength.

The photographs record Lynndie England's power. She is a soldier. She has weapons. She commands. She is obeyed. She wears, as few women do, the uniform of her country's military. She serves with men. Her presence at Abu Ghraib testifies to the inclusion of women in the American military, to the equality of men and women. Her presence testifies that women have access to military power. Several of the photographs show England in Freudian poses of sexual power. She stands, clothed, before a line of naked men, pointing to their genitals. She points, a cigarette in her mouth, to another prisoner's penis. She has the phallus, and the phallus is hers.

The camera lies: or more precisely, it speaks with a forked tongue. Lynndie England's performative claims to power could not survive knowledge of her rank, her class, her relation with a man who was both an exploitative superior and an exploitative lover. The photographs portray England as a woman with power over a man; men had power over her. She presented herself to be read as a woman with power, as evidence for the equality of women in the West, serving with men as their equals, but she is formally and informally, publicly and privately, subordinated to Spc. Graner. She is free to exhibit her own sexuality, her sexual power, and her power over the sexuality of men, yet the use of her sexuality as a tool of state, by her superior officers, testifies to her subjection.[18] Emancipatory struts or structures reach their ends, are diverted and transformed to serve as supports for old established structures of hierarchy and abjection. Affirmations of the equality of women were diverted into supports for a system that renders Arabs and Muslims abject; and in this transformation women were rendered abject as well.

Critical readings of the photographs from Abu Ghraib made Lynndie England's subjection visible, but they did little to undo this architecture of abjection, or to disable the narrative that set white women against brown men. They tended, on the contrary to affirm narratives of female weakness, and to conceal the political processes that so elegantly served several chauvinisms simultaneously. England, a *Newsweek* reporter wrote, "came from a poor town in the hollows of West Virginia and lived for a time in a trailer."[19] ABC News asked "Is Lynndie England Victim or Victimizer?" quoting her defense psychologist on her failure to speak before she was eight, her special education classes.

ABC's account placed England in the narrative of failed romance, noting her early unsuccessful marriage and foregrounding her slavish devotion to Spc. Graner. "Graner took pictures of her—not only nude pictures of her—he took pictures of her having sex with him," Lynndie England's counsel Amador said. "He had another soldier who was older and outranked her take a camera and they had sex together while this soldier took a picture. She felt humiliated. She thought it was perverted. She felt it was wrong. So I asked her why she did it, and she said, 'I didn't want to lose him.'" Amador's account puts England in the position of the prisoner, placed in humiliating and perverted settings and photographed. The force of Amador's narrative depends on undermining England's consent, casting her in the role of a woman powerless before an exploitative lover. Casting Spc. Graner as England's lover rather than her supervisor placed enquiry into the chain of command outside the narrative. The narrative of women betrayed was echoed in the self-exculpating literary effort of General Janis Karpinski. Karpinski, however, cast the betrayal as a political rather than a personal one.[20]

Amador's narrative also required the absence of the Arab. Amador shifts the scene, from the photographs of the Arab prisoners to those of Lynndie England. His narrative draws a veil over their presence, and so over the acts that made England notorious. Amador's narrative thus conceals the way in which invidious constructions of the Arab and the Muslim and narratives of the power of women in the West were used to conceal the mutual reinforcement of sexual and civilizational hierarchies. Karpinski similarly erases the Arab, especially Arab women, in presenting herself as the victim of male deceit and exploitation.

Our Women . . . and Theirs

The conditions cited in defense of England and Karpinski may not be adequate to exculpate them, but they have unsettled the narrative of the progressive empowerment of women in the Western state. They should also impel interrogation of the uses of sexuality by the state and capital.

Americans were forced, in Abu Ghraib and in Guantanamo, to confront the use of women soldiers as agents of sexual humiliation. The employment of these techniques of torture depends upon employing American women not as intelligence officers, but as women paid for the performance of specific sexual acts. The tactic demonstrates the continuing importance of American female sexuality as a tool of the state. The question at issue in the camps is not only the treatment of the enemy, of the other, but the treatment of one's own. This strategy turns on—and turns over—the inclusion, equality, and freedom of the woman soldier. She is differentiated, marked out by her sexuality and reduced to it.

The abuse of Iraqi women at Abu Ghraib was hidden in the United States and made visible abroad. The visibility of the abuse abroad redoubled the abuse visited on these women. They were humiliated and, in some cases further endangered, by the circulation of their photographs in newspapers and on the Internet. Hiding the abuse in the United States preserved the fiction of Americans as the liberators of Arab and Muslim women.

Rather than liberating women—Arab or Western—the effects of the United States' invasion and occupation have been to reduce the status of women and increase their peril. We might look instead to another series of photographs taken at Abu Ghraib. In these photographs Lynndie England is shown with an Arab woman identified as a prostitute. England is fully clothed in all the photographs I have seen, but reports cite the presence of others in which she is shown not as a soldier, but as a sexual object, not clothed in the uniform, but naked and sexually available. The series of photographs that pairs England with the prostitute presents them as equals. They are about the same height and weight, they stand with their arms around each other. Both wear Western clothes.[21] These photographs put the opposition of the West and Islam, Arab and American, in question. The identification of the Arab woman as a prostitute or (still more tellingly) as "prostituted by her husband" speaks against the claims to equality and power staged in the photographs of England abusing male prisoners. These photographs stage England as one prostitute with another. They cast her simultaneously as victim and transgressor, and they point to the presence—outside the space of the photograph—of men more powerful than she who are responsible for her degradation.

The Man in the Hood

The photograph of the hooded man became an icon within days of its appearance. The image, like all icons, is full of meaning. Among these meanings is a series of references that are iconic in a sense that is at once richer and more troubling. The image echoes religious images. The pointed black hood recalls the customary garb of Spanish penitents to a European eye. In any American lexicon of images, the pointed hood belongs to the Klan. This image was seized by cartoonists who took the hood off the prisoner and restored it to the torturer.[22]

Placing the hood on the head of the prisoner might seem to identity the prisoner with the Klan, and so with the forces of bigotry. This effort has been central to those who sought a license for American antisemitism. The campaign against the Arab and the Muslim has identified Arabs and Islam with bigotry against Jews and Christians, and made the bigotry the license for invasion, war, and war crimes. The fascist sympathies of Charles Lindbergh and Ezra Pound are remembered rarely and mentioned only in passing. They figure as anomalies and aberrations in their cultures, and indeed, in themselves. Lindbergh's heroism and Pound's poetry are thought to be at odds with their fascist sympathies, and one is permitted, indeed encouraged, to honor the men and their work while condemning this defect. Flying and poetry, whiteness and Protestantism, are not tarnished by Pound and Lindbergh; Judaism is not tarnished by Jabotinsky or Meir Har Zion, but Muhammed Amin al Husseini, the Mufti of Jerusalem, has become a metonym for Arabs and Muslims, and his antisemitism a comprehensive cultural indictment. Given the endemic accusations of cultural intolerance, the photograph of the man in the hood might seem to speak of an assault on Arab antisemitism.

The performance of violence recorded in the photograph of the man in the hood testifies against this reading. The hoods the Klansmen wore were white, like the race they claimed. Here the hood is black and the man is dark. The Klan wore their hoods to claim power in the name of race and culture, to assault those who challenged that power, and to hold fast to their own supremacy. Here the dark hood marks a dark man, held in the grip of power, assaulted, the abject subject proving another's supremacy. The fire the Klansmen used to fuel their crosses and light their lynchings was primitive and hot. Here the flaming cross is replaced by a small black box, and the fire runs through cold wires.

The posture of the prisoner evokes, above all, the crucifixion. In an atmosphere of millenarianism and eschatology the image directs a series of imperative challenges and questions to Christians, religious and secular. The staging of the prisoner's electrocution evokes the crucifixion. Neither Christ nor the prisoner is alone. The prisoner who stands, covered with dirt and feces before a military guard, stands in the form of Christ crucified. The prisoners handcuffed to the cell doors and photographed sag, arms outstretched.

Fernando Botero, in a significant departure from the characteristic references and emotional valences of his work, painted the tortured of Abu Ghraib as Christ and the saints were painted: in their suffering. His *Abu Ghraib 53* (2005) recalls the "dog piles" but it also refers to a photograph of a prisoner wounded by "non-lethal weapons fire." The painting recalls the wounds of St. Sebastian. The canonical portraits of that saint show a body wounded many times, bound and open. Botero cites and reverses the conventions. The body of the saint was lithe and upright, the body of Botero's prisoner is cramped and downcast; the face of the saint drew the eye, the face of Botero's prisoner is hidden; the saint stood alone, Botero's prisoner is one of many. The eroticism of these portraits of the bound and open body of St. Sebastian has been often noted in art criticism; Mishima Yukio wrote of its erotic power in *Confessions of a Mask*. The eroticism of the painting may have been an effect of the hagiographic impulse that transformed a scene of delayed and tortuous death into epiphany and jouissance. Seeing sainthood transformed the abject, suffering human into an object of desire. In Botero's portrait, the perverse eroticism of the Abu Ghraib photographs is reversed again. The erotic is stripped away by the hagiographic citation. The link between human and divine is found in suffering and abjection.[23]

Botero's *Abu Ghraib 66* echoes paintings of Christ carrying the cross, bearded, lips parted in pain. Botero heard the divine in the photographs of suffering humanity. He had canonical warrant. "As you did it to one of the least of these, my brethren, you did it to me."[24]

Primo Levi wrote of another set of Muselmanner, "If this is a man." Stripped of dignity, the once man may be man no longer, may be something more or less, may be a dog. And then, one might ask, what is a dog? An animal, the philosophic animal, a domesticated animal. The philosophic animal, who knows the difference between friend and enemy. (Those of us who've watched the dog bark at the postman might view this capacity, and the Schmittian theory it anchors, with a suspicious eye.)

Perhaps the dog is that animal at home with us. Perhaps there is an ethics of domestication. Perhaps that ethic is called forth in the question "When you made the dog your own, what did you make of it? Friend or enemy? Guardian or predator? Teammate or servant?" Insofar as domestication entails making the animal one's own, it provides a text of that which is one's own. The dog made predator is the text of the master's depredations; the dog made servant, the text of the master's need, the master's lack, the master's desire for dominion.

Domestication reveals more than this. The dog made predator testifies to a desire for predation allied to a failure of capacity. The dog made a weapon testifies not only to the desire for depredation but to the inability to accomplish it. The dog that is badly used testifies to the master's practical as well as ethical failings, to weakness in action as well as weakness of will. Neither all failures nor all lacks are shameful. A desire for friendship that is not complete, a desire for friendship that is not satisfied with the human alone; a desire for cooperation, for common work that binds animals together: these are not occasions for regret.

The process of domestication is in one sense a process of utterance: of making visible one's own, of giving form to lack and desire, of making these take form in the world. The process is also, in practice as it is in etymology, the making of a household. It might remind us that the household is not only a site of intimacy and affection, but also of tyranny and animality; that the warmth of the "companions of the cupboard" is shadowed by the dark father, by patriarchal tyranny. One is reminded that the idea of the dog comprehends the guardian and the predator, the friend, the servant and the enemy, the companion and the tool. Because domestic relations are crafted, the process of domestication raises the questions concerning diverse forms of making: making friends, making enemies, making use, making trouble.

There is, of course, an older place where the human and the animal meet. The animal who becomes one's own in domestication carries its animality with it. The animal that is one's own is also, always, the animal carried in the self. The abjection of bare life carries within it an affirmation of the sweetness of life. Insofar as the prisoner is shown to be an animal and abject, he is also shown to be our own. The condemnation of that abjection carries with it a question concerning the treatment of animals, of *zoe*, of a sweet life still more broadly shared.

But there is also, in the image of abjection, an image of the divine. The Jew saw in the bodies of other Jews, more reduced, more abject than he, the Muslim bowing before God. Botero saw, in the images of men tortured by animals in the hands of other men, the image of the divine. When the human is stripped of humanity what is left? A beast or a god? The animal or the divine?

Three figures animate this essay: the woman, the dog, the divine. They are bound together in the suffering of the body, the sweetness of life, the passion of incarnation. Perhaps it is the experience of life in the flesh that opens to the divine. Life, bare life, and the sweetness of life testify to a divinity indiscriminately incarnate.

NOTES

1. The first phrase is attributed to Jesus on the cross, and is commonly translated as "My God, my god, why have you forsaken me." The second comes from the Latin liturgy of the Catholic church, in which the speaker confessed "my fault, my fault, my most grievous fault." The third is a line taken from a poem by Mahmoud Darwish which has become an iconic expression of Palestinian identity, "Record: I am an Arab."

2. See Marie Gottschalk, *The Prison and the Gallows* (Cambridge: Cambridge University Press, 2006).

3. The canonical locus of this concern with concealment is that set of practices and conventions concerned with women's dress, especially the veil, *hijab*, *burkha*, or *niqab*. Joan Scott has furnished a powerful critical study of the controversy over these in *The Politics of the Veil* (Princeton: Princeton University Press, 2007).

4. The Public Affairs Officer at Guantanamo refused my request for research access.

5. Susan Sontag notes the use and effects of editorial cropping of the photographs from Abu Ghraib in her essay "Regarding the Torture of Others," *New York Times*, May 23, 2004.

6. Sheldon Wolin, *Democracy Inc.* (Princeton: Princeton University Press, 2008).

7. Sontag, "Regarding the Torture of Others."

8. Ted Olson, "More Christian Organizations Respond to Abu Ghraib Scandal," *Christianity Today*. www.christianitytoday.com/ct/2004/mayweb-only/5-10-42.0.html. *Christianity Today* condemned the Abu Ghraib abuses as torture early on, as did Fr. Richard Neuhaus of *First Things*, and the Vatican.

9. www.salon.com/news/abu_ghraib/2006/03/14/introduction/index.html.

10. Sontag, "Regarding the Torture of Others."

11. Tzvetan Todorov, *The Conquest of America* (New York: Harper and Row, 1987).

12. There is an extensive and invaluable literature on the animal, the human, and post-human, which I am only beginning to explore. I am particularly indebted to the work of Donna Haraway, Vicky Hearne, Yi-fu Tuan, Kennan Ferguson, and Peter Singer. On the subject of Abu Ghraib, I have benefited from discussions with Alex Danchev, and from his paper "Like a Dog! Humiliation and Shame in the War on Terror," presented at the Political Theory Workshop, University of Pennsylvania, October 2006.

13. Adam Zagorin and Michael Duffy, "Inside the Interrogation of Detainee 063," *Time* 20 June 2005, www.time.com/time/2006/log/log.pdf. Also quoted, with ellipses, in Jane Mayer, *The Dark Side* (New York: Doubleday, 2008), 182.

14. Danchev, "Like a Dog!" 2006.

15. Sontag, "Regarding the Torture of Others."

16. *The Abu Ghraib Investigations: The Official Reports of the Independent Panel and the Pentagon on the Shocking Prisoner Abuse in Iraq*, ed Steven Strasser (New York: Public Affairs Press, 2004), "Investigation of the Abu Ghraib Detention Facility and the 205th Military Intelligence Brigade," 144–45. This also provides an account of the ambiguity over "who owned the dogs," Col. Pappas's claims to authority over interrogations, and the refusal of Navy dog handlers asked to participate in "fearing-up" inmates. See also James Sturck, "General Approved Extreme Interrogation Methods," *The Guardian*, March 30, 2005. Salon.com reported that "At least two other military memos referenced exploiting many Arabs' known fear of dogs, including an October 11, 2002, review of potential interrogation tactics for Guantánamo Bay, which Defense Secretary Donald Rumsfeld drew from for his Dec. 2, 2002, memo authorizing harsh tactics at that prison." Salon.com, "Working dogs," chap. 8: December 12–30, 2003.

17. Seymour M. Hersh, *New Yorker*, May 24, 2004.

18. Peter Nicholson of *The Australian* (May 6, 2005) has furnished a visual critique of this reading of England. In his cartoon, England is leashed as well: she stands over the prisoner, Graner looms over her. One might ask who held Graner's leash, or who loosed him? www.nicholsoncartoons.com.au_3616/html.

19. Evan Thomas, "Explaining Lynndie England," *Newsweek*, May 15, 2004, www.newsweek.com/id/105054

20. Janis Karpinski, *One Woman's Army: The Commanding General of Abu Ghraib Tells Her Story* (New York: Miramax Books, 2006).

21. See www.salon.com/news/abu_ghraib/2006/03/14/introduction/index.html

22. There are many examples of this use of the image, including Peter's Kuper's censored 2004 version, showing the wires connected to the White House. See David Wallis, "Cartoons Deemed Unfit to Print" *Los Angeles Times*, May 20, 2007. www. latimes.com.

23. The Botero paintings can be seen at marlboroughgallery.com.

24. Matthew 25. The philosophic corollary may be Antonio Negri's account of his imprisonment in *Job, la force d'esclave* (Paris: Bayard, 2002).

5

Passionate Performance
26/11, Mumbai

Veena Das

In his acute observations on Austin's theory of performative utterances, Stanley Cavell notes with some regret that Austin gave up too soon on the drama of perlocutionary effect of statements and instead came to take illocutionary force as the privileged example of performative utterances.[1] Cavell feels that Austin's "skimpishness" whenever he mentions emotions is another symptom of philosophy's refusal to engage with passion as essential to the human form of life. A crucial paragraph in Cavell reads as follows:

> The explicit reason he (Austin) gives for ruling out the perlocutionary as relevant to performativity (and thence to a certain picture of human speech and intelligibility) is this: "Clearly *any*, or almost any, perlocutionary act is liable to be brought off, in sufficiently special circumstances, by the issuing, with or without calculation, of any utterance whatsoever, and in particular by a straightforward constative utterance (if there is such an animal)." ... *Any? Almost? Liable?* Why is that roughly the end of the story rather than the (new) beginning of one? (pp. 172–73)

The new beginning for Cavell is in the thought that perlocutionary acts might make room for, and reward, imagination and virtuosity, while illocutionary acts do not, in general, need imagination. Thus while the typical words I speak in illocutionary acts (I declare, I name, I promise to pay the holder . . .) are formulaic, legal, or ritualistic in character; the words I call on to persuade (you to marry me?), or warn (you that a friend is betraying you?) all require thought, tact, or talent. Thus Cavell calls attention to the fact that "perlocutionary-like" effects can be achieved without saying anything—the urgency of passions is expressed, he says, before and after words. While illocutionary acts are anchored on the picture of law and convention, perlocutionary effects occur in the scene of disorder of desire for better or for worse.

The fate of words or the fatedness of words in the scene of disorder was the subject of earlier work I did on panic rumor, where I noted that in the urge to pass on rumors that become lethal, language took on the feature of something infectious.[2] I further noted that what accounted for the perlocutionary effect of rumor was its very absence of signature. Rumor did not cause violence, but it certainly authorized it in the way it enabled consolidation and circulation of passions of hatred and revenge. Cavell offers a careful enumeration of "felicity" conditions for perlocutionary effect that are matched with the similar conditions enumerated by Austin for illocutionary force. He points to the occurrence of both illocutionary verbs and perlocutionary ones in a passage from Jane Austen's *Emma,* and suggests that it is in its movement between these two contrasting field of forces, that of law and that of desire, that speech may be said to perform. The commerce between these two forces becomes evident in the scene of violence that I will analyze in this essay—the scene in which the figure of the "terrorist" bursts into light and makes violence completely "public." My claim is that there are no standing languages available in such cases through which we can analyze how illocutionary force or perlocutionary effect is achieved. At one level this might be read as the failure of representation, but I am less interested in how representation performs its failure, and more in how words that seem quite conventional nevertheless in combination become lethal—their force lies in the very fact that the access to context is lost. It is this absence of standing languages—in the sense that no reliable map on how to interpret or move within this kind of language game is available—that makes such traditional questions as those of standing, consent, and representation come to the fore. However, I claim that—rather than making political engagements recede into the background—this very absence of standing languages opens up the possibility of engaging with politics from a stance of uncertainty and doubt.

Before I go into a discussion of the specific nature of the event that took place in Mumbai (India) in November 2008, I will make a brief detour into a theory of fear and its relation to forms of governmentality proposed by Brian Massumi that is perhaps inspired in part by recent claims of neurosciences to render emotion as a movement between bodies occurring below the threshold of language and representation. Sympathetic though I am to attempts at understanding how the singularity of corporeal experience is to be integrated into new forms that violence and responses to it are taking, I feel that the steps taken within this framework are far too rapid and close off political possibilities rather than opening them up for further reflection and action.

Let me take the example of Massumi's influential essay on fear which analyzes the manner in which the color-coded alert system introduced by the Department of Homeland Security became a system of affective modulation of the population.[3] "The system," says Massumi, " addressed the population immediately, at the presubjective level: at the level of bodily predisposition or tendency . . . Each body's individuality performed itself reflexively (that is to say, non-reflectively) in an immediate nervous response" (p. 33). Aligning this "nervous" response to the central role of television in creating the affective event of, say, a terrorist attack or anticipation of one, Massumi argues for a new kind of politics in which government-media function is geared toward production of a new kind of power. "Government gained signal access to the nervous systems and somatic expressions of the populace in a way that allowed it to bypass the discursive mediations on which it traditionally depended and to regularly produce effects with a directness never before seen" (p. 34). Massumi qualifies the claim of direct affective modulation of a whole population by his later statement that these modulations lacked both content and form, and thus they could not produce effects that were entirely predictable. He also concedes that in a complex social environment made up of heterogeneous groups and a polity distanced from any meaningful interaction with political leaders, the state cannot produce the immediacy of effects that the notion of direct access to the nervous system of the population as a form of governmentality initially assumed. My sense of this mode of argumentation is that the elements it acknowledges in the making of new political subjectivities are correct but the analysis does not give us the fuller geography of the courses that the relation between passion, governmentality, and individual response can take. For example the color-coded system works on the body in the United States in very different ways on different kinds of subjects. If instead of bearing a Christian name and Eurasian features, your name is a recognizable Muslim one, you speak Urdu or Arabic and thus are the object of suspicion—you are likely to become watchful that your actions in public do not draw attention to these features of your biography. Representations, experiences with the history of being this kind of person in these public places (such as airports) stand along with the reactions felt at the level of the body—these together produce the perlocutionary effects about which Cavell says that my expressions can be before and after the words—they are not exhausted by the words spoken. It is time to take the reader to the scene of violence with reference to which I will take my analysis in more specific directions.

India's 9/11?

Many pictures of the terrorists in the act of shooting people circulated on media sites, but one of them, of a hooded man with gun cocked and his figure lighted by burning orange flames in the background, became an icon of the defiant terrorist. It visually condensed the series of coordinated terrorist attacks that occurred in Mumbai, India's financial capital, on 26 November 2008 and continued till 29 November.[4] A number of places including the highly populated railway station Chhatrapati Shivaji Terminus were attacked by a small number (ten) of armed young men—it appears that all of them were Muslims from neighboring Pakistan.[5] Eight of the attacks occurred in South Mumbai: with the focus on Chhatrapati Shivaji Terminus, two elite hotels—Oberoi Trident and the Taj Mahal Palace and Tower—a hospital (Cama Hospital), and the Orthodox Jewish–owned Nariman House. By the early morning of 28 November, Mumbai Police and security forces had secured all sites except for the Taj Mahal Palace. Commando action by India's National Security Guards on 29 November put an end to the attacks at the Taj Mahal Palace.[5] It was here that the violence had taken the form of a spectacle with the ten attackers moving from room to room and setting the building on fire. The attackers had commando-like training and were able to hold their own not only against the police but also against the highly trained commandos who had to be flown in from Delhi to offer combat. In all, 173 people died in this highly publicized event, and more than 300 others were injured. The media and political commentators were quick to characterize these killings now named 26/11 as India's 9/11. The only surviving person among the attackers was captured and was interrogated to create a dossier for action against Pakistan for its alleged support to the terrorist action. He is being tried in the civil courts in India.

Some commentators on this event have characterized it as part of a pattern of revenge for repeated anti-Muslim violence in different parts of the country, referring especially to the anti-Muslim pogrom in the state of Gujarat in 2002. Thus Arvind Rajgopal gives an analysis of the "lesson" from the attacks. "As the Indian state fails to provide justice, private parties have sought to settle accounts through public violence."[6] This is a comforting narrative that would somehow domesticate the violence within well-recognized categories of rights, justice, revenge, but it is difficult to know how the motives of the terrorists were discerned since there was little communication from any known militant or terrorist outfit claiming any responsibility for the attacks. Other more careful readers of the event have noted what they call the "voicelessness" of the terrorist attacks—as compared to earlier history of terrorist attacks in which a group took responsibility for the attack, or put demands on the State to exchange, for instance, prisoners for hostages—this time there was only killing and the final submission to being killed rather than surrendering to the armed forces.[7]

It seems necessary therefore to pause, to hesitate before reading motives, or even to fix this event into stories that rely on a framework of causes and consequences. Let us, instead, pay close attention to the kind of spectacle that the violence created and the affects that circulated around the event.[8]

Mediation or Immediacy?

Talking, about a month after the event, to a friend who hails from a low-income Muslim locality in Delhi in which some of my ethnographic work was located, I was stuck by his dismissal—"some people just want to be heroes for the media (*media par hero banane ks shauk hai kuch logon ko*)." There was no mention of martyrdom, or of Muslim grievances, or of revenge. Yet I know how relieved my friends and acquaintances in these localities were that it was not the Indian Muslims but Pakistan that was implicated in the attacks. My friend's comment comparing the terrorists to "media heroes" was to suggest that the attacks were in the nature of a parody despite the tragic deaths. The locutionary forms *bada hero banta hai,* or, *chala tha hero banane* (a big hero, eh? Wanted to become a hero, did you?) are often used in everyday life to admonish boys or to express mild censure for someone's mannerisms as theatrical or melodramatic— anyhow, not quite grounded.[9] There was something unreal, simulated, not quite believable in these events for my friend, though, according to his wife, he himself was glued to the TV while they were going on. I believe we could take this comment seriously and explore what kind of media effects were created by the kind of representations that were made available to the watching and participating public.

First let us take the telecast by India TV, a private Hindi-language news channel, that presented "interviews" with two of the attackers in Nariman House, the orthodox Jewish Center in which both the rabbi and his young wife were killed.[10] The entire spectacle of crowds surrounding the two hotels and the Nariman Center, clapping and cheering the police and later the commandos, trying to get into conversation with the attackers, transmitting news to others with their cell phones, while shots from AK-47 rifles and grenades were being launched and people were dying, had the kind of effect that my friend was describing when he made the disparaging reference to the "media hero."[11] The alleged conversation between the television anchor and the two attackers went as follows.[12]

The title line of the telecast is *"atankiyon se muthbheda—a confronta-tion with terrorists."* A text line at the bottom informs us that there are five terrorists in Nariman House and that the telephone conversation is taking place with one of them named Imran Babar. In the background we can see images of fire raging in Nariman House and people running around and shouting.

MALE VOICE *(presumably Imran Babar, reciting in a monotone)*—We are trying to tell you that we have come to raise our voice against the oppression—to talk of peace.

FEMALE VOICE *(high pitched, urgent)*: You say you have come to talk of peace but you are killing people.

MALE VOICE: That is what we are trying to tell you—see what you have done to our Muslims. You bomb our mosques and then you declare us, our ulla-mas, to be terrorists, you are playing a bloody *holi* [colour festival].[13] . . .

FEMALE VOICE *(interrupting)*—But if you have complaint against someone, complain to them; why are you killing other, ordinary people?

MALE VOICE: That is what we are trying to tell you—that see what you have done to our Muslim brothers in Kashmir and what you are doing to Muslims . . .

FEMALE VOICE: The people you are killing—they too are someone's brother, someone's wife, someone's child.

MALE VOICE: You are telling us this—we have come because we have been compelled by all the violence against Muslims to do this . . .

The female voice tries several times to interrupt with questions such as— where have you come from, whom do you represent, which organization do you belong to, how do we know you are in Nariman House . . . but the male voice continues in the monotone of someone delivering words that seem to have no relation to the immediacy of the situation—they are recited like frozen scripts.

It is interesting that the terrorist/militant voice here as well as the an-chor both use a vocabulary through which humanist projects are often discussed in the political rhetoric of India. Thus references to rights of minorities; the appeal to the "human," not as an abstract entity but as "someone's brother or someone's son"; demands for justice—all these phrases circulate in political discourse and in humanist writings against violence. We might be tempted to think along with Feisal Devji that this is analogical to Al Qaeda's rhetorical use of the vocabulary of human rights, which, he interprets as the aspiration not only to belong to a global community but also to show the hypocrisy of those in the West who claim to embody such discourse.[14] Indeed militants from Pakistan or from the Indian organizations sympathetic to outfits such as Lashkar-e-Taiba, like Sikh militants earlier, use the human rights vocabulary to publicly proclaim the hypocrisy of the Indian government at least in the kind of discourse that is intended for national or international audiences. But to see these statements as expressions of belief is to miss the point that constative statements acquire perlocutionary effect by becoming embedded in the kinds of conditions, gestures, pitch and tone of voice that constitute for Cavell the felicity conditions for such acts. When a terrorist is proclaiming that he is demanding peace while in the middle of a public shooting spree and shifting the agency of his actions to the audience as the proxy for Indian government, Hindus, moderate Muslims ("see what you people have made us peace-loving Muslims do," as one terrorist proclaimed) then our analysis must take into account how speech performs and not simply how it represents. Indeed, to use Judith Butler's acute formulation, representation must be seen here as performing its own failure, but not surely to recover "the human," as she seems to suggest. Of course the same observations apply to the speech of colonial officials, soldiers killing and raping while they are on peace missions, or heads of state demonstrating the benefits of civilization to primitive polities by having judicial public executions to punish human sacrifice.[15] The hold over the real becomes precarious, as my conversations with my friends in low-income Muslim localities revealed to me.

Simultaneously, at the level of image, the picture of the hooded terrorist defiantly cocking his gun at the sky illuminated by the fire behind, stands in complete contrast to the publicly circulated pictures of the crouching, naked, and terrorized Muslim bodies that gained an iconic place as the sign of the power and brutality with which captured Muslims were treated at Abu Ghraib.[16] It also carries a different affect than that of the picture I will discuss later, in which the mother of a dead Muslim soldier mourns in a pieta-like position, and which announces the price at which Muslims might be integrated into the body politic of the nation, in this case the United States.[17]

The Irreality Effect

One month later, when I was back in Delhi, I asked various people what they thought of the attacks. While some people I talked to told me that they had been mesmerized by the conversation and the live coverage, many more said that what was being shown during the attacks was just a "drama"—they simply did not believe that the dialogue was anything other than a simulated package, delivered with the burning hotels as the mis-en-scene. Christian Metz argued that the dreamlike effect in cinema that is created through "process effects" in an image track depends upon the distance it establishes from *"photographicity."*[18] The interesting difference here is that the tele-audience knows that it was in the presence of an event taking place in complete synchronicity between the time of the event and the time of viewing, yet doubts were cast over the nature of the "real," which accounts for the feeling that the attacks were both real and unreal. Related to that is the understanding of news as a commodity—the suspicion that the television station had simply used the opportunity to put up a melodramatic show to increase its viewer rating. At one point the male voice of the supposed terrorist when informed that the commandos had surrounded the Nariman Center and that it would be better to surrender, said, "It is better to die the death of a lion than to live this life of ignominy (*zillat*)." Some people I talked to in both Muslim and Hindu neighborhoods pointed to the inappropriate affect with which this line was repeated twice—there was no passion, they said, only a flat, dead rendering of a line as if learned by rote in school.

Now it might be that the conversation was completely simulated—many Hindi news channels now dramatize newscasting, adding special effects and a bit of scenery. On the other hand, how are we to know in advance what affect is appropriate and can be rendered effectively in a situation such as I am describing? It seems that the relation between violence, horror, fear, tragedy, comedy, pain, laughter as expressions has become completely unhinged from the assumed inner states of which they are outward expressions. Said otherwise, our standing languages through which we connect, say, laughter with joy, or tears with sorrow, are put into question. It is a scene of skepticism that makes the terror of imagining that I might be, after all, all alone in the world as Descartes imagined, a realistic description of the situation rather than the unnatural doubt of a café skeptic. We do not know what experience means or how in our experience the outer behavior and inner states are stitched together.[19]

The sense of "irreality"[20] is amplified by the serious tone in which different "security experts" speak, analyzing the situation on PTV from Pakistan. For example, in a program on Politics and Pakistan (*Siyasat aur Pakistan*), the 9/11 template was used to suggest that both 9/11 and what happened in Mumbai were staged "dramas," but whereas the Americans had been sophisticated and suave in the manner in which they executed the supposed conspiracy of staging an attack and using it as a pretext for invading Afghanistan and Iraq, the Indians had simply bungled the whole show. As proof, there was a close reading on Pakistan news channels of the minutest details of body, gesture, or clothes to discern if the person was a Muslim, a Pakistani, or a counterfeit agent of the Research and Analysis Wing, the Indian secret service (RAW). For example, some commentators on PTV said that a wristband identified as saffron or yellow worn by one of the attackers showed him to be a BJP (Hindu nationalist party) supporter. Another asked spectators to look at the picture of one of the terrorists that had been captured by a passer-by and was being telecast—look at him, does he have the features of a Pakistani and a Muslim? At another time supporting his theory of the terrorist killing as a bungled staged operation of RAW, one commentator said, pointing to the picture of the terrorist walking with a gun slung on his shoulders, "see his face—it does not show any fear—this is because he is a RAW operative who has been assured that he will not be killed but the Indians have so bungled the operation that they will end up killing their own operatives."

What is interesting in these forensic readings is that they show a great intimacy with Hindu cultural symbols but the representations are just a little off-key. For instance, a saffron or red thread is sometimes worn on the right wrist by Hindus as a sign of ritual commitment, but is not necessarily a sign of allegiance to BJP. Yet one does not know what this thread, on this person, meant in terms of ritual commitment or any other kind of commitment (dancers, singers, and disciples of various art forms, whether Hindu or Muslim, wear such threads too as a sign of a vow to complete a mission or a course of learning from a teacher). Or take the assumption that the features of the man shown on television are not Muslim enough, which must remain a puzzle, since South Asians look quite alike if they are wearing jeans and tee shirt, as this man was. To distinguish Muslims and Hindus one would have to look for other signs such as the type of beard, or the clothes, or the name of the person. One commentator even identified the two men as a Sikh and a Hindu with names respectively of Amar Singh and Hira Lal.

In one sense such representations simply participate in the structure of rumor; at another level they point to profound skepticism about the ability to believe what is before one's eyes. The terrorists split and multiply into a chimera of representations—Muslim terrorist, militant mujahidin, Hindu or Sikh masquerading as Muslim, mercenary, soldier, commando, martyr, victim of manipulations of ISI (Pakistan Intelligence Agency) or RAW (the Indian Intelligence Agency.) For the observer and the analyst such as myself, the signs are too many and too confusing to interpret except as an indication of representation staging its own failure in a mood of parody.

The fact that one's experience of the terrorist attacks was a heavily mediated one came home to me when listening to or reading the accounts of the "intercepted" messages that terrorists are supposed to have sent to their organizers located in Pakistan. I take one example. When news that among the first casualties was the highly regarded police officer Hemant Karkare came out, one of the intercepted messages was about this event. In its English rendering, which was made available to the media, one of the terrorist is supposed to have reported to his superior, "Among the dead are two high-ranking police officers," and the person on the other side of the conversation is reported as replying—"that is icing on the cake." Now the conversation was taking place in a street language, a mixture of Urdu and Punjabi, since the attackers did not speak English, but I know of no expression in either language that could be translated to refer to cakes and icings. So my first thought was that this was a "made-up" story. But then I have seen the truly poor translations in the subtitles that are provided on both public and private TV channels (telecast for international viewers) for the speech of the commentator on news channels or of actors in soap operas. Hence the technique for the provision of "truth" that can be communicated through translation might itself lead to doubt; or else the fact of intercepted communications might in time turn out to be pure fiction.

A very different alignment between fact and fiction was available in videos circulated on the Internet and also watched by a couple of Muslim families I know in which attempts were made to align the Mumbai attacks within the genre of the "sword of Islam" stories that, however, were quite innocent of the-sword-versus-the-word dichotomy. The videos produced within this supposed genre assumed a direct inheritance marked both by such verses as "we are the inheritors of the sword of Karbala" and by such titles as *"allah ki talwar hai hum"*—we are the swords of Allah. For instance one of the videos renders the well-known song *"dushmmanon tum nein kis kaum ko lalkara hai"* (oh, enemies, which community have you challenged?) with images of Muslim leaders from different parts, flags of Islamic countries, and pictures of men in various warlike formations, presumably the mujahidin in Kashmir and Afghanistan.[21] Political commentators such as Zaid Hamid appeared on Karachi TV and declared that Pakistan was going to crush Israel and India, drawing historical analogies, and stating that Indians could never look Pakistanis in the eye since they (the Hindus) had been ruled by Muslims for a thousand years and were a race of cowards.

While such comments are mirrored in some street-level popular tracts in Hindi against the Muslims and in the literature of the Hindu right, the rhetorical excess marks it as literature which bears superficial resemblance to the medieval tracts in this genre as well as to the hate literature of the late colonial period, which was specifically produced to attract publicity by adopting the genres that the British censor recognized as "communal" literature likely to disturb public peace.[22] When and how such literary renderings might take lethal forms, as for instance in panic rumors, or in speeches to recruit young men for the "cause" of Hindu or Muslim militancy is unpredictable but causes great concern, especially among ordinary Muslims in India—on which I will have more to say later.

It is important to recognize that the strident discourse of imagining a future conquest of India by Pakistan was not the discourse of either Pakistani politicians or the government, nor of several other citizen groups in Pakistan. The Pakistani government while denying for a long time its involvement in the Bombay attacks, settled on the language of non-state actors who were acting without support from any official agencies. Similarly some political commentators in India (e.g., Swapan Dasgupta and Arun Shouri) talked of civilizational conflicts and the need for strong action (a euphemism for war), but the government scaled down its own rhetoric. Still, the Congress Government ended up passing anti-terrorism legislation (Unlawful Activities Prevention Act, 2008) which resembled the earlier POTA (Prevention of Terrorism Act, 2002) that the United Progressive Alliance Coalition of which the Congress was a major partner had repealed in 2004. The one important difference between POTA and the new legislation that is a small victory for human rights groups is that under the new law, the confessions obtained by the police will not be admissible in court.[23] Human rights groups and academic researchers had consistently shown the abuse that such a provision on the admission of confession made to police under POTA could lead to.

The point I am trying to make is that while rhetorical excess and melodramatic special effects were the order of the day in media reports and discussions, generating a deep skepticism about what was being observed, there were real effects of the attacks in both countries. For India there was the passing of antiterrorism law that the BJP had demanded for a long time, and in Pakistan there was the ban imposed on some militant organizations such as the Jamaat-ud-dawa, widely believed to be the front organization of the banned Lashkar-e-taiba. There was also the real threat of a war that could lead to deployment of nuclear weapons on both sides. Finally the strong war rhetoric that the attacks generated in India allowed the supporters of the army, especially the ex-general Parvez Musharraf, to claim that the stability of Pakistan depended entirely on its army and on the ISI and not on democratically elected government.[24]

To sum up my argument in this section, I have proposed that in the reporting of a catastrophic event such as the Mumbai attacks the urgency and immediacy try to hide the processes of mediation—yet, they generates a tempo of skepticism in which the senses become or are experienced as "untrustworthy." While the literature on media recognizes the privileging of the present in television as compared to photography, the close kinship between television and the temporality of rumor merits more sustained attention. The availability of a plurality of viewing channels, the juxtaposition of reportage on TV with circulation of videos, the blurring of fact and fiction in the commentaries of those constructed as "experts"—all this generates an excess in which the relation between emotions and their expressions becomes completely unstable. Yet the effects generated by the event as well as its representations are real and have grave political and personal consequences. In the next section I ask how we might understand the relation between aesthetic and political representation considering the modality through which the real was portrayed. How does the individual experience the mix of attachment to and detachment from political community as the media portrayal of catastrophic events seeps into everyday life?

Aesthetic and Political Representation

The impressive literature on political representation that has grown since Hanna Pitkin's seminal work inspired by Stanley Cavell's doctoral dissertation on Wittgenstein and Austin has contributed considerably to our understanding of formal processes of representation.[25] More specifically, it has deepened our understanding of the centrality of context for understanding how political communities are created and sustained; of the place of temporality as in the distinction between promissory representation and anticipatory representation; and also of the plurality embedded within any rendering of community and its attendant processes of representation.[26] Also drawing from Pitkin's original insight, scholars have asked how the gap between aesthetic representation and political representation might be occupied.[27] Underlying these questions, it seems to me, is the deeper question of how we determine what it is to consent to "belong" such that one can agree both to being represented and to represent others. In his simultaneous reading of film and texts of political philosophy, Cavell puts the issue as that of understanding the difference between expressed consent and tacit consent.[28] What does Locke intend, asks Cavell, in suggesting that, as distinct from expressed consent to membership in a political community, tacit consent is something that is assumed for anyone who simply happens to be in the space in which laws of a political community are applicable? In Cavell's own remarkable reading, expressed consent allows one to withdraw from membership in a political community and is meant for those whose ties are forged by a whole way of life, whereas tacit consent assumes shallow contacts with a political community, as of a stranger who is simply in proximity to that community. The latter form of consent might be nothing more than a single-arm, offhand contact. Such is the example of a stranger's relation to the law of the highway on which she is driving in an alien country. Yet the act of strangers in the terrorist case becomes the occasion for assuming tacit consent with far more lethal consequences for the Indian Muslims and invites us to contemplate this region of thought further.

Thus, I want to take Cavell's creative reading of consent in a somewhat different direction. However theatrical the manner in which the terrorists declared their act as vengeance or as a form of popular justice and however might Indian Muslims in the kind of neighborhoods I work in try to render the speech of the terrorists as simply "filmy dialogue," the question of whom the terrorists represented puts pressure on the political community. Bano Begum, one of my friends living in the single-room low-income locality of Abdul Azad Nagar, said *"karte wo hain, marte hum hain"*—they do, we die. Bano Begum was referring to years of experience in which an event such as this, or a communal riot elsewhere, or even such global events as the protests over the Danish cartoons are slowly folded into the experience of having to explain yourself to some interrogating public. While the literature on representation has rightly raised the question of how marginal or subaltern groups might find voice,[29] here the problem is somewhat different . Simply because you are a Muslim, your tacit consent to acts of terrorism is taken for granted. How one expresses one's distance, or gives a different rendering of the simultaneous sense of having been unjustly treated within the Indian polity and yet feeling distant from those who assume to represent your grievances through acts of violence, is the key issue for many Muslims. The sense of "irreality" that I mentioned nevertheless has real consequences. Within the excess of speech that has rumor-like quality in that it makes language itself suspect, how do Muslims strive to find a voice?

In an interview on the private TV channel NDTV, the anchor, Barkha Dutt, pressed Shahrukh Khan, the charismatic Bollywood actor and director, to explain his silence after the Mumbai attacks. In order to publicly signal their distance from the terrorist projects, various famous Muslim personalities in Mumbai had tied black bands on their arms as part of a protest on Eid on December 8, observing it as "Black Eid."[30] Shahrukh's answer about this silence was to say, "Like everyone else, I was just very scared." On being pressed to articulate what he was scared of, Khan replied that he was scared that anything he might say might be interpreted in ways he had no control over. Interestingly, he then moved the narrative to the voice of his children—his fear becoming one with their fears, which were easier to articulate. What languages does God hear prayers in, how are they to deal with the fact of a Muslim father and a Hindu mother?

At one level this terror of speech when there were too many words flying around is the vulnerability of the human to the fact of language—the fact that my utterance might be cited by another, distorted, made to carry affects that are foreign to me, parodied, or simply quoted out of context.[31] At another level this is the terror: that I do not have the means to annul my assumed and tacit consent as in the case of anxiety that circulated around the figure of the Indian Muslim. The performance of non-consent had to be repeated and public in order for Muslims in India to signal their distance from the acts of the killers.

The most dramatic expression of this "non-consent" was the decision by various Muslim organizations in Mumbai such as the Muslim Jama Masjid Trust, the Dawat-i-Islami, and the Muslim Council Trust to deny burial to the bodies of the terrorists on the basis that their brutal acts of killing women and children were testimony of the fact that they did not have the right to be called Muslim. This clearly went against the obligation of pious Muslims to provide burial to unclaimed Muslim bodies or to

the bodies of those who die by suicide. Yet the powerful effect of national
solidarity that this action created showed how each such act of terrorist
violence creates greater demands for Muslims to perform publicly their
allegiance to India. The story of Antigone and the question of whether the
allegiance to the polity must transcend even death continue to cast a shadow and are in complete contradiction, for instance, to the idea that bodies
of dead warriors, whether one's own or of the enemy, deserve a proper
funeral.[32] Political belonging is here publicly displayed and overcomes religious obligation—the dead are too dangerous to handle. The dramatic
effect is similar to that of Colin Powell's speech on the right of a young
Muslim boy to the dream of becoming the president of the United States,
which was framed in the context of Obama's candidacy and rumors about
his being Muslim. It might be recalled that Powell was commenting on
the moving image of a Muslim mother grieving at the grave of her dead
son, the tombstone with a crescent and star proclaiming his Muslim identity. Though powerful in its affirmation of Muslims belonging to the U.S.
polity, Powell's speech depended for its affective force on not only the sacrifice made by an American Muslim soldier who died in the Iraq war but
also on the image of his grieving mother, further "domesticating" through
the pietà-like tableau in the image that so moved him, the foreignness of
Muslim presence on American soil.

The Muslim in Powell's speech becomes a full citizen not by the rule of
law but by the right he earns by sacrifice understood through a Christian
language of sacrificial death and witnessing.[33] In the context of Mumbai
the effect of national inclusion was created through public repudiation of
the dead terrorist bodies by the Muslim leaders, thereby making public
the project of the nation as not simply a legal concept but a theological
one as well.

But in the end, one might ask, might one not—what is the standing of
those who demand that Muslims repudiate their assumed and tacit consent to acts of terrorism? Cavell puts the matter of standing thus: "Moral
standing is pushed to the center of the stage in perfectionism. Where the
morally good is calculated, say in a revised tax code; or where the morally right is derived from Kant's categorical imperative, say in the case of
abortion or capital punishment, if an act is bad or wrong, then it is bad or
wrong period: that is, no matter who you are. But if you tell me 'Neither a
borrower nor a lender be' or 'To thine own self be true' you had better have
some standing with me from which you confront my life, from which my
life matters to you, and matters to me that it matters to you."[34] Yet, those

who expressed disappointment that Muslims did not take to the streets in protest, such as the journalist Thomas Friedman of the *New York Times*[35] or the various members of the political parties in India, did not ever ask themselves what standing they could claim with the Muslims given that, after the Gujarat carnage, neither the Gujarat Government nor the Hindu Right groups offered a public apology. By assuming that they had the right to demand an explicit disavowing of terrorism from Muslims, but sidestepping the question of who has standing to examine Muslim lives, Hindu groups came to represent themselves as "naturally" connected to the nation while others had to demonstrate that they had earned the right to be part of the nation.[36]

A Conversation from the Past

I reproduce here a conversation I had regarding a "small" event in the Abdul Azad Colony,[37] a low-income neighborhood in Delhi, after a terrorist bombing in Delhi in 2004. Two children from the locality (one Hindu and one Muslim) decided on the spur of a moment to play a prank. They called the police emergency number from a public telephone in a shop, with the warning of an imminent bomb attack on a nearby cinema. To their utter surprise,[38] a siren-blowing police van turned up at the shop within minutes, but instead of catching the children, they arrested a young Muslim man who was standing nearby and accused him of being a terrorist. The children were pleading that it was not the man but they who has played the prank, but the police saw a lucrative opportunity and were not going to let go easily. Within the next hour the people in the locality, both Hindus and Muslims, had collected ten thousand rupees that were handed over to the policemen as a prize for their leaving the man and the children alone.

Soon after this event, while we were discussing the fact that Muslims were constantly being asked to prove their allegiance, one of the men recited the following verse:

> *Tere ishk mein ji-jaan ko lutaya ham ne*
> *Teri zameen pe ghar apna basaya hum ne*
> *Phir bhi gila hai ke wafadar nahin*
> *Hum wafadar nahin tu bhi to didldar nahin*

Freely translated this would read:

For your love we squandered life and heart
On your earth we made our home
Yet the complaint that we are not faithful
If we are not faithful you too are without a loving heart[39]

I realized that this was an improvisation of one of the verses of the poet Iqbal, regarded as the national poet of Pakistan,[40] from his famous poem *Shikwa* (complaint), but also that the last two lines were recycled and embedded now in Qawalis and popular songs. Yet the manner in which this man recited the poem brought the discussion to a point where nothing remained to be said. In this improvisation he had expressed both the sense that he claimed India as his country and the sense that if Muslims could not be fully faithful, India too was unable to welcome them with full heart. This combination of belonging and alienation, of acknowledging that there was a larger Islamic community spread in the world to which Muslims did belong and yet that their particular Islam authorized them to claim India as their own—to me this summed up the combination of antagonism/agony through which Hindu-Muslim relations are expressed within specific local worlds.[41]

In her remarkable reflections on ordinary affects, Kathleen Stewart meditates on how what she calls extreme trajectories "take root and then take off with a life of their own." Using the example of multiple personality disorder, she shows the tempo of events that included movement between various points defined by experts and by ordinary people that morphed into such experiences as "childhood abuse," "false memory syndrome," and "satanic rituals." In her words, "Such trajectories and metamorphoses are not just dead social constructions that we can track back to a simple origin, but rather are forms of contagion, persuasion and social worlding."[42] So, following the kinds of extreme events that the Mumbai spectacle of violence represented, one expects there will be the sprouting of a story here, a police action there, a report in a neighborhood newspaper, suspicion of a tenant, the elopement of a girl with a man across the Hindu-Muslim divide, and that these then could become flash points for a number of small skirmishes or might generate effects out of proportion to what one might have thought their potential was. In this sense it is the fact of holding the memory of the event, the new anti-terrorist legislation, and the whisperings around people and places as pure *potentia* that one needs to analyze in the manner in which terrorist violence becomes part of everyday practices through which relations are negotiated. In that sense the time of the event cannot be determined in advance but must await its unfolding.

Let me speculate that this unfolding will take different courses at the national and the local level. The sense of "irreality" I noted in the creation of media representations, and especially the sense that the internal states and their expressions had become unhinged from each other, continue to hold the possibility that Muslims will have to perform their allegiance to India in more strident terms even as the grief of a community that does not recognize itself in what is propagated in its name finds little expression. At the level of small neighborhoods, the possibility of violence that could morph from national events into purely local ones and circulate through these neighborhoods in daily fights and daily acts of reclamation now defines the work of the everyday. The "eventologies of the ordinary," as Shane Vogel calls them, move beyond the suddenness of the event to describe practices and performances that disperse and multiply the event as it is threaded in everyday life.[43] The example I gave of the children's prank, the police response, and the readiness of the local community to ward off the danger of police atrocity by a collective act of bribery is one example of the slow shifts by which the local is reorganized. There are other examples through which the fear of terrorism folds into relationships, as Muslim mothers become more watchful of their sons or Hindu landlords refuse to take in Muslim tenants, deepening the divide of Hindus and Muslims in everyday life. I do not hold out the picture of the everyday as organically stitched together that would keep violence at bay, for the everyday is not simply the time of routine and familiarity that lies between events. The kind of spectacular violence that terrorist acts perform become like seeds in the world that could sprout in many different ways. In the favorite words of Kathleen Stewart—Or Something.

NOTES

For comments and reflection on an earlier account of the Mumbai attacks, I am grateful to Talal Asad and Naveeda Khan for their incisive comments and to various commentators who responded with criticisms and comments, especially Devraj Singh. See "Jihad, Fitna and Muslims in Mumbai," The Immanent Frame, SSRC Blog on Religion and Public Culture, posted December 9, 2008, and the responses that followed. I thank the participants in the seminar "Performing Violence" for their helpful suggestions, and especially Amy Huber for her detailed response to the paper. Bhrigupati Singh, Sylvain Perdigon, Deepak Mehta, Roma Chatterji, Pratiksha Baxi, Michael Moon, and Anad Pandian opened up possibilities for exploration that I gratefully acknowledge. Comments from an anonymous referee were very useful in the finetuning of the essay.

1. Stanley Cavell, "Performative and Passionate Utterance," in *Philosophy the Day after Tomorrow* (Cambridge: Harvard University Press, 2005): 155–92.

2. See Veena Das, *Life and Words: Violence and the Descent into the Ordinary* (Berkeley: University of California Press, 2006).

3. Brian Massumi, "Fear (The Spectrum Said)," *Positions* 13 (2005): 31–48.

4. This picture circulated on television programs and YouTube and became the lead photo in many journalistic accounts.

5. Although Pakistan initially denied that the attackers were from Pakistan, it later conceded that they were "non-state actors" after the only surviving terrorist identified himself as a Pakistani citizen. The story continues to develop as the case of murder registered against Ajmal Amir Kasab, the surviving twenty-one-year-old attacker, proceeds in the Indian courts. The now routinely televised picture of Kasab, who appears as a young, poorly educated man being tried for a crime, stands in complete contrast to the defiant Muslim body captured in the image discussed here. This "normalization" of the figure of the terrorist through allowing normal law to operate deserves a separate treatment that I am unable to provide here.

6. Arvind Rajgopal, "Violence, Publicity and Sovereignty" Paper posted on SSRC Blog, The Immanent Frame: Secularism, Religion and Public Sphere, December 15, 2008.

7. See especially Faisal Devji, "Attacking Mumbai," SSRC Blog, *The Immanent Frame*, December 19, 2008.

8. On the close affinity between television and mythic experience, see James W. Carey, ed., *Media, Myths, and Narratives: Television and the Press* (London: Sage Publications, 1988); on the blurring of the fact/fiction dichotomy as a feature of television, see M. Doane, "Information, Crisis, Catastrophe" in *Logics of Television*, ed. P. Mellencamp (Bloomington: Indiana University Press, 1990); and on the impact of 9/11 on the construction of news on television, see Wheeler W. Dixon, *Film and Television after 9/11* (Carbondale: Southern Illinois University Press, 2004). The spectacular aspect of television reporting of terrorism was captured in an earlier study, Michel Wieviorka and D. Walton, *Terrorisme à la une* (Paris: Gallimard, 1987).

9. Such expressions—hero, lion—can also convey the pathos of one who has been defeated by life especially as part of autobiographical statements. Bhrigupati Singh captures this when he relates the story of a Cinema Workers Union leader who is now reduced to managing the workers on behalf of the owners and who says to him, "*Yaar mein sher hua karta tha—par ab circus ka sher ban gaya hun*—buddy, I used to be a lion but now I am merely the circus lion." See Bhrigupati Singh, "Adamkhor Haseena (The Man-Eating Beauty) and the Anthropology of the Moment," *Contributions to Indian Sociology* 42 (2008): 239–47.

10. I had access to this and some other telecasts from recordings made by research assistants and from the archives of the media, some of which were available from the Web.

11. It is characteristic of street life in India that crowds gather round any event almost in a moment.

12. The conversation takes place in Hindi and Urdu—all translations are mine. I provide some extracts as examples.

13. Notice how medieval metaphors of war—for example, *khun ki holi*, the spring festival of color imagined as played with blood—migrate from festival to war to suggest that the bloodiness and cruelty of war, especially for victims, are transported here and make the speech of the terrorists both "dramatic" and part of popular culture.

14. Faisal Devji, *The Terrorist in Search of Humanity: Militant Islam and Global Polity* (New York: Columbia University Press, 2008).

15. See Felix Padel, *The Sacrifice of Human Being: British Rule and the Konds of Orissa* (Delhi: Oxford University Press, 1991).

16. See Steven C. Caton, "Coetzee, Agamben, and the Passion of Abu Ghraib," *American Anthropologist* 108, no. 1 (2006): 14–23.

17. There is a considerable literature analyzing the photographs at Abu Ghraib and their significance. I discuss this literature in Veena Das, "Violence, Gender and Subjectivity," *Annual Review of Anthropology* 37 (2008): 283–99.

18. Christian Metz, "*Trucage* and the Film," trans. François Meltzer, *Critical Inquiry* 3 (1977): 657–75. Trucage is translated as trick photography in the singular and special effects in the plural. Hent de Vries has analyzed the resonance between special effects and miracles and the implication of this resonance for an understanding of mediation in relation to religious experience: Hent de Vries, "Of Miracles and Special Effects," *International Journal for Philosophy of Religion* 50 (2001): 41–56.

19. This was an important theme in Wittgenstein's thought on animal life, as in the case of the dog who can express expectation but not hope.

20. I use the term "irreality" rather than unreality to suggest that the commerce between fact and fiction, truth and delusion, is something akin to the Sanskrit term *maya* that covers this kind of semantic joining. Unfortunately my English vocabulary is too limited to find an exact equivalent—or perhaps this range of thought is not easily captured in English.

21. It is not possible to inherit this or any other form of speech without the signs of the contemporary marking the text. Thus for instance, the hagiographic literature on the conquest of Hindu kingdoms by Muslim kings or chiefs, beginning in the thirteenth century, carries various references to infidels, and the breaking of idols as Islamic obligation. However, these texts also have chapters which describe how alliances were forged with Hindu kings in the course of battle. Similarly, the Muslim conquest of a region was marked by the promise that the khutba (sermon) read during the Friday prayers in the mosque in that region would thenceforth include the name of the Sultan who secured it in the glory of God against Hindu idolaters. The videos make no such references either to alliances or to any particular Sultan on whose behalf a battle is launched—the subject becomes the collective "quom"—community of Muslims. The question of "secular" versus "communal" histories has become so fraught with present forms of political discourse in India that it has become impossible to receive that history without inserting into it the present-day politics of the region. For an account of the difficulties of addressing this literature from a historian's perspective, see the excellent work of Shahid Amin, "On Retelling the Muslim Conquest of North India," in *History and the Present*, ed. Partha Chatterjee and Anjan Ghosh (Delhi : Permanent Black, 2006). Amin writes, "The narratives of Muslim warrior saints retailed by balladeers, which bear a complicated relationship with the more standard hagiographies, are evidence of the refashioning of sagas of 'religious' conflict in order to create communities in the past and in the present" (24). My point is that to claim inheritance from this literature one can draw upon both the stories of iconoclasm, the plunder of Hindu kingdoms, and the reworking of these stories for creating communities of tolerance or cohabitation. Thus representation does much more than simply re-present—it also marks time in terms of the signature that time leaves on the text.

22. Deepak Mehta, " Words That Wound: Archiving Hate in the Making of Hindu and Muslim Publics in Bombay," in *Crisis and Beyond: A Critical Second Look at Pakistan,* ed. Naveeda Khan (Delhi: Routledge, 2009). One important feature of this literature on both the Muslim and Hindu side is the use of rhyming prose.

23. On the manner in which the passing of anti-terrorism laws enables local police to apply categories of danger along sectarian lines, see Julia Eckert, "POTA and the Categories of Danger," Paper presented at the Law and Social Science Network Inaugural Conference, New Delhi, December 2008. For a documentation of abuse of POTA see Ujjwal Kumar Singh, *The State, Democracy and Anti-terror Laws in India* (Delhi: SAGE Press, 2007).

24. See Parvez Musharraf's interview with Wolf Blitzer on CNN, January 23, 2009.

25. Hanna F. Pitkin, *The Concept of Representation*, (Berkeley: University of California Press, 1967).

26. Concepts of temporality are built, for example, into the distinction between promissory representation and anticipatory representation as proposed by Jane Mansbridge, "Rethinking Representation," *American Political Science Review* 97 (2003): 515–28. On representation and mediation for marginalized communities and its implication for thinking about plural communities, see Melissa Williams, "The Uneasy Alliance of Group Representation and Deliberate Democracy," in *Citizenship in Diverse Societies*, ed. Will Kymlicka and Wayne Norman (Oxford: Oxford University Press 2000), 124–55.

27. See F. R. Ankersmit, *Aesthetic Politics: Political Philosophy beyond Fact and Value* (Stanford: Stanford University Press, 1997); William Connolly, *Neuropolitics* (Minneapolis: University of Minnesota Press, 2001); and the remarkable recent book by Thomas Dumm, *Loneliness as a Way of Life* (Cambridge: Harvard University Press, 2008).

28. Stanley Cavell, *Cities of Words: Pedagogical Letters on a Register of Moral Life* (Cambridge: Harvard University Press, 2004). See especially the discussion in chap. 3.

29. The classic paper is Gayatri Chakravorti Spivak, "Can the Subaltern Speak?" in *Marxism and the Interpretation of Culture*, ed. Cary Nelson and Lawrence Grossberg (Urbana/Chicago: University of Illinois Press 1988), 271–313.

30. See report in *Outlook*, December 4, 2008, on the appeal to all Indian Muslims to observe December 8th as Black Eid by wearing black arm bands.

31. See Das, *Life and Words*, especially regarding the fate of language in rumors.

32. I am struck by the unconscious mimesis of colonial acts of denying religious funerals to those defined as traitors.

33. I owe this point to Nadia Khan, "Rumor, Narrative Ambiguity, and the Obama-Muslim Myth in the 2008 Presidential Campaign," term paper for the course Logic of Anthropological Inquiry, Fall 2008, Johns Hopkins University, 18 pages.

34. Cavell, *Cities of Words*, 50.

35. Thomas Friedman, "Calling All Pakistanis," *New York Times*, December 2, 2008, as in the following passage: "When Pakistanis and other Muslims are willing to take to the streets, even suffer death, to protest an insulting cartoon published in Denmark, is it fair to ask: Who in the Muslim world, who in Pakistan, is ready to take to the streets to protest the mass murders of real people, not cartoon characters, right next door in Mumbai?"

36. I do not wish to imply that this "natural" relation to the nation works without mediation—there is indeed an invented history of the natural, as Wittgenstein tells us. I also reiterate that there is no givenness to the term "Hindu" and not all Hindus are similarly placed vis-à-vis the nation.

37. Names of places and people are pseudonyms used to protect privacy and anonymity.

38. The surprise is worth noting because people, especially in poorer localities, do not expect to get a quick response from any institution related to public service provisions.

39. An alternate translation of the last line suggested by a scholar of South Asian Islam is "if [you say] we are faithless, it's you who has no heart." My own translation tries to capture the feeling of many Muslims in low-income neighborhoods that they cannot

completely avoid responsibility for acts of terrorism and yet there is no easy way for them to speak about these matters. This feeling is at odds with both the Hindu right's representation of Muslim responsibility and secular discourse that attributes the appeal to violence to a response to economic or political discrimination alone.

40. This not to imply that Iqbal is not claimed by Indians as one of their, own since much of his poetry was written for a mixed audience. Even now some of his poems that can fall into the category of edifying literature are used in school recitations. An example is his poem "dua" or prayer.

41. This theme is explored in detail in my forthcoming essay "Moral and Spiritual Striving in the Everyday: To Be a Muslim in Contemporary India," in *Ethical Life in South Asia*, ed. Anand Pandian and Daud Ali (Bloomington: Indiana University Press, forthcoming).

42. Kathleen Stewart, *Ordinary Affects* (Durham: Duke University Press, 2007), 65 and 66.

43. Shane Vogel uses this expression as condensing both the ethnography of everyday life in Stewart and the character of everyday affects. Shane Vogel, "By the Light of What Comes After: Eventologies of the Ordinary," *Women and Performance: A Journal of Feminist History* 19 (2009): 24–60.

6

Ordinary Violence on an Extraordinary Stage
Incidents on the Sector Border in Postwar Berlin

PAUL STEEGE

On June 19, 1962, the *New York Times* described how nine East Berliners attempted to tunnel under the Berlin wall and escape to West Berlin. Four people succeeded. East Berlin police caught five more and inadvertently killed one of their colleagues as they fired on the escapees. The article concluded, "The shooting, the escape, the five who did not get away, the dead policeman—all were discussed for a moment [by a crowd on the western side of the wall]. Then the talk turned to other matters, matters that are supposed to help make people forget that nothing is really normal in Berlin these days."[1]

Even the most cursory exploration of news reports on escapes, attempted escapes, and shootings at the Berlin wall encounters repeated references to the "dramatic" nature of these events, a characterization that proclaims their separation from "normal" daily life.[2] The wall's presence in the city reflected—it has been presumed—the geopolitical realities of a macrohistorical conflict, the Cold War. For the rest of the world, that global confrontation had transformed Berlin into something other than a normal city. It had become an icon, defined by the recurring dramas that overwhelmed Berliners' ordinary life. Divided Berlin's iconic status as the capital of the Cold War depended in no small part on a wall of "theatricality" behind which ordinary life seemed to disappear.[3] But that vanishing act was illusory. Already years before the wall set Berlin's division in concrete, ordinary Berliners had rehearsed the meanings of that Cold War border, learning to make room for it in the midst of their everyday life.

This essay examines how Berliners helped make normal the practices that divided Berlin during the Cold War. In this reading of Berlin's division, the wall serves as more than the physical manifestation of Cold War politics. It also reflects and fits within Berliners' journey through the twentieth century, their stories of collaboration and resistance, complicity and endurance with which they negotiated shifting political regimes and the violence of total war. Focusing on violent encounters on the occupation sector boundaries in early 1949, this essay locates the production of an evolving border regime in everyday practices that transcend any one political system. It thus highlights the blurred lines between history as event, that is, a history demarcated primarily by interruptions to the normal flow of everyday life, and history *as* everyday life, in which normalcy is visible as a human construct that ordinary people impose on everyday life.[4]

Erected over night from 12 to 13 August 1961, the Berlin wall served East German authorities as they sought to halt the exodus of East Germans to the West,[5] but it also fit into a longer genealogy of efforts to impose order on the disorder of everyday life in Berlin. With the wall, East German authorities attempted to codify—to set in stone—the particular regime they imagined for the city and by extension all of East Germany. Looking into that future, they fantasized about an orderly Berlin that looked similar to the city imagined by their Cold War antagonists in the west, but would also have seemed familiar to many who sought to defend and conquer the diverse bulwarks of power in a bygone Berlin. Municipal police protecting the "street scene" during the *Kaiserreich*, Communists and Nazis defending and assaulting "Red Berlin" during the Weimar Republic, but also New Left activists and police who imagined potential revolution among the street demos and occupied apartment blocks of West Berlin in the 1960s and '70s: they all operated with a paradoxical sense of their own power and powerlessness.[6]

These competing visions of order and disorder played out in the dynamic interaction between rhetorical and physical practices on display in the city streets—performances that for all of their stagecraft almost always threatened to slip out of control. At first glance the wall seems to have been an instrument of total control, but that vision depends on a willingness to detach it from the ordinary life of which it remained a part. When one looks more closely at a version of that everyday life before the wall came to anchor the hegemonic image of Cold War Berlin—a city divided by a concrete barrier—it is still possible to recognize the extraordinary and ordinary elements that will remain part of that Cold War structure—even if no longer so obviously.[7]

Normal Policing, Normal Violence

Recent work on German policing continues to wrestle with the extent to which the Nazi regime at the center of the twentieth century represented a continuation of, a departure from, or a rupture in the midst of longer traditions of policing, "authoritarian," "modern," or otherwise.[8] In particular, work describing the Gestapo's dependence on denunciations has demolished the popular view of that Nazi-era secret police as an all-powerful, totalitarian force.[9] But I am no less convinced that popular willingness to be complicit in Gestapo terror (most explicitly through denunciation) draws, as well, on a readiness to participate in the exercise of police power that predates the Nazi seizure of power and operates under the veneer of normal policing even as those police practices eventually joined in the work of war, annihilation, and genocide.[10] To the extent that the practices of policing operate across and around the edges of society and the state—sustaining internal order also become a necessary precondition for defending the state's boundaries externally, even if that is not generally the job of the police.[11]

In 1949 Berlin, a defeated capital occupied by the four victors of World War II, the internal and external boundaries of the state overlapped, and the obligation to defend those borders often fell to the police (although occasionally these efforts also depended on the support of one or the other of the occupying military powers). Despite the growing political and administrative divides and notwithstanding the accelerating preparations for separate East and West German states, Berlin in early 1949 was not a divided city. Berliners continued to move back and forth between West and East sectors to work, shop, trade, and seek out culture and entertainment. Even in the face of Soviet Zone and East sector transportation restrictions, border crossing remained a vital part of Berliners' everyday life and also a critical way in which they collaborated (even if unintentionally) to "stage" the border between East and West Berlin, to craft the iconic forms that came to define Berlin as capital of the Cold War, and to stage the divide that would become concrete twelve years later.[12]

The genealogy of the controls that Soviet sector police formulated in March 1949 extended back beyond the start of the Berlin blockade in June 1948, and they functioned as part of a long-running effort by Soviet Zone authorities to assert control over economic activity in the territory they administered.[13] Officially, Berlin and the surrounding Soviet Zone operated according to a ration economy in which scarce goods were allocated in a tightly regulated distribution system. Individuals could purchase food, fuel, and other rationed goods only after presenting the requisite coupon from their ration card. Merchants dutifully pasted these coupons into sheets with which they accounted for the goods they received from wholesalers and municipal supply depots.

In practice, however, nearly everyone's survival depended on participation in an illegal economy, the black market. In Berliners' everyday lives, black marketeering represented both an ordinary practice of everyday survival and an extraordinary and dangerous act that threatened to embed its practitioners in an at times draconian punitive regime. In spring 1949, authorities in the Soviet Zone underscored their fundamental anxiety about this pervasive practice of black marketeering and its role in undermining their ability to control the Soviet Zone economy by proposing the death penalty for some economic crimes.[14] This broad context of economic crime formed the backdrop within which Soviet sector police sought both to define and to manage the sites where this crisis seemed most visible: Berlin's sector borders.

Formulating an Extraordinary Crisis

On March 3, 1949, more than twelve years before construction of the Berlin wall, the commander of the East sector's municipal police articulated a policy that claimed an extraordinary status for the evolving border within the city. His "Instructions for Checkpoints on the Sector Border" concluded with "Special Rules of Conduct" (*Besondere Verhaltungsmassregeln*) that sought both to explain and to manage the material encounters between the diverse actors—police, border crossers, passersby—who came together in the interstitial spaces of the sector borders in the heart of Berlin. Even as these special regulations proclaimed the means by which police sentries could assert and maintain their control over the sector border, they also articulated the operational sources for a fear that success would elude them.

Special Rules of Conduct

1.) Every checkpoint must be informed of the password and should demand it from controlling bodies before distributing any information to them.

2.) After darkness falls, sentries may not stand next to each other [. . .] The 2nd as well as the 3rd sentry should stay under cover at a measured distance in order to the defend the investigating policeman in case of particular incidents. The broad headlight of a car represents a particular source of danger for the sentries. They should take care not to be blinded and thus rendered incapable of action.

3.) Sentries should keep the service pistol continuously loaded with the safety on and ready to hand so that it is impossible to lose the weapon without an exchange of fire. Every loss of the service pistol—regardless of how it occurred—will be punished to the full extent of the law [. . . .]

4.) Checkpoint duty absolutely requires a *precise knowledge of the area* (*genaue Ortskenntnis*). To the extent that such knowledge is absent, the course of the sector border should be studied—if possible with the help of a map or sketch—before going on duty. During the night as well, the sentry must be familiar with the area and be informed about particular danger points (building ruins, walls, etc.). Any inattentiveness—especially in the dark—can bring immediate danger for the sentries.[15]

These special regulations focus in particular on the need to confront limits on seeing and knowing. While the specialized knowledge of the border area was to be secured behind a wall of passwords, the remainder of the regulations put into question the acquisition of that knowledge. The fall of darkness and blinding headlights both threaten to render border sentries incapable of action. And such action is to be expected—weapons are to be kept ready to hand. During January 1949, Soviet sector police on the sector border fired their weapons on sixteen occasions (a total of fifty-nine shots) when vehicles refused to stop and continued on without decreasing speed.[16]

At the same time, the document expresses skepticism about individual policemen's readiness to fire their weapons or even to hold on to them. Warning that "every loss of the service pistol [. . .] will be punished to the full extent of the law," the police commander demonstrates his uneasiness with his men, although the document hedges whether this concern derives from fears of the policemen's incompetence or their political unreliability. Critically, then, this directive imagines the possibility of threats coming both from within and without.

The directive's final call for police to cultivate a "precise knowledge of the area" asserts the desirability of mastering the physical and rhetorical space of Berlin's borders. But such optimistic claims to total control (even absolute local knowledge) belie the shifting and fragmented character of this particular urban place.[17] As point four acknowledges, Berlin remained quite literally shattered, full of ruins that simultaneously obstructed (sightlines, streets, etc.) and opened up new passageways, hidden from plain sight. The physical reconstruction of the city eventually reshaped this border area but also necessitated modifications in regimes with which police and other Berliners negotiated that terrain. Following this initial warning that police need precise local knowledge, the directive provides two examples that give us a street-level view of the heated contests for control of the sector border or at least of those venturing into and across it. These two examples underscore how police anxiety about border crossers also extends to quite explicit fears about physical assaults and even death at the hands of those who challenge the regimen of border controls.[18]

The first example describes a midnight incident in late January 1949 in which "armed bandits" managed to disarm a series of four double sentries on the border between the American sector and the surrounding Soviet Zone (Treptow) and made off with six service pistols.[19] Only one of the sentries resisted, and he was severely wounded with a shot to the chest. The perpetrators escaped without being recognized. The report emphasizes the extraordinary nature of the perpetrators by naming them in a way that asserts their presumptive place outside the normal boundaries of society: "armed bandits"—a designation underscored by the location of their criminal activity on the border.

While the presence of "bandits," even "bandits in Russian uniform," made regular appearances in police reports in the first two years after the end of World War II, they marked out lines of continuity to the pervasive violence that characterized the initial arrival of Soviet troops at war's end and thus put into question the degree to which the war had, in fact, been relegated to the past. At the same time, this case serves as a foundation for regular behavior on the sector border more generally. Including this example in a set of guidelines, even for extraordinary situations, articulates a pervasive fear that police could expect to detect "armed bandits" even among ordinary passersby walking down the city streets near other border checkpoints.

While the second example in this document presents the violent threat to police in less exotic terms, it nonetheless draws traces of the first case's frontier flavor to a working-class district in the heart of the city:

In the Prenzlauer Berg district on 25.2.49 a car modified as a delivery vehicle and carrying women's underwear was stopped at the sector border. As he was being directed toward the checkpoint, the driver did not turn into the street indicated to him and attempted to reach the French sector. The vehicle was again brought to a halt. Police officer K. advanced with his weapon drawn in order to force the driver to get out. As he approached, the sentry [K.] was attacked by the passenger in the truck bed. Taking advantage of this situation, the driver grabbed the service pistol and drove on into the French sector.[20]

The relative weakness of the individual police officer figures throughout this account. His attempt to "force" the driver to stop failed; and while the passenger attacked the officer, the driver ripped his service pistol out of his hand. Here, the drama of "armed bandits" from the preceding example plays out with a slightly absurd flavor: a battle over a truck full of underwear. Of course for the women and men of postwar Berlin, undergarments were no laughing matter. Pervasive clothing shortages and the general disrepair of clothing and footwear made the availability and pursuit of off-ration clothing a vital concern.[21] But for our purposes, the Soviet sector police's juxtaposition of these two examples helps render visible the blurred lines of association between these two encounters. While we get dramatic encounters with "bandits" and what we might imagine as cinematic battles on the back of trucks crossing the border, we also get the mundane, a truck full of underwear. If the first example describes an explicit assault on the police and their action of standing sentry, the second case locates the bandit-like activity (the taking of the officer's weapon) within an action that is not an assault on the police per se. This "theft" occurs in the midst of a drive across the city, albeit a drive that gets invested with additional implications in the course of the truck's attempt to drive from one city district into another.

During the eight months before this report appeared, the first overt clash of the Cold War, the Berlin blockade, cast a new light on the act of crossing this district—but also since summer 1945, occupation sector—border. At the end of June 1948, the Soviets imposed restrictions on ground transport from Germany's Western zones to Berlin. Within days the British and Americans responded with an improvised airlift to ferry supplies to the city's western sectors. While these supply efforts claimed to confront an absolute Soviet blockade that threatened West Berlin with starvation, Berliners' normal practices of everyday survival continued unabated. Foraging trips into the countryside (in the surrounding Soviet Zone), under the counter deal-making, and black marketeering sustained Berliners, just as they had before the blockade began.[22]

In early 1949, while British and American planes roared overhead and American and Soviet diplomats began secretive conversations in New York to craft a diplomatic end to the confrontation, the political and economic situation on the ground had already achieved a de facto resolution. Since the end of 1948, Berlin's municipal government had been split into eastern and western halves, and the two sides were struggling to come to grips with the process of jointly, if often antagonistically, administering the former German capital. The two administrations competed for personnel and resources (even on the level of files and office furniture) but also waged an ongoing struggle to articulate the terms with which to explain the significance of these evolving administrative and jurisdictional shifts.

The Berlin police had fractured even before the administration. In August 1948, the SPD's Johannes Stumm, set up an alternative Police presidium in the American sector. From that point the two Police Presidents (Stumm and his eastern counterpart, Paul Markgraf) each claimed authority over the entire Berlin police even as their police operations worked according to East-West sector boundaries. On some level, these new constraints built on postwar restrictions that pre-existed the split of the police. As part of the four-power administration of Berlin, police in each of the four sectors were restricted from pursuing suspects or carrying weapons into other sectors without prior authorization (each of the four sectors possessed a liaison from the respective occupying power whose intervention could trump the decrees of the central police administration; thus from the beginning of the postwar period, the Berlin police offered a telling example of the fractures/boundaries that ran along and across district and municipal administration, playing out in both geographic and organizational terms).[23] In the face of a public rhetoric of antagonism, the police forces still found wide areas of operational agreement in the need to battle vigorously and occasionally violently against the black market, for example. But, as we will see shortly, these assertions of a shared commitment to defending the public order incorporated different political perspectives and dramatically different interpretations of the same events.

This document from March 1949 locates the problems facing checkpoints on the sector border, especially threats to police sentries' physical safety, within a broad context of black marketeering ("economic crime").

It continues, "The experience gained up to now has shown that Economic criminals often seek to reach the western sectors with loaded vehicles without paying any attention to the life or health of police sentries." Positioned on the sector border, they faced challenges, as they interpreted them, from both internal and external foes. As a foundation for their interpretive work on the border, the document argues, police must understand the importance of their task and "possess the necessary *political awareness.*" Claiming personal "political awareness" as a basis for successful policing suggests the possibility for future performance improvement (by means of political schooling) but also articulates an explanation for potential failures that could reaffirm the sense of danger that made these police controls necessary in the first place.

The directives governing these control measures underscore the need to explore the obvious (look in car trunks) but also an expectation of deviousness and underhandedness on the part of those who seek to cross the border. Thus police should watch for false bottoms and other parts of vehicles in which goods could be concealed in an effort to smuggle them out of the Soviet sector. One directive extends these regulations to the personal interactions between police officers and the people they encounter. By expressing concerns about the popular perception of police control measures, the police leaders acknowledged the real limits on police power (and authority) and anxiety about the legitimacy of police in the Soviet sector:

> Unnecessary discussions with vehicle drivers or passengers are to be avoided. During a control all police personnel should maintain a definitive but nonetheless polite tone. The use of [familiar] forms of address 'Du' and 'Ihr' toward civilians should be avoided in any case. The sentries' proper conduct in public will make the greatest contribution to promoting public understanding for these control measures.

This insistence on politeness, that is, on the proper forms of personal interaction, implicitly acknowledges the power retained by the persons passing the checkpoint. The document goes on to articulate the police authorities' fears about this power and the likelihood that people will subvert the police controls. Although the checkpoints were responsible for controlling vehicles crossing the sector border:

> The checkpoints should at the same time pay attention to *passersby (Strassenpassanten)* who cross the sector border with baggage. If they are carrying large packages, backpacks, suitcases, etc., they should be subject to inspection. This also goes for conspicuous smaller pieces of luggage. If persons,

for example, are carrying several of the same boxes or if several people appear one after the other with one of these boxes, a control is necessary. The accompanying receipts have often proved to be forged.

In its iteration of particular behaviors to be watched for, the report likely provides a glimpse into practices that have already confounded these police control measures. The police's reaction to popular innovations in circumventing the evolving controls suggests that border crossing functioned as a kind of game, albeit a very serious one, in which all participants strived for a degree of predictability in their encounters but also anticipated the need to adapt to and defend themselves from shifting situational contexts.[24] The later more visible façade of these hegemonic structures (the Berlin wall) concealed how ordinary practices of control preceded the normalization of more explicit forms of violence. In other words, while Berliners of the 1970s and 1980s may have learned to live with the wall, they cultivated the conditions for its normalcy even before it had been built. And the traces of wartime violence remained central to their efforts to make sense of a postwar world in which the war had not really disappeared.

Violent Practices between War and Postwar

Nearly four years after the Second World War ended in Europe, Berlin remained a city of ruins. The city had been a regular target of British and American bombers since fall 1943, and the Soviet Army's final push to conquer it proved particularly destructive. By war's end, Berlin had absorbed more bombs and shells than any other city in the war, but it never assumed the iconic stature of a Hamburg or Dresden (or more broadly, Rotterdam, Coventry, or Tokyo) as a city destroyed by bombs. In just two weeks, the final Soviet assault took half a million German and Soviet lives.[25] While the end of the war put a stop to this scale of totalizing violence, the boundaries between war and not war proved less definitive.[26]

Wartime violence continued to project itself into the postwar present— buried munitions exploded, weakened walls gave way—and these were only the most explicit ways that the war continued to claim more victims. Unlike after World War I, Berliners (and Germans more generally) suffered no illusions that this war had ended with anything other than total defeat. But for many Germans, the intense violence of that defeat began to detach the war's end (Germans as objects) from the war's beginning (Germans as subjects).[27] For Berliners in particular the mass rapes that accompanied the Red Army's entrance into the city—and lasted in varying degrees until Soviet forces were confined to barracks in 1947—defined the brutality of defeat more than any other act of violence.[28] This collective experience (of as many as one in three women in Berlin) mattered not only for its place in an evolving and highly gendered articulation of German victimhood in postwar Germany but also as an interpretive lens that shaped popular engagement in postwar struggles for social and political power.[29]

At their wartime and postwar meetings, the victorious allies decided to divide Berlin into four occupation sectors. Located over one hundred miles within the Soviet Zone of Occupation, the city seemed (and has generally been represented) to be an island in the midst of Soviet domination. The fact that the Soviets were the city's sole occupier from May to July 1945 and installed its first postwar administration—subsequently endorsed by the four-power administration in Berlin—suggests that they had created structures designed to reinforce their position of strength. Walter Ulbricht, the future leader of East Germany, infamously declared to the young communist Wolfgang Leonhard, "It's got to look democratic, but we must have everything in our control."[30] This optimistic communist vision of Berlin's political future never materialized. When Berliners voted in municipal elections on October 20, 1946, and soundly rejected Soviet-sponsored German communists (in the form of the new Socialist Unity Party or SED), they rendered explicit something that otherwise remained embedded in the practices of everyday life: Berlin was a site of Soviet weakness, not Soviet strength.[31]

Central to Berliners' political rejection of the SED was their understanding of the party as little more than the German arm of the Soviet occupier. The struggle for control of the municipal administration was thus never just about post-1945 politics. There was no 1945 zero hour at which the city's history restarted after World War II. Berliners' readiness to associate the SED with the Soviets also linked this postwar political contest to what was still the defining German experience of Soviet occupation: mass rape. To the extent that they facilitated popular efforts to renounce any role in wartime violence or Nazi-era crimes, "honest" discussions about the scale of these rapes helped to define this particular violence as needing political and cultural scrutiny and, by extension, to neglect conversations about (Nazi) violence in which Berliners' complicity or even responsibility might figure.[32] For the purposes of this essay, the struggle to locate this collective experience of sexual violence matters because it shows how, at the same time that police and Berliners were putting into practice an increasingly restrictive (even violent) border regimen, Berliners were also struggling to explain how their experiences of wartime violence mattered for their postwar present.

Narrating these experiences of violence in public and private helped Berliners shape postwar Berlin's political terrain in ways that both German politicians and occupation forces recognized. In an effort to confront anti-Soviet attitudes even within the communist-dominated SED, the party organized a campaign in late 1948 and early 1949 to hold a discussion "about 'the Russians' and about us." Some 700 persons assembled in December 1948 at the House for the Study of the Culture of the Soviet Union in Berlin and took part in a surprisingly frank examination of popular concerns about rape. The discussion recapitulated for those in attendance familiar phrases that recalled how Soviet soldiers initiated acts of theft or rape when they arrived in the city in 1945. Their broken German had come to stand in for the acts of violence their speaking initiated. The phrase "Uri, Uri"—a Russian plural of the German *Uhr* (watch) recaptured the image of Soviet soldiers posing with multiple, confiscated wristwatches reaching up their arms.[33] More ominously, "Frau, komm" (woman, come!), offered an invitation that helped to conceal for the speaker the violent sexual act for which he called out the (or more likely any) woman in the room.

At the SED forum, however, one of the speakers linked these two terms in a rhetorical gesture that (intentionally or not) served to conceal the violence of rape behind the "small" act of taking a watch. This double performance took place just beneath the public surface. On the one hand, the speeches contained frank if generally metaphoric discussion in language needing no interpretation for the knowledgeable crowd: for all of the discussion of watches and stolen bicycles, it was clear that participants were talking about rape. On the other, the SED officials seeking to guide the discussion were quite aware of the ways that their formulations slipped out of their control and facilitated an implicit public critique of the SED and its Soviet patrons. Even as Soviet and SED officials made efforts to soft-pedal the brutal violence with which the Red Army took Berlin, their declarations that simultaneously acknowledged and concealed the recent past marked a politically charged form of Berliners' (and especially Berlin women's) struggles to narrate their shared experiences of rape.[34] While most German communists sought to explain Soviet "excesses" as a small detail in a necessarily brutal campaign to defeat Nazi Germany,

many German women in Berlin also adapted their day-to-day language and practices to accommodate the changed normalcy in which rape, too, came to fit.

One particularly matter-of-fact recorder of events from late April to late May 1945 describes the new vocabulary that women in Berlin appropriated to explain their experiences of sexual violence and, particularly, their declaration of agency in the context of their battles to survive: "sleeping for food," "rape shoes," "my major's sugar," and "coal filching."[35] This "specialized jargon" (her term) interjected and contextualized these acts of violence within the shifting normalcy of their changed everyday lives. But she also acknowledged how this discourse of survival strategies evolved in the transition from war to postwar. She describes how her fiancé reacted with shock and discomfort at the frank and explicit ways that she and other women related their stories from the weeks during and after the battle for Berlin. "You've all turned into a bunch of shameless bitches, every one of you in the building. Don't you realize? [. . . .] It's horrible being around you, you've lost all sense of measure."[36] Her experiences confronted him with the implications of the extremes of violence embedded in "normal" war and challenged the somewhat more comfortable idea of war as an extraordinary event that is simply lived through and thus has no connection to the "ordinary" life that continues once the war is over.[37]

For the anonymous diarist, war was not elsewhere, and could not be relegated to the past. Historians of Germany and Berlin in particular face similar challenges as they seek to negotiate the contentious and politically charged relationships between past and present in their effort to address the overlapping and to some extent competing choices about twentieth-century chronology. The choices include, among others, long or short twentieth centuries; "crisis years" that range from the beginnings of German military collapse at Stalingrad in 1942 to the re-establishment of normalcy with the currency reform of June 1948; a long Cold War, as well as the "zero hour" that sought at least in part to facilitate a clean break with the Nazi era.[38]

Border Crossing Rituals

The large dramas of these macrohistorical formulations found parallels in small tragedies in people's daily lives. If one disconnects the totalizing explanations of the dramatic narrative from the daily practices in the midst of those dramas, it becomes possible to reclaim for individual human beings the power of individual actions.[39] People's claims to be subject to small tragedies often serve to conceal the implications of everyday life. They deny the individual and collective complicity in crafting structures of hegemony and conceal the performance of particular (small and large) acts of violence.[40]

In trying to approach the everydayness at the heart of this tension, I use the term "ritual" intentionally; to get at the repetitive nature of my sources (the police reports at the center of this essay represent but a small sample extracted from a larger series of this type) but also to get at the way in which these police reports interact with the practices they attempt to describe in a collaborative undertaking that strived to give form to the uncircumscribed actions of daily life.[41] Walter Benjamin describes ritual as "an experience which seeks to establish itself in a crisis-proof form."[42] By tearing these examples out of their larger context (a series of reports, on the one hand, and the component pieces of a big "event," on the other), I reject the conviction that these systems of dominance (*Herrschaft*) can exist without the murky complicity of those who are also subjected to such hegemony.

This sort of complicity often coexists with and even reinforces acts of stubborn self-will (*Eigensinn*) and thus facilitates individual actors' room for maneuver. But Eigensinn also serves to blur the lines between collaboration and resistance and to unsettle easy claims to distance, noninvolvement, or nonconfrontational noncompliance.[43] Benjamin describes two different kinds of experience that help to make this tension visible. On the one hand, people organize and explain moments of lived-through time (*Erlebnis*) in coherent structures of normalcy. On the other hand, moments of experience (*Erfahrung*) produce a "shock" that helps people to recognize the ways that individual practices are, in fact, implicated in fabricating the smooth veneer under which one's *Erlebnisse* comfortably shelter.[44]

This collection of police reports on "events" (*Ereignisse*) elaborates a series of happenings for which, by dint of including them in these reports, the reporting officer has claimed a level of (historical?) significance. They have entered (or rather been placed) into the official record as part of a collection that defines (from a policing perspective) the events of each day. The language of the individual cases, however, offers a somewhat greater sense of ambiguity. Here, the happenings appear as *mere* "incidents" (*Zwischenfälle*), a term that while still connoting some sense of interruption (of normal routine, perhaps) also suggests a greater level of spontaneity; they appear as occurrences without clearly crafted intent. The spatial component of their naming (*zwischen* = between) provides, as well, a suggestion of their conceptual location "betwixt and between" while also underscoring the socially mediated construction of these locations in which the diverse participants—police, spectators, and especially the border crossers (*Grenzgänger*)—shape their encounters.[45]

The figure of the Grenzgänger dominated public disputes in East and West about control and transgression of Berlin's borders throughout the 1950s. For western authorities, West Berliners willing to shop for cheaper staples in East Berlin betrayed the democratic principles of the city's ideological battle against the communist system. For communist authorities in the east, Berliners armed with the more valuable West Mark comprised a fundamental threat to the evolving planned economy in East Berlin and the surrounding Soviet Zone.[46] For most Grenzgänger these macropolitical arguments proved less compelling. West Berliners pursued inexpensive bread and rolls on the other side of the border. East Berliners watched American movies in West Berlin cinemas, and an entire economic infrastructure developed in Berlin to cater to those moving back and forth within the city.[47]

In analyzing the encounters described in police reports from early 1949, however, the border crossers underscore the conditions of scarcity that dominated human interactions in the immediate postwar period (and in East Germany, at least, for decades thereafter).[48] The border crosser as a typology emerged as people's practices of survival encountered and interacted with Soviet sector authorities' control efforts. For the Soviets and their German supporters, the imposition of control measures in and around Berlin had relatively little to do with the desire to confront and challenge the West, its ideologies, or its political control of any particular territory (West Berlin). Instead, it reflected their real and pervasive anxiety about their inability to exercise control over the territory ostensibly already under their authority. The more explicit marking of borders helped to define and reinforce the scope of that authority, but the embodiment of these formal claims depended precisely on ongoing and regular interaction with those persons whose actions threatened East sector claims to understand and explain the situation. The ability of Berliners to recognize and articulate the "meaning" of the border depended on the interaction between the authorities' formal claims and the vital practices of daily life that sought to break through those formal constraints.[49] That dynamic is articulated in the police event reports.

At around four p.m. on February 17, 1949, members of the Soviet sector police attempted to stop a vehicle approaching the sector border. Even though one officer jumped onto the vehicle, the driver brought it to a stop only after it crossed into the French sector. As the officer left the car, "a fight broke out" between the populace and other members of the Soviet sector police who hurried across the border to support their colleague. One of these officers fired a shot, but nobody was hurt. When officers of the French sector police station 51 arrived, their eastern counterparts returned to their own sector.[50]

This "incident on the sector border" comes from a report submitted by police in the working-class district of Wedding (French sector). In a brief paragraph, we get the details of this late winter afternoon. The driver of this Tempowagen (a hybrid passenger/transport vehicle) faced the efforts of an East sector police officer to halt the vehicle before it crossed the sector border. As he leapt onto the vehicle, the officer unintentionally joined in its flight across the boundary, and faced—along with his police colleagues who also followed across the sector line—the small-scale violent force of the crowd on the street. The appearance of West sector police (a reminder of organizational division that framed the spatial demarcation of Berlin before the construction of the wall) reasserted the power of those institutional lines (or perhaps the West sector police report seeks to underscore its own authority and its ability to master the space of its jurisdiction). In the midst of a big confrontation that largely constituted the ritual practices of the Cold War—the Berlin blockade—this less dramatic encounter makes visible a different relationship between everyday life and the violent marking of divided Berlin. Here, the quotidian act of driving down Swinemünder Strasse at the corner of Bernauer Strasse is still visible as such and not just as the everyday life object of a Cold War predicate.

A report from police in Neukölln (American sector) also describes an "incident at the sector border": February 25, 1949, between nine and eleven in the morning. The passive bureaucratese of the report explains how the incident arose between two East sector police officers and a policeman from Police Department 215 in Neukölln ("*es [kam. . . .] zu einem Zwischenfall*"). The confrontation started when the Soviet sector police attempted to compel a truck that had driven into the American sector to return to the "Russian sector," because it had allegedly failed to obey the police order to stop. The two Soviet sector officers climbed onto the truck—even though the West sector policeman had directed them to return to their own sector (in general, Berlin police were prohibited from crossing sector lines in pursuit of suspects). When the western policeman pushed one of those from the east, "fisticuffs ensued." A group of street car workers intervened and "distracted" the eastern police, and the truck continued on its way.[51]

This example again describes the individual rejection of police authority (failure to obey an order to stop), the almost spontaneous generation of physical violence (*"es [kam] zu einem Handgemenge"*), and the intervention of the bystanders, who distracted the police from their efforts to fulfill their duty (although in a location across the sector boundary and thus technically beyond their jurisdiction).[52] This interaction suggests the extent to which police violence incorporates both "law-preserving" and "law-making" properties and blurs the relationship between ends and means.[53] The report's concluding remark embeds this encounter in an additional layer of bureaucratic meaning production, in this instance with the transmission of the report to the American Office of Public Safety.

More important, the small scale of violence in this instance (fisticuffs) maps the efforts by almost all the participants to delineate the boundaries of authority with respect to the sector border. While these physical interventions worked as acts of self-expression, they served less to challenge the existence of an evolving border regime than to create room for maneuver within that border area. In the report, the "battle" to mark, control, or impose the sector border assumes a ritual quality: the various participants play their roles in a brief interruption of the normal drive across the city (the report explicitly describes the truck's ability "to continue its trip into the American sector"). One can imagine the crossing of the sector border as the occasion for a brief exertion (the eastern policemen jumped onto the vehicle, the West sector policeman pushed one of them away, pulses inside and outside the vehicle raced briefly). "Nobody was injured."

One month later, on March 26, 1949, another incident ended with slightly greater violence. In just a few short lines, the police in Kreuzberg (American sector) describe the seizing of an East sector policeman: "around 22.50 hours, after a baggage check at the S-Bahn Station Potsdamer Platz, the 47-year-old east sector policeman Walter D—— from Police Station 1 was prevented from getting out of the S-Bahn train. On board the train and in the Anhalter Station, D. was beaten by the passengers and injured about his head. Passersby brought him to Station 103; after questioning (*Vermehmung*), he was released again."[54]

This case has at its center a more extended process of crossing the border. The commuter railway makes explicit the interstitiality (betwixt and between-ness) of the act of border crossing.[55] What on street level was essentially a line to be crossed was here the much lengthier passageway between the last train stop in the east and the first stop in the west. That at least some of the violence directed against the police officer takes place en route is not surprising. The passengers existed in a self-contained world and created an alternative set of power relationships that undermined any purely geographic border designation but marked individuals' place within the symbolic geography of the evolving political contest for the city.[56] For Berliners, the division of the police into east and west remained somewhat ambiguous. Without the context of a particular practice (conducting a baggage check in the last station of the Soviet sector), the passengers described in the report would likely have found it difficult to physically distinguish between East and West sector policemen. Until summer 1948, Berlin police still served under a single Police President, and in all sectors continued to make do with the same rather limited uniform stock.[57] While West sector police, too, conducted raids on illicit economic activity (black marketeering)—sometimes even in close cooperation with their eastern colleagues—it was precisely the act of carrying out these control measures in the context of crossing the border that would have marked the individual officer as coming from the "east."

The Soviet sector police officer conducting baggage inspections on public transport passengers at the last stop before the train left the Soviet sector was forced by those passengers to accompany them across the border. This inversion of power had physical consequences (the passengers beat him) and subsequently resulted in his temporary subordination to West sector police officials. The brief expression, "released after questioning" (*nach Vernehmung* [. . .] *wieder freigelassen*) conceals a great deal about this interaction among (former) police colleagues. We can't know if this exchange (in the context of "questioning") was friendly, confrontational, sarcastic, or sympathetic. After the police split into east and west branches, individual officers had to choose where to serve. Policemen residing in the Soviet sector risked losing their apartments if they chose to serve in the western police branch. They would, however, be paid in the more valuable western Mark. Additionally, the occasional seizure of police officers for detention in camps in the Soviet Zone or even in the Soviet Union underscored the heated competition for policemen but also the physical risks that voluntary or involuntary border crossing potentially posed for the individual members of the police.[58]

Police in both East and West sectors feared the possibility of attacks on or across the sector border. In articulating these fears, they defined them in terms of ends, primarily as politically motivated assaults on police or the political territory they ostensibly defended. Border crossing, especially as captured in these reports, is instead about means, about the tactics, processes, and physical mechanisms by which individuals made their way across or through the border regime. In Cold War Berlin, this "how" is generally taken for granted because the political "why" remains so over-determined. Focusing on the how relocates these stories to claim Berliners as historical actors, not mere objects.

This essay has attempted to wrestle with the ways in which authoritative and popular claims about what seems to be in plain sight (here the sector border in occupied Berlin) are, in fact, products of convoluted interactions between people in particular times and places. Competing claims about what these interactions mean—at the time and in retrospect—tend to conceal as much as they reveal. The various participants in these "incidents" on the sector border—East and West sector police, border crossers, passerby, etc.—become players in an almost ritualized conflict that denies power to act/know even as it describes involvement. A small, but telling example: in the series of reports submitted by West sector police on vehicles crossing the sector border, the inability to detect the license plate number seems a remarkably consistent occurrence. Whether the numbers were obscured by night or dirt, or consciously ignored by individual policemen, the open-endedness of the description creates room for maneuver within the evolving border regime—for both the police reporters and border crossers. The point is not to claim that all participants are equally responsible for the individual acts of violence but rather to consider how the integration of even small acts of violence into a narrative framework of grand (political) significance helps to render these and other violent acts normal.[59]

Too often, in trying to make sense of divided Berlin, the tendency has been for historians to project the wall backwards, to assert an absolute split even before its concrete iteration. The collapse of the wall in 1989 and the post-reunification anxieties about the ongoing "wall in the head" between former East and West Germans have facilitated questions about the ways that Berlin's split into east and west was less about technology than daily practices of division.[60] Already in 1982, Peter Schneider's imaginative novel, *The Wall Jumper* (not insignificantly the source of the term "wall in the head"), begins with the description of an airplane's shadow crossing over the zigzag of the wall ("more a civic monument than a border") from East to West Berlin.[61] While the wall jumpers in the novel move back and forth between east and west and operate in a fantastic world somewhat at odds with the real violence that confronted hundreds of persons who attempted to cross the wall, Schneider's narrative suggestively reminds readers that borders, no matter how heavily armored, are made by people. Interjecting human agency back into the story also serves to undermine a sense of fateful tragedy imposed on individual victims (actors) in the service of some larger meaning.

Rather than asking only why the wall fell and why the German Democratic Republic (East Germany) collapsed in 1989, historians need to understand that state's relative stability. In a German historical context, this state outlasted the Weimar Republic and the Third Reich combined. It survived not only due to the communist state's coercive apparatus and the lingering presence of Soviet tanks in the background, but depended on widespread complicity in a regime that also sought to accommodate popular desires.[62] This essay has adopted a similar perspective, looking beyond the technological apparatus of sector borders in Berlin and focusing instead on broad if at times unintentional complicity in crafting the border regime in Cold War Berlin. Border crossing in the postwar years before the wall's construction in 1961 was still a routine act. If we look at what that routine contained—not least the potential for violent performances at the border—it is possible to recognize within normal, everyday life the divide that will, after 1961, be proclaimed to be so dramatically set apart from normal life in Berlin, or anywhere else. Thus, we can reclaim for Berlin a place in the normal course of quite ordinary history and relegate timeless tragic dramas to the literal theaters where they belong.

NOTES

The research for this essay was supported by the Friedrich Ebert Foundation and the Villanova University Department of History.

1. Sydney Gruson, "Red Guard Killed at Berlin's Wall," *New York Times*, June 19, 1962, 1, 3.

2. E.g., "Berlin Wall Is Scene of Drama and Gunfire," *New York Times*, April 10, 1984, A9, and "Drama at the Berlin Wall: A Wild Drive to Freedom," *New York Times*, August 30, 1986, 2.

3. Patrick Wright, *Iron Curtain: From Stage to Cold War* (Oxford: Oxford University Press, 2007), 18. Also Andrew J. Webber, *Berlin in the Twentieth Century: A Cultural Topography* (Cambridge: Cambridge University Press, 2008), David Clay Large, *Berlin*

(New York: Basic Books, 2000), and Paul Steege, *Black Market, Cold War: Everyday Life in Berlin* (Cambridge: Cambridge University Press, 2007).

4. Andrew Stuart Bergerson, *Ordinary Germans in Extraordinary Times* (Bloomington: Indiana University Press, 2004), 8. On the History of Everyday Life, see Paul Steege, Andrew Stuart Bergerson, Maureen Healy, and Pamela Swett, "The History of Everyday Life: A Second Chapter," *Journal of Modern History* 80, no. 2 (June 2008): 358–78. For a different discussion of "eventfulness," see Veena Das, *Life and Words: Violence and the Descent into the Ordinary* (Berkeley: University of California Press, 2007), 1–17.

5. Patrick Major, "Innenpolitische Aspekte der zweiten Berlinkrise (1958–1961)," in *Mauerbau und Mauerfall: Uursachen—Verlauf—Auswirkungen*, ed. Hans-Hermann Hertle, Konrad H. Jarausch, and Christoph Kleßmann (Berlin: Chronos Links Verlag, 2002), 97–110, and Hope M. Harrison, *Driving the Soviets up the Wall: Soviet–East German Relations, 1953–1961* (Princeton: Princeton University Press, 2003), 99–102.

6. Belinda Davis, "The City as Theater of Protest: West Berlin and West Germany, 1962–1983," in *The Spaces of the Modern City: Imaginaries, Politics, and Everyday Life*, ed. Gyan Prakash and Kevin M. Kruse (Princeton: Princeton University Press, 2008), 247, 255; and Belinda Davis, "Polizei und Alltagsgewalt in Berlin im 20. Jahrhundert," in *Polizei, Staat, Gewalt. Historisch-vergleichende Studien zur Polizeipraxis im 20. Jahrhundert*, ed. Alf Lüdtke and H. Reinke (Opladen: Leske and Budrich, 2009).

7. Thanks to Veena Das, who raised this point during the conference discussion of this essay. The extent to which acts and representations of violence simultaneously reveal and conceal their implications figures in several of the essays in this volume.

8. Hsi-Huey Liang, *The Rise of the Modern Police State and the European State System from Metternich to the Second World War* (Cambridge: Cambridge University Press, 1992); Jose Canoy, *The Discreet Charm of the Police State: The* Landpolizei *and the Transformation of Bavaria, 1945–1965* (Leiden: Brill, 2007).

9. Robert Gellately, *Backing Hitler: Consent and Coercion in Nazi Germany* (Oxford: Oxford University Press, 2001), and Klaus-Michael Mallman and Gerhard Paul, "Omniscient, Omnipotent, Omnipresent? Gestapo, Society, and Resistance," in *Nazism and German Society, 1933–1945*, ed. David F. Crew (London: Routledge, 1994), 166–96.

10. Sace Elder, "Murder, Denunciation, and Criminal Policing in Weimar Berlin," *Journal of Contemporary History* 41, no. 3 (2006): 401–19; Paul Steege, "Looking for Russian Murderers in Berlin: An 'Ordinary' Criminal Case, December 1941" (unpublished manuscript).

11. Liang, *Rise of the Modern Police State*, 8–9.

12. Peter Sahlins, *Boundaries: The Making of France and Spain in the Pyrenees* (Berkeley: University of California Press, 1989). Also, Andreas Glaeser, *Divided in Unity: Identity, Germany, and the Berlin Police* (Chicago: University of Chicago Press, 2000), esp. the section on "rhetorical readings of space" that starts on p. 47

13. These control structures are perhaps most visible in the expansion of the powers of the Soviet sector's German Economic Commission and the creation of a series of checkpoints known as the "Ring around Berlin" in spring 1948. Steege, *Black Market*, 155–61, 178–86.

14. See the 4th Draft of a Verordnung über die Bestrafung von Schiebern und Spekulanten, dated February 12, 1949, SAPMO, NY 4062/80, Bl. 79.For additional context, see Steege, *Black Market*, 265.

15. Instructions for Checkpoints on the Sector border from the Kdo. d. schupo, dated 3.3.1949, Landesarchiv Berlin (LAB), Rep. 26, Nr. 143, Bl. 63.

16. Monthly report (January 1949) from the Kdo. Schupo (Pech) to the Police Pres., dated 3.2.1949, LAB, Rep. 26, Nr. 215, Bl. 6.

17. Edith Sheffer, "On Edge: Building the Border in East and West Germany," *Central European History* 40, no. 2 (June 2007): 307–39; Glaeser, *Divided in Unity;* Pamela E. Swett, "Political Networks, Rail Networks: Public Transportation and Neighbourhood Radicalism in Weimar Berlin," in *The City and the Railway in Europe*, ed. Ralf Roth and Marie-Noëlle Polino (Aldershot: Ashgate, 2003), 221–36.

18. West sector police expressed parallel anxieties about the threat of seizure or kidnapping and subsequent detention within the Soviet Zone or even deportation to the Soviet Union. See, e.g., Arthur L. Smith, Jr., *Kidnap City* (Westport, Conn.: Greenwood Press, 2002).

19. Eric J. Hobsbawm, *Bandits*, rev. ed. (New York: Pantheon Books, 1981).

20. Instructions for Checkpoints on the Sector border from the Kdo. d. schupo, dated 3.3.1949, LAB, Rep. 26, Nr. 143, Bl. 63.

21. See, e.g., the photographs submitted to the mayor's office in October 1947, LAB, C Rep. 101, Nr. 121, Bl. 265–6.

22. Steege, *Black Market.* For examples of the way that mythic accounts of absolute blockade continue to trump the messy experience of porous Soviet controls and the independent survival strategies of individual Berliners, see Andrei Cherny, *The Candy Bombers: The Untold Story of the Berlin Airlift and America's Finest Hour* (New York: Putnam, 2008) and Richard Reeves, *Daring Young Men: The Heroism and Triumph of the Berlin Airlift June 1948–May 1949* (New York: Simon and Schuster, 2010).

23. See Norbert Steinborn and Hilmar Krüger, *Die Berliner Polizei 1945 bis 1992: Von der Militärreserve im Kalten Krieg auf dem Weg zur bürgernahen Polizei?* (Berlin: Verlag Arno Spitz, 1993), esp. 34.

24. Greg Eghigian, "Homo Munitus: The East German Observed," in *Socialist Modern: East German Everyday Culture and Politics*, ed. Katherine Pence and Paul Betts (Ann Arbor: University of Michigan Press, 2008), 37–70.

25. Wolfgang Schivelbusch, *In a Cold Crater: Cultural and Intellectual Life in Berlin, 1945–1948*, trans. Kelly Barry (Berkeley: University of California Press, 1998), 1–2. Norman Naimark, *The Russians in Germany: A History of the Soviet Zone of Occupation, 1945–1949* (Cambridge: Harvard University Press, 1995), 11. More generally, Peter Fritzsche, *Life and Death in the Third Reich* (Cambridge: Harvard University Press, 2008).

26. Roger Chickering, Stig Förster, and Bernd Greiner, eds., *A World at Total War: Global Conflict and the Politics of Destruction, 1937–1945*, Publications of the German Historical Institute (Cambridge: Cambridge University Press, 2005) and Tony Judt, *Postwar: A History of Europe since 1945* (New York: Penguin, 2005).

27. Fritzsche, *Life and Death*, 301.

28. Atina Grossman, *Jews, Germans, and Allies: Close Encounters in Occupied Germany* (Princeton: Princeton University Press, 2007), 48–86. Naimark, *The Russians in Germany*, 69–140.

29. Elizabeth Heineman, "The Hour of the Woman: Memories of Germany's 'Crisis Years' and West German National Identity," *American Historical Review* 101, no. 2 (April 1996): 354–95.

30. Wolfgang Leonhard, *Child of the Revolution*, trans. C. M. Woodhouse (Chicago: Henry Regnery, 1958), 301.

31. Steege, *Black Market*, 64–104.

32. Heineman, "The Hour of the Woman," and Maja Zehfuss, *Wounds of Memory: The Politics of War in Germany* (Cambridge: Cambridge University Press, 2007), especially chap. 6.

33. See the photo in Naimark, *The Russians in Germany*, following p. 140.

34. Ibid., 132–40.

35. Anonymous, *A Woman in Berlin: Eight Weeks in the Conquered City*, trans. Philip Boehm (New York: Henry Holt, 2005), 190. Also, Heineman, "The Hour of the Woman."

36. Anonymous, *A Woman in Berlin*, 259.

37. Walter Benjamin, "On Some Motifs in Baudelaire," *Illuminations: Essays and Reflections*, ed. Hannah Arendt, trans. Harry Zohn (New York: Schocken Books, 1968), 163.

38. Martin Broszat, Klaus-Dietmar Kenke, and Hans Woller, eds., *Von Stalinsgrad bis Währungsreform: zur Sozialgeschichghte des Umbruchs in detuschland*, Quellen und Darstellungen zur Zeitgeschichte 26 (Munich: R. Oldenbourg Verlag, 1988). Webber, *Berlin in the Twentieth Century*. Andreas Huyssen, *Present Pasts: Urban Palimpsests and the Politics of Memory* (Stanford: Stanford University Press, 2003). Walter Benjamin, "A Berlin Chronicle," in *Reflections: Essays, Aphorisms, Autobiographical Writings*, trans. Edmund Jephcott (New York: Schocken Books, 1986), 3–60.

39. Benjamin, "On Some Motifs in Baudelaire." On the fragmenting of German history in the twentieth century, see Michael Geyer and Konrad H. Jarausch, *Shattered Past: Reconstructing German Histories* (Princeton: Princeton University Press, 2003).

40. Gyanendra Pandey, *Routine Violence: Nations, Fragments, Histories* (Stanford: Stanford University Press, 2006). More generally see Antonio Gramsci, *Selections from the Prison Notebooks*, ed. and trans. Quintin Hoare and Geoffrey Nowell Smith (New York: International Publishers, 1971).

41. In wrestling with how to articulate this process, I imagine that the meanings of everyday life are a kind of aesthetic construct, the product of a tension-filled interaction between form and (material) practice. This thinking has been broadly influenced by Friedrich Schiller, *On the Aesthetic Education of Man: In a Series of Letters*, ed. and trans. Elizabeth M. Wilkinson and L. A. Willoughby (Oxford: Clarendon Press, 1989), and Friedrich Nietzsche, *The Birth of Tragedy*, in *The Birth of Tragedy and the Case of Wagner*, trans. Walter Kaufmann (New York: Vintage, 1967).

42. Benjamin, "On Some Motifs in Baudelaire," 182.

43. On the complicated historiography of resistance in German history, see Ian Kershaw, *The Nazi Dictatorship: Problems and Perspectives of Interpretation*, 4th ed. (London: Arnold, 2000), and Michael Geyer, "Resistance as Ongoing Project: Visions of Order, Obligations to Strangers, and Struggles for Civil Society, 1933–1990," *Resistance against the Third Reich 1933–1990*, ed. Michael Geyer and John W. Boyer (Chicago: University of Chicago Press, 1994), 325–50.

44. Benjamin, "On Some Motifs in Baudelaire," 163.

45. Victor Turner, *Blazing the Trail: Way Marks in the Exploration of Symbols*, ed. Edith Turner (Tucson: University of Arizona Press, 1992), and Turner, *The Forest of Symbols: Aspects of Ndembu Ritual* (Ithaca: Cornell University Press, 1967).

46. Sylvia Conradt and Kirsten Heckmann-Janz, *Berlin halb und halb: von Frontstädtern, Grenzgängern und Mauerspechten: Berichte und Bilder* (Frankfurt am Main: Luchterhand, 1990), Erika M. Hoerning, *Zwischen den Fronten: Berliner Grenzgänger und Grenzhändler 1948–1961* (Cologne: Böhlau, 1992), and Katherine Pence, "Herr Schimpf und Frau Schande: Grenzgänger des Konsums im geteilten Berlin und die Politik des Kalten Krieges," in *Sterben für Berlin: Die Berliner Krisen 1948 : 1958*, ed. Burghard Ciesla, Michael Lemke, and Thomas Lindenberger (Berlin: Metropol Verlag, 2000), 185–202.

47. Frank Roggenbuch, *Das Berliner Grenzgängerproblem: Verflechtung und Systemkonkurrenz vor dem Mauerbau*, Veröffentlichungen der Historischen Kommission zu Berlin 107 (Berlin: Walter de Gruyter, 2008). Hoerning, *Zwischen den Fronten*, and Uta G. Poiger, *Jazz, Rock, and Rebels: Cold War Politics and American Culture in a Divided Germany* (Berkeley: University of California Press, 2000), 32.

48. Mark Landsman, *Dictatorship and Demand: The Politics of Consumerism in East Germany* (Cambridge: Harvard University Press, 2005).

49. In Nietzsche's terms, one could imagine the Grenzgänger as a Dionysian figure, closely tied to primal, material pursuits. In Berlin, these bodily desires included above all food and coal. Nietzsche, *The Birth of Tragedy,* 37–38.

50. Kdo. d. Schutzpolizei: Ereignismeldungen, dated 18.2.1949, LAB, Rep. 2, Acc. 888, Nr. 452.

51. Kdo. d. Schutzpolizei: Ereignismeldungen, dated 26.2.1949, LAB, Rep. 2, Acc. 888, Nr. 452.

52. On physicality as central to self-assertion and to challenges to authority, see Alf Lüdtke, "Cash, Coffee-Breaks, Horseplay: *Eigensinn* and Politics among Factory Workers in Germany, circa 1900," in *Confrontation, Class Consciousness, and the Labor Process: Studies in Proletarian Class Formation,* ed. Michael Hanagan and Charles Stephenson (Westport, Conn.: Greenwood Press, 1986), 65–95.

53. Benjamin, "Critique of Violence," *Reflections: Essays, Aphorisms, Autobiographical Writings,* trans. Edmund Jephcott (New York: Schocken Books, 1986), 285–87. The intervention of the crowd and its rejection of police claims to authority offer parallels to E. P. Thompson's formulation of the "moral economy" of the crowd: E. P. Thompson, "The Moral Economy of the English Crowd in the Eighteenth Century," *Customs in Common* (New York: The New Press, 1993), 185–258.

54. Kdo. d. Schutzpolizei: Ereignismeldungen, dated 28.3.1949, LAB, Rep. 2, Acc. 888, Nr. 452.

55. Turner, *Blazing the Trail.*

56. This experience foreshadows the strange post-1961 phenomenon of subway stations on West Berlin subway lines that were physically located in East Berlin. Passengers traveled through these "ghost stations" and encountered a subterranean world in which they passed under the wall in a setting that blurred temporality as well as geography. In the 1980s, the stations still retained the décor and even the advertisements of 1961 while staging the "present" threat of violence in the form of machine gun–carrying border guards standing on half-lit subway platforms. Christopher Links, *Berliner Geisterbahnhöfe: The Berlin Ghost Stations: Les gares fantômes* (Berlin: Ch. Links Verlag, 1994). On the historicity of threats, see Judith Butler, *Excitable Speech: A Politics of the Performative* (New York: Routledge, 1997), 3.

57. Arthur Schlegelmilch, *Hauptstadt im Zonendeutschland: Die Entstehung der Berliner Nachkriegsdemokratie 1945–1949* (Berlin: Haude and Spener, 1993), 125–30.

58. Smith, *Kidnap City.*

59. Pandey, *Routine Violence.*

60. Edith Sheffer, "Burned Bridge: How East and West Germans Made the Iron Curtain" (Ph.D. diss., University of California, Berkeley, 2008), discusses the permeability of the border between East and West Germany. On the "Potemkinism" of the Iron Curtain, see Wright, *Iron Curtain.*

61. Peter Schneider, *The Wall Jumper: A Berlin Story,* trans. Leigh Hafrey (Chicago: University of Chicago Press, 1983), 3.

62. Andrew I. Port, *Conflict and Stability in the German Democratic Republic* (Cambridge: Cambridge University Press, 2007), 2–3.

Contributors

MARY WELEK ATWELL
Professor of Criminal Justice, Radford University

CARLEEN BASLER
Assistant Professor of Sociology, Amherst College

VEENA DAS
Krieger-Eisenhower Professor of Anthropology,
Johns Hopkins University

THOMAS L. DUMM
William H. Hastie '25 Professor of Political Science,
Amherst College

RUTH A. MILLER
Associate Professor of History, University of Massachusetts
Boston

ANNE NORTON
Professor of Political Science, University of Pennsylvania

COREY ROBIN
Associate Professor of Political Science, Brooklyn College
and the Graduate Center (CUNY)

AUSTIN SARAT
William Nelson Cromwell Professor of Jurisprudence
and Political Science, Amherst College

PAUL STEEGE
Associate Professor of History, Villanova University

Index

Abbott, Lyman, 57
Abu Ghraib, 8, 12–13, 98–117; and dogs, 105–9, 117n.16; history of, 99; and hooded man, 113–14; images of, 124; paintings of, 114–15; and pornography, 102–3
abuse: child, 81, 88–89; of Iraqi women, 112
accountability, 78
Adams, John, 24
Addington, David, 37
agency, 2, 7, 43–68, 64n.18; abandoning, 52–56; and Berlin Wall, 159; critique of, 45–46; elimination of, 62; and Judith Butler, 49–50; and rhetoric of violence, 61; and violent speech, 48–49; voters without, 56–62
Aileen: The Life and Death of a Serial Killer, 87–88
Aileen Wournos: The Selling of a Serial Killer, 71, 78, 85–87
Amador, Xavier, 111
Amin, Shahid, 137n.21
Anthony, Susan B., 60
anti-Muslim violence, 14, 121
antisemitism, 113
anti-terrorism legislation, 128, 138n.23
Antonio, Walter, 77
appellate attorneys, 77, 88
Arendt, Hannah, 4
Aristotle, 106
Arrigo, Bruce A., 82
Asad, Talal, 45–46, 64n.16
atrocities, 102
attorneys, 77, 88
Atwell, Mary Welek, 6–8, 11–12, 69–97
Austin, J. L., 65n.24; and agency, 47; and performative speech, 52, 54, 118; and

representation, 129; and speech acts, 2, 10
authority, 154, 156

bandits, 145–46
Basler, Carleen, 1–17
beauty, 25
Benjamin, Walter, 15, 153
Berlin, 15–16, 140–63; blockade of, 146–47, 155; and the Cold War, 141; Wall, 140, 159. *See also* borders; police
Berry-Dee, Christopher, 79
black market, 147–48
blood justice, 1
Bonaparte, Napoleon, 32
borders, 140–63; and bandits, 145–46; crossing, 142, 152–59; incidents at, 155; meaning of, 154; and police, 143–46; and rules of conduct, 143–44
Botero, Fernando, 114–16
Botkins, Dawn, 79–80
bourgeoisie, 27, 31
Broomfield, Nick, 71, 77–79, 84–88
Brown, H. Rap, 7
Burke, Edmund, 8–9, 19–41, 44
Burress, Troy, 77
Bush, George W., 38, 103
Bush, Jeb, 79, 89
Butler, Judith, 47–51, 64n.18; and gender, 69, 84–85; and hierarchy, 93; and physical effects of speech, 10, 12; and representation, 124

Calhoun, John C., 28
capital: defendants, 77; punishment, 6, 11
capitalism, 27–28, 101–2
Carksaddon, Charles, 77